LEANability

Practical Kanban

From Team Focus to Creating Value

Klaus Leopold

This version was published on 2017-12-28

Stay up to date!

 practicalkanban.com

LEANability.com

youtube.com/c/LeanBusinessAgility

twitter.com/klausleopold

facebook.com/LEANability

ISBN: 978-3-903205-00-0

Other ISBNs
  Kindle   978-3-903205-04-8
  EPUB   978-3-903205-05-5

Leanpub ISBNs
  MOBI   978-3-903205-03-1
  EPUB   978-3-903205-02-4
  PDF   978-3-903205-01-7

Contents

CONTENTS

Why did I write this book?

"In theory, there is no difference between theory and practice. But, in practice, there is." [1] This book offers practical solutions for the most significant problems, which could arise when using Kanban. For Kanban practitioners, this book offers motivation to expand Kanban within your business.

Why another book about Kanban when there is already "Kanban Change Leadership"? Good question! In our first book, Kanban Change Leadership, Sigi Kaltenecker and I presented a short introduction of Kanban with an emphasis on establishing Kanban within your company. Our priority was to discuss, in practical terms, the essentials of change management and how to design and implement a Kanban system. Implementing a Kanban system, however, is only the beginning of a long journey towards continuous improvement in your organization.

The title, *Practical Kanban: From Team Focus to Creating Value*, is a good indication of what you can expect from this book. I am a Kanban practitioner. I was not completely happy doing pure research at the university despite the work being very satisfying, because the results of the research were never implemented in the "real world". I often thought that I had great solutions without a corresponding problem. Once I started working as a Kanban trainer and consultant, this was no longer an issue. In 2015 alone, I was involved in over 100 Kanban System designs and implementations. Since 2008, when I started my Kanban career, I have worked on several hundred Kanban Systems. After the implementation of a Kanban System, I often return to the company some time later,

---

[1] see also Klaus Leopold & Siegfried Kaltenecker. *Kanban Change Leadership: Creating a Culture of Continuous Improvement*, John Wiley & Sons Inc, 2015.

analyze the system and hold improvement workshops. Experience has shown me there are typical problems that continually occur within Kanban implementations. When I understood the problems, I was able to offer better solutions. I began to catalog the solutions for these problems, and eventually had a library of solutions for all possible issues. This book brings structure to my experience and solutions and makes them available for everyone to use.

Which problems seem to continually pop up in Kanban implementations? The following questions provide a good summary:

- Are we using Kanban properly?
- How can we improve our Kanban?
- How can we scale our Kanban?
- How can our work become more predictable?
- What should we work on next?

Chapter 1 reviews the fundamentals of Kanban. Advanced users may roll their eyes and think, "Yeah, we know this already." Regardless, take time to review the basics because lack of improvement in your Kanban implementation could be rooted in a misunderstanding of these fundamentals. The questions

- Why are we using Kanban?
- What is a workflow?
- Why should we limit the work in the system?
- Where can I use Kanban in my company?

are answered in this chapter.

Chapter 2, Using and Improving your Kanban, dives into the practical side of Kanban. The road to poorly implemented Kanban is paved with good intentions, as perhaps you have experienced within your organization. Complaints are made about a project taking too long, Kanban is implemented, WIP (Work in Progress) limits are established and it is assumed the work will automatically be finished sooner. When project completion time doesn't improve, the culprit is almost certainly based on the wrong work being limited. In this chapter, I discuss properly setting WIP-limits and give you tips and tricks about Kanban visualization, WIP-limits and workflow. I'll also show you, through personal experience, how to learn from obstacles, how to deal with bugs and how to avoid bottlenecks. The end of this chapter answers the question: Which Kanban meetings are useful and how can we organize them effectively? This chapter should bring ideas for improving your Kanban system and help you determine if your Kanban system is implemented correctly.

Kanban is rarely implemented with a "big bang", meaning there are not, all of a sudden, hundreds or thousands of people in a company working with Kanban. More often it begins with pilot teams who gather experience using Kanban, and if they are not completely inept in their undertaking, the first positive changes occur. The thinking often goes; if a little Kanban is good, more must be better, right? The Kanban consultant/trainer cries tears of joy at the prospect of so many billable hours, because dozens (maybe even hundreds) of teams will need to be converted to the Kanban system. This is great for the consultant, less so for the company. In the best-case scenario, the company's performance levels remain the same, although more likely the performance levels will decrease. In **Chapter 3**, I'll discuss why this is the case and present a typical example of how to better implement Kanban on a large scale.

Chapter 4 is completely dedicated to forecasting. Customers and employers want to know, and rightly so, when they can expect work to be completed. This requires predicting the future, which is never easy, because there can be so many different outcomes based on factors which we cannot control. Fortunately, some outcomes are more probable than others, and we can use this to our advantage when preparing a forecast for work completion. The beauty of this approach is no time is wasted on guessing. With a little data, you can prepare a forecast which is far more accurate than most estimations.

In principle, a good situation is one where there is a lot of work in the idea pool, backlog or option pool of a Kanban board, meaning demand for your products and services are higher than your capacity to supply them. Hopefully there will always be more demand than supply, because more supply than demand, i.e. employees without work to do, will inevitably lead to personnel reductions. We need to appreciate the circumstance of having more demand than the capacity to meet it, which immediately leads to the question: What should we work on first, and which work can wait? I answer this question in **Chapter 5**. I do not claim, however, to present the only proper method of prioritization, as there are many different approaches, each with their own advantages. In this book, I use Cost of Delay as my favorite approach. At the beginning of a Kanban implementation, I recommend using the Cost of Delay prioritization method because it shifts the focus to the value of the results rather than the cost of development. Time receives a price tag, which allows economically sound decisions to be made. When the idea of economy of delay has been completely embraced by the entire group, you can begin to expand your toolkit of prioritization methods and risk evaluations. The bottom line: Prioritization is nothing more than making a decision based on your risk assessment.

In **Chapter 6**, I give a report about the eventful Kanban journey of the STUTE Logistics Company. Their IT manager, Holger Reith, transformed his department within 18 months into a high-performing group. Before implementing Kanban, they were a "typical" IT department: lots of open tickets and requests, long waiting times and an improvement process in need of improvement. Today, tickets arrive in a regulated workflow and the automated forecasting informs the customer when the work will be completed. Employees can bring ideas for improving the order of tasks to be completed which ultimately determine the Cost of Delay. The improvement process of the IT department at STUTE Logistics mirrors many of the topics in this book and I am pleased to be able to share their story. This practical example of a Kanban implementation, which shows the ideas presented in this book being used on a daily basis, is the perfect conclusion to my book.

By the way: You can find supporting materials to help you implement the ideas presented in this book at www.practicalkanban.com.

Klaus Leopold

Vienna, April 2017

1. Why do we use Kanban?

A participant from our Applying Kanban training in Bangkok tweeted, "Increased team performance can lead to decreased system performance". At such moments, I breathe a sigh of relief because the participants truly understand the message: Kanban is not a method for optimizing teams. Assuming Kanban is a team optimization tool already limits the possibilities of using Kanban for your organization. This is, without question, the biggest misunderstanding which continually manifests itself when I'm working with companies or doing workshops and trainings. Although the biggest, it is only one of many. I get called in by companies to help them with their Kanban implementations and see their Kanban boards. I observe how the employees build their boards with gusto and, unfortunately, false supposition, and know it's time to take a step backwards. At such times, it's necessary to gather the users, review the principles and practices, and clarify exactly what it means to use Kanban.

Like any new method, Kanban has become a trend, which in itself brings risks. Whether brought on through their own actions, or through greater economic crises and upheavals, companies search for the next magic elixir which can solve all of their problems in economically unstable times. The elixir being used at the moment is Agile. Companies hope to find success by implementing Agile practices and, at some point, realize just following the rules of a few practices is not the same as using them. Behind every method stands an abundance of knowledge and insights from principles and assessments which need to be understood in order to use the method successfully.

This is exactly what I experience with Kanban; all hopes are put into one method. Several times a month, I observe highly motivated people in their various companies develop, within two days, the most amazing Kanban systems. These works of art, composed of colorful Post-It® notes, perfectly drawn columns and swim lanes, hang on the wall and are proudly observed by the team. "I really hope Kanban can make us faster" or "Hopefully Kanban will help us somehow" are statements which commonly follow. While these statements slowly move to the back of my mind, I imagine the daily routine in such a company. The team sits in a semi-circle in front of the Kanban board as a member takes a red Post-It® and writes "Block: Test Infrastructure not ready" and proceeds to the board and places the Post-It® on a ticket in the Test column, turns around and sits down again. His colleagues confusedly look at him, often followed by an awkward silence, until someone finally asks, "How does that help?"

Surprisingly, or perhaps not so surprisingly, it doesn't help anything. Just because you have visualized something with creativity and colorful pieces of paper does not mean the weak points in your system magically disappear. Have you ever been able to lose weight by just sitting next to an exercise machine? Whether it's a treadmill or a new method for working more effectively, the effectiveness does not come from the purchase. To be effective, it must be used. People are the driving force behind every transformation. The other parts, whether it be the home trainer or Kanban, are nothing more than tools. This is the point I wish to convey about Kanban. It is a tool to help you see the weak points in your system and generate better value for your customer. Sometimes the Kanban board immediately reveals the problem, and often the solution, at the same time and sometimes the sticking point reveals itself more slowly. The Kanban board is only as useful, however, as the people who are willing to see the problems and understand that they must invest time and energy to bring about the change they seek. When they have understood this, they can think about improvements, and make precise and deliberate decisions about their system under two conditions:

1. The participants develop their own process instead of blindly implementing "Best Practices". "Best Practice" is, in any case, a dubious concept because it assumes to have explored every single option and determined the best of all of them. Even if you've attended many Kanban workshops or trainings to understand how to improve your system, you still must do the work yourself.

2. The participants understand their problem before they start thinking about the solution.

Nevertheless, one of the greatest weaknesses in management today is the haphazard installation of a solution without truly understanding the underlying problem. The focus on solutions does not make the company more adaptable to the uncertainties and emergencies of a complex world. When Kanban doesn't hold up to the expectations of management, the problem is not with Kanban, but rather with lazy management and their preconceived notions about improvement. If you are searching for a To-Do list, or a few simple steps to remedy your issues, don't even bother trying Kanban and move on to the next trendy method.

Toyota Production System: What is correct?

Many ideas of Kanban in knowledge work originated from the Toyota Production System (Ohno & Bodek, 1988). Toyota willingly showed their production system to anyone interested. However, the production system is only a snapshot of the current solution to the given production requirements, problems and challenges. Many visitors did not understand this point.

Mike Rother, in his book "Toyota Kata", tells the story of a friend who traveled to Japan several times to visit a Toyota factory (Rother, 2010). On his first visit, he observed how the assembly line workers took pieces off of rolling shelves which were filled with parts from different car models. The worker could pull the appropriate components from the shelf based on the model of car which was rolling down the assembly line. Through the use of these rolling shelves, several different models of cars could be assembled on the same line, and many automakers copied this system.

Several years later, Mike Rother's friend returned to the same factory, but the rolling shelves had been removed. The component parts for each car were arranged in a kit which rolled down the assembly line with the appropriate car. When the car arrived at an assembly point, the worker need only reach into the kit to retrieve the necessary part.

Mike Rother's friend was indignant. He asked his Toyota host which approach was the correct one, but the host didn't understand the question. The host answered, "When you were here the first time many years ago, we were assembling four different car models on this line. Today we assemble eight different models on the same line - it was not possible to hold the various components for each car model on one shelf. Not to mention that we wanted to achieve a one-piece flow. Whenever you visit us, you see the solution which we developed for a specific situation at a given point in time."

What problems are we trying to solve?

When I get a request for consulting, I try to steer the conversation so the following questions are answered: Why does the company want to implement changes? What problems are they trying to solve by implementing these changes? As long as these questions remain unanswered, every method - Kanban or not - will run into a brick wall. Without answers to these questions, it is impossible to define the parameters which measure improvements after implementing the method. Look at Figure 1.1 and ask yourself which system you think is better.

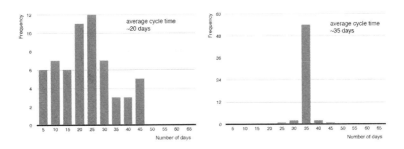

Figure 1.1: Which system is better?

In both charts, the x-axis is the cycle time in days and the y-axis show the frequency of each cycle time. By calculating the average cycle time, we see that System 1 makes a delivery every 20 days and System 2 makes a delivery every 35 days, so clearly System 1 is faster than System 2. Faster is always better, correct? What if speed is important, but something else was more important than speed? Let's look at the two systems again from a different angle.

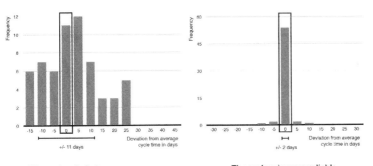

Figure 1.2: Speed versus Predictability - what is better?

In Figure 1.2, the x-axis shows the deviation from the average cycle time in days, giving us a different aspect of the systems being compared. System 1 makes a delivery every 20 days on average, but with an uncertainty of +/- 11 days. On the other hand, the owners of System 2 can deliver in 35 days, and the customer can be assured that they receive their product within +/- 2 days of their delivery date. Thus System 2 is more predictable. So, which system is better?

You probably have already noticed that neither system is better unless we know in which context and in which industry these systems are used. In the automobile industry, for instance, the production start of a new model begins on a target date. Before this target date, all of the components - which can be as many as 10,000 individual components - for the new model must be developed. Once in production, the result of this development is reproduced. Any additional delay to beginning production would cost an arm and a leg. Predictability is, in this case, the only criteria to evaluate the fitness of the development department for the purpose of developing a new model. In contrast, speed of delivery would be more important for a software start-up because the customers want to see new features more quickly, even if quality is perhaps still slightly lacking.

The real question is, what is important for the customer? Each company, and each entity within a company, fulfills a specific purpose. For some companies, the purpose is to make money as fast as possible. Other companies prefer to be in the market long-term and believe in offering the customer - whose purchases pay the bills - better service. The internal processes of the company should be aligned to whichever purpose they serve, thus giving the customer what they want and need. In addition, a company must recognize what type of service a customer values. By which fitness criteria (Anderson, 2013) does a customer evaluate the type of service? The fitness criteria often are, but not limited to:

- Delivery time

- Predictability/Adherence to delivery schedules
- Quality
- Security
- Compliance with regulatory requirements.

Good fitness criteria, from the customer's view, are those which are definable and measurable. In reality however, such criteria - for example, efficiency, agility or quality - are terminologies which each person defines and understands differently. When I set up Kanban in a company, I often hear the employees discuss their expectation of increasing efficiency in the organization. Great, but at what point is the company more efficient? Efficiency is a general term that needs to be specifically defined since the idea of efficiency is different not only for each company, but for each person. In such cases, I pose the following question: What do we want to improve with Kanban and how can we measure our improvement? By persistently repeating this question, the empty umbrella terms of efficiency give way to tangible, quantifiable metrics.

In the intensive process of determining objectives and their related fitness criteria, it also becomes clear that you cannot have everything, and priorities must be set. From an insider's point of view, quick delivery and high employee workload are rarely achievable, even if it appears that way when compared to other companies. Even shorter delivery time and predictability are polar opposites - flight traffic is the best example of this. Pilots typically fly slower than what is technically possible because flying faster brings no advantage. The airlines must hold to their flight plans and adjust their flight times according to the air traffic at the destination. Therefore, the airline does not use flight speed as a measure for successfully completing a flight; rather, the pilot must fly at the correct speed so he can land at the destination airport at the planned time. In the automobile industry, a supplier would permanently damage the customer relationship by delivering component parts a week earlier than requested and needlessly using up precious storage space. Just because something can be done doesn't mean it makes sense to do so.

Good customer service provided by a company is always linked with a deliberate decision to define the focus points of that customer service without sacrificing improvements to their development. This assumes that you know your customer, first of all, and understand them, second of all. Understanding the customer is usually where the company invests the least amount of energy. I often observe this in companies where the customer is never mentioned in meetings, and if they are, it is in the context of being a nuisance. In classical change management, the customer receives her 15 seconds of fame through the prominent placement of her name on the first Power Point slide - by the Org Chart slide, the role of the customer has been forgotten. Wanting to understand the customer is the basis of every improvement and, therefore, is also the point of the question as to why we want to work with Kanban.

If a company wants to make themselves ready to use Kanban, they need to find their own answers to the following questions:

1. How do we find out what the customer wants?
2. Once we know what our customer wants, how will we fulfill the requirements? What must our workflow look like to generate value for the customer?

The answers to the first question are addressed by methods such as Discovery Kanban www.discovery-kanban.com or practices like Lean Startup, Lean UX and Design Thinking. This is fascinating material and highly recommended if you truly want to understand your customer. The focus of this book, however, is to answer the second question. We assume that a company has already answered the first question and knows what the customer values. The next step is to build a work system which can fulfill these customer values in the best way possible.

We have already established, that Kanban - like any other method - cannot work wonders just by existing. No method or framework could ever be suitable for every single company in the world. Why, then, should Kanban be an appropriate tool for solving question 2?

1.1 Building Ships in a Workflow

Kanban is not always intuitive. Occasionally at the start of a Kanban training, before the participants can settle into a comfortable state of listening and learning, I will tell them... nothing. Instead I begin with an exercise - difficult to describe in writing, but I'll give it a try. For the next few minutes you can feel like Aristoteles Onassis: time to build a ship!

A Workflow Experiment: Folding Paper Ships

What you will need:

- A stack of paper
- A stopwatch
- At least six people, but no more than 12 people, in a single row (designates the work system)
    - The first person in the row (work system) is responsible for passing the paper into the system one piece at a time.
    - The last person in the row (work system) is responsible for timing the work.

How to proceed:

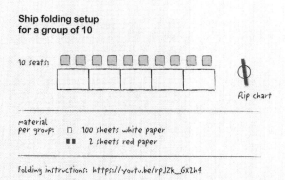

Folding instructions: https://-youtu.be/rpJZk_GX2h4

Figure 1.3: Ship Building Setup

- The people in a work system sit side-by-side at a table (make sure the table is long enough).
- With the exception of the next-to-last person, each member in the work system is responsible for a maximum two folds of the ship, regardless of the total number of people in the system, and each fold (activity) is distinct for each work system member. I **define an activity to be the individual steps or actions which are executed in a work system that at the end produces tangible value.** An activity can have many different forms - in this experiment it denotes the various folds needed to form a paper ship.
- The next-to-last person must complete several complicated folds.
- The last person time-stamps each completed ship.

The experiment is done in two rounds:

- Round 1: There is no limit to the work which flows into the system. The members work according to the push principle and, as soon as their work (fold) is completed, move the ship to the next member.

- Round 2: This round demonstrates the pull principle. Only one ship at a time can be worked on in each individual activity (WIP limit of 1). This means, as soon as a participant has completed her activity, she raises her hand and leaves her ship on the table in front of her. She can only take a new ship into her activity when her ship has been pulled into the following activity and the ship in the previous activity is finished and waiting to be pulled.

The following rules are used for both rounds:

- Ships will be worked in a strict First In, First Out (FIFO) order; i.e, the ships will be worked on in the order that they enter the system.
- Team members are not allowed to help one another or improve the process. This might seem strange, but it is important since we want to measure the difference between the two rounds. If the process would be improved in the second round, we could not compare the measurements between the first and second round.
- Work needs to be done quickly because we want to maximize output. In economic terms, if each ship produced can be sold for ten dollars, then the goal is to produce as many ships as possible in each round.

Push it! Everyone knows this situation well. There is endless amount of work to finish and the salespeople pull in one order after another. Ursula, from today's training, gets the roll of Sales Manager. Her job is to fold the piece of paper in half and pass it into the work system. In the first round, she does this without pause. At the beginning, everyone is still having fun and Harald, the next one in line, only has to fold the paper in half. He's pretty swift and manages to pass the paper within half a minute on to Anna, whose activity is a bit more complex because she needs to fold the corners towards the middle. The next member, Lisa, also completes her activity deftly, but slowly a backlog of work starts to pile up. As the pile gets larger, the laughter dies down and a concentrated silence takes over the room. Everyone hastily folds their ships to reduce their pile as quickly as possible, but before a ship is even completed, two more have landed on the pile. Tom, who sits at the end of the row and has to complete three activities, has it the worst. I joke with him, "Hopefully you don't break your fingers," as he continuously folds the ships one after the other. For the first few seconds he keeps up the pace fairly well, when all of a sudden two ships pile up, then three, then five until he has a vast pile next to him: a textbook example of a bottleneck. Too bad for Tom - everyone else is so busy doing their own activity that nobody has time to help him. John, on the other hand, has an easy job. He measures how many ships per minute are completed, starts the stopwatch at the beginning of the round and each time a ship leaves the final activity, he notes the time. I motivate the members to work faster and faster because I can sell each completed ship for ten dollars and I want to get rich!

After two minutes, I send a red piece of paper into our ship building enterprise and give notice that it will be the last ship. Gradually each member finishes her work, but Tom has a few minutes of work left. While the members are waiting for Tom to finish his work, I give them some food for thought. I tell them, "Don't forget, in reality you would need to continue working because there are always new customer orders being placed." Finally, Tom finishes the red ship and sends it to John, at which point I say "Stop!" John measures the cycle time (see the formula below) of the red ship:

$$Cycle\ Time = Arrival\ Time - 2\ Minutes$$

Arrival time is 5 minutes 18 seconds, so the red ship was completed in the first round with a cycle time of 3 minutes 18 seconds. Everyone gets a short break (Tom can shake his hands out), and then we're off to the second round.

Pull it! The second round begins under different circumstances. In each activity, only one ship can be worked on at a time, which denotes a WIP limit of 1. Ursula, our Sales Manager, holds to the guidelines exactly and sits calmly in front of her pile of paper. She folds the first piece, then raises her hand. Harald pulls the piece of paper from Ursula, completes his fold, then raises his hand. This is the signal for Anna to pull the piece of paper from Harald, complete her folds, then raise her hand. It reminds me a bit of a human "wave" moving through a football stadium - a rhythm is established in the assembly line: complete the fold(s), raise your hand, then pull the next ship. Tom, who is the process bottleneck at the end of the row, has less stress in this round because he can steadily fold his ships to completion without ships piling up in front of him. However, since Tom must make four folds to complete the ship, his tempo determines the speed of the entire production line. That means, at some point during the exercise, everyone must wait for Tom to complete his activity before the next ship gets pulled. When this happens, I comment (again) how each ship can be sold for €10 and if the workers in our "factory" are staring at the ceiling instead of working, we will soon go bankrupt. It is interesting to see what the participants do while they are waiting for the next ship. Some closely observe what is happening in the production line. Others use the time to improve the quality of their work by carefully going over the folds again. After two minutes, I send a red piece of paper in to the system. At 2 minutes and 45 seconds, the completed ship arrives at John - the cycle time is 45 seconds. Stop.

1.1.1 We Cannot Complete More Work, Even If We Work Faster

Let's review shortly: In the first round using the push principle, everyone worked as fast as they could. In the second round, several people had time to relax and just look around or used the time to improve their work. This can only mean the second round was less productive, or-? I asked the participants how they felt after working with the pull principle and I received the following answers:

- It was more relaxed.
- I was able to concentrate.
- We could work on quality.

These observations are interesting. I immediately note (since I'm the boss of the ship company) that I believe I made more money in the first round. In the second round, I claim that I had to declare bankruptcy in because everyone spent their time staring at the ceiling instead of working. How can we find out the amount of money we made in each round? We examine the throughput. Throughput tells us how much work - in our case the number of ships - is completed within a given time. When I take, for example, an average throughput of four ships per minute, and I sell each completed ship for 10 dollars, I earn 40 dollars per minute. Now the moment of suspense: we calculate the measurements from John together. Can you guess how many ships were completed per minute in each round? I draw a table on the flip chart. We need to remove the first result from both rounds because the system was not completely filled at that point. The final result is removed as well, since it was a partial minute when the final ship was completed. We are searching for the average throughput per minute, and the first and last measurements would skew these results. We can now calculate the average throughput of each round.

Minute	Push with no Limit	Pull with WIP 1
0	3	3
1	5	6
2	6	5
3	6	
4	5	
5	2	
Ø Throughput	5.5 ships per minute	5.5 ships per minute
Cycle time of the red ship	3:18 minutes	0:45 minutes

I love this moment - the participant's faces are filled with looks of bewilderment. How are these results possible?

- In both rounds, approximately five ships leave the work system every minute.
- The second round using the pull principle was completed more quickly, since the red ship was delivered after 2 minutes 45 seconds versus 5 minutes 18 seconds in the first round. The cycle time was reduced by a factor of four, from 3 minutes 18 seconds to 45 seconds.
- Stress in the first round, free-time in the second round.

The participants understand the results as soon as I look towards the end of the row in our ship building enterprise: there was the bottleneck in the process (mind you, only the process - people are not usually the bottlenecks).

Whether working in a push system or in a WIP limited system, the **bottleneck** determines the throughput, because the work is deadlocked latest at this point in the system. It doesn't matter how much work we dump into the system or how fast the previous activities are finished: at the end of the day the

> amount of work completed is the same.

For managers in manufacturing plants, this is rudimentary knowledge. Even when folding our ships - our "manufacturing" plant - it was easy to identify the bottleneck. In the area of knowledge work the concept of a bottleneck is well-known, but it is often difficult to easily identify the bottleneck. In knowledge work bottlenecks tend to occur temporarily in one area and then move on to another area because each piece of work done is almost never the same, i.e. a different "ship" is produced each time. There are no two identical customer orders in knowledge work, thus each requires different amounts of work in the various areas each time value is created. For example, one work item may require a majority of effort in the analysis phase and less effort in the development phase, so you might assume the analysis phase is the bottleneck. However, this can change with the next work item.

Often too much energy is invested trying to overcome perceived bottlenecks, when the obvious solution is usually overlooked: The inflow of work can be limited and the resulting available resources can be used to ease the bottleneck. Bottlenecks are discussed in more detail in section 2.4.

1.1.2 We Have Enough Time for the Work We Never Have Time For

Let's look at it from an economic perspective: When we can sell each ship for 10 dollars, we will earn the same amount of 55 dollars per minute (5.5 ships/minute x 10$ per ship) whether we use a push system or a pull system. Or think about the usual situation in companies, where although employees are already working to their limits, work continues to be added. Such a heavy workload is, ironically, perceived positively within many companies. Since the bottleneck determines the throughput of the system, however, it makes absolutely no sense to continuously increase the workload because the system will not become faster or more productive; not to mention in a push system, a large amount of capital is tied up in the backlog of work in progress. In knowledge work, there is a lack of awareness of this tied-up capital because the backlog is invisible - mostly it is stored data which is no longer worked on.

W. Edwards Deming would say, "It's not about working harder, it's about working smarter" (Deming 2000). This is exactly what happens in a pull system, because the work flows in only as fast as the bottleneck allows. For one thing, workers in the system can budget their time accordingly and second, they still have time left over (which is, ironically, automatically interpreted as a bad sign). So I ask my training participants, "What could we do with the free time available while waiting for the bottleneck to clear?"

1. **We could assist our colleagues at the bottleneck**. In practice, one of the most common objections to this idea is "We are not specialists for the bottleneck work." The good news is, that is beside the point of helping a colleague! It's going about easing the burden of work and this can be done in many different ways. For example, you could take over some administrative duties or go as a substitute to meetings - those wanting to help don't necessarily need to perform specialized work. More important is that the colleagues in the bottleneck can concentrate on completing their work. What are the consequences? Even when a non-specialist assists at the bottleneck, the throughput increases (see also section 2.4). It may be slower than a specialist (who is presently unavailable) stepping in to help, but it still improves.

2. **Is this even an optimal process?** When everyone in a department is working at full speed and, nevertheless, work is being completed slowly, the fundamental question about balance needs to be asked. It is possible that the manner in

which the work is distributed and performed is not ideal. In our experiment the imbalance was readily seen. While every other process step only had one task to complete, at the bottleneck there were three tasks to complete. Distributing the work more evenly would resolve the bottleneck and the throughput increases.

More throughput means more product can be delivered in the same amount of time. As we saw in the ship experiment, the free time can also be used to improve the quality of the work. One person would be extremely happy when more product of better quality can be delivered: the customer. The beauty of it is, quality improvements stemming from employees reflections on the process during the available free time, cost the company nothing. There is no need to engage expensive process engineers or consultants (such as myself) to take over contemplating what can be improved.

> **Slack** offers an opportunity, with the same amount of output, to identify and evaluate the weak points in a system, as well as working on quality and finding ways for improvement. In a non-limited system, these opportunities do not exist due to chronic overload.

1.1.3 When We Set Limits, We Become More Predictable

The stability and hence the reliability of a system are directly associated with one of the least favorite topics in the business world: estimation. In the classical overloaded push system with - you guessed it - employees working to capacity, someone is given the thankless job of making a project plan. So, the project planner goes to the individuals, teams or departments and to each one in turn says, "I have a question. When will you be finished?" Each one picks a number then doubles it as a precaution. The experienced project manager adds the partial estimations together and multiplies it by three, just to be safe, and finally arrives at the delivery date on which the product or project will most certainly not be finished. Consequently, because the delivery date is so often missed, the project manager preoccupies his colleagues, while in a system where no work seems to get completed, by constantly asking, "How much do you have left to do?" This question manifests itself in supervisory measures, such as status reports, which require more administrative work and prevents the employee from getting to the real work, thus exacerbating the problem further. On top of this, the employees are sent to an estimation workshop so they can finally learn how to do estimation correctly, although the employees and their estimating capability are not really the problem. **The cause of incorrect estimations is the amount of work in the system is constantly changing. A reliable prediction method, regardless which one, can only function on the basis of a stable system.**

Nobody can give a valid estimation for when work will be completed in an unlimited system where new work is continuously added that needs to be worked on immediately. In addition, people are conditioned to estimate effort. They ask themselves the question "How long do I need?" instead of focusing on the cycle time by asking "When will it be finished?"

Think once more about our flow experiment: What would have happened if I had placed the red piece of paper into the system after 15 minutes instead of two minutes?

- In the push system, a massive backlog would have formed and we wouldn't be able to say when the red ship would be completed. We would only know that it would take much longer - but how much exactly? In other words, this system is *unstable*. The customer receives no reliable statement as to when he will see his ship in the water.

- In the pull system, the answer is simple: We know how much work is in the system. This system is more stable. Therefore, it is possible, through the use of estimation or forecasting for example, to say when the work will be completed. Utilizing a pull system for folding ships does not change the cycle time. On account of this stability, the ship building enterprise can themselves, after 15 minutes, give their customers reliable information about the completion time of the ship. In knowledge work it's not quite that easy because the scope of the work varies, rather than the same object being built over and over again. Nonetheless, in knowledge work a limited system is a prerequisite for being able to say when a job will be completed.

> One of the greatest advantages of WIP limits for both the worker and the customer is **predictability**. On-time delivery is only possible when the amount of work which gets started is limited, which results in a stable system.

1.1.4 When Everything is Important, Then Nothing Is

Let's assume the customer puts the red ship into our unstable push system at the 15-minute mark. As a result, the cycle time increases dramatically and after an hour the ship is only approximately 80 percent complete. The following exchange is what typically follows in real world companies everyday:

Customer: "I could fold the ship together myself in two minutes and you are telling me that after one hour it still isn't finished? Hurry it up!"

Manager: "As you know, we place our focus on the customer."

Which means the red ship gets top priority and is sent past all other ships in the assembly line. Bad luck for the customers waiting for white ships; they now have to wait longer. Thank goodness, the red ship will be finished before the others - at least the impatient customer is somewhat satisfied.

However, a company usually has more than one customer. The possibility increases within an unlimited push system that there are many unhappy, waiting customers who want their orders pushed forward. At some point the system is flooded with red ships. What happened?

- The advantage of priority at some point turns into a disadvantage. If more high priority red ships need to be built, the normal priority ships will need even longer to complete, although this is already the case due to the individual process steps. Not only will the white ships take longer, production of the red ships will also gradually slow down.
- When the system is eventually filled with nothing but high priority red ships, priority no longer exists. If everything has priority, then nothing has priority. The red ships now have the same cycle time which the white ships had before, and the white ships will most likely never be finished - at least until someone makes it top priority. The entire system becomes slower, again.

You would not believe the bizarre excesses which can occur from an uncontrolled prioritization in the real world. In many companies, I have seen not only priority 1, but also priority 1+ and 1++. When a company reaches this stage, a task force is established, which itself gets prioritized - a fascinating endless circle.

> If **priority** should be guaranteed to a customer, it is necessary
> to limit not only the system, but also the priorities.

1.1.5 The Later We Begin, The Better For the Customer

Let's go back to our special customer who gave the order for a red ship at the 15-minute mark. Since the ship building enterprise hasn't delivered anything and the world has continued turning in the meantime, the customer wants something new after the fourth activity. Now he wants a green ship. Remember our experiment: in the first round the red ship entered the system after 2 minutes and had a cycle time of 3 minutes 18 seconds. If the ship had entered the system after 15 minutes, the cycle time would have been approximately one hour. This means the longer you work in an unstable system, the longer the cycle time becomes. On the other hand, in the second round the cycle time remained the same because the ships already in the system were completed before something new was started.

In a push system, the following would occur: the customer's red ship would be taken out of the process and instead a green ship would be placed at the beginning of a system which is already overloaded. Not to mention the work already performed on the red ship is wasted. That hurts the bottom line.

What would happen in a WIP limited pull system? Nothing. The work on the red ship would have not started when the customer changed their mind, thus there would be no economic loss.

One of the fundamental principles of a limited system is to keep the work outside of the system as long as possible (Late Commitment). The simple reason is once a job is started, it should be finished as fast as possible. Work that is being planned will not be stuck in the system, because this would increase the cycle time. Instead, the planned work is put on hold before entering the system. In Kanban, this is known as the Option Pool. For the work system, the effects can be advantageous:

- In the case where the customer changes their mind, the likelihood of wasted work due to the Late Commitment is reduced.
- The lower the WIP limit of the system is set, the shorter the cycle time. Shorter cycle times reduce the probability that the customer wants or needs to change something in the job while it is being worked on.

> With a **limited system**, we strive to keep the cycle time short and at the same time start the undertaking of a job as late as possible (Late Commitment). Thereby we reduce the risk that job changes requested at a later time would make the work already performed useless.

1.1.6 Local Optimization Brings Global Sub Optimization

Imagine the individual activities of our unlimited push system for building paper ships were performed by a team versus just one person. With everything else remaining the same, management decides to perform a team optimization. The first two teams are chosen for the optimization to use a new process to deliver faster than before. Each week the selected teams improve their performance, their throughput increases and the cycle time decreases. Management happily pumps more jobs into the system - a reason to be satisfied with their decision. Why, however, does the cycle time of the entire system suddenly increase?

The local optimization of the teams at the beginning of the process has the effect that more jobs can be pushed into the system. As more work is shoved into the system, the amount of work in progress (WIP) increases. More work in progress means longer cycle time. If a bottleneck is present in the system somewhere (and there is always a bottleneck), it determines the total throughput of the work system. The local improvement of individual teams results in the entire system slowing down.

It is a firmly held belief in many companies that local optimization has a positive effect on the entire system. In the Agile way of thinking, the team is the focal point of optimization because the value stream consists of building a team with representatives of each required discipline. This leads to a false conclusion, because rarely can a single team cover the entire value chain. In the current theme of Agile scaling is this particularly clear: many companies wanting to become agile believe they merely need to educate their teams on agile methods to become an agile business. By no means is this true. I am a fan of the organization theorist Russell L. Ackoff from whom this timelessly valid statement stems:

> "And therefore, the performance of the whole is never the sum of the parts taken separately, but it's the product of their interactions." (Ackoff & Gharajedaghi 1984).

Unless the newest miracle work improvement weapon is currently being tested (such as Scrum or Kanban), the false belief of local optimization manifests itself often in the form of objectives for a single person or teams tied-in with bonuses or other perks. With this indirect attempt at optimization, the pressure on the work system is merely increased. In the best case, this has no effect on the overall performance of the system. Normally, however, a decrease in performance over the entire system will occur. What would the motivation be to help a colleague (in a different team or department) at the bottleneck when the team itself is measured exclusively on accomplishing their local objectives? The fact that a team is only one element along the path of producing value for a customer goes completely unnoticed. Local optimization is for me a clear case of failed vision: the understanding of the system as a whole is missing. Let's look at local optimization from the customer's point of view. For them, it is completely irrelevant if Team 1 or Team 2 works faster. Referring to the example of ship building, this form of performance improvements brings no value to the customer because a) they still have to wait for the entire ship regardless of how quickly the individual activities are completed and b) they have to wait longer for the ship to be finished because Team 1 and 2 slow down the entire system with their performance. Local optimization leads to global sub-optimization.

Perhaps you understand now why I get ruffled when Kanban is described as a team method. Using Kanban solely for individual teams or departments is, in many cases, shooting yourself in the foot. Kanban best reveals its potential when initiatives for change are removed from the team level and instead the optimization considerations are applied at the highest overall level possible (more on the Kanban Flight Level theme is discussed in section 1.4). Visualizing is a central practice in Kanban for good reason. Above all, at the beginning of a change initiative, visualizing helps to see as much as possible from the system in order to answer two basic questions:

1. How do we generate value for our customers?
2. Where do the problems lie in our system?

Had the management of our imaginary ship enterprise looked at the overall picture, one thing would have become clear: The bottleneck is the point in the process where optimizations should be implemented. In the ship experiment, the idea was proposed that a single individual was the bottleneck. In reality, the same thinking occurs. When people work in a system, then the optimizing must occur at the people level. Thus, trainings and workshops are given with the goal to make each person work faster, not the system as a whole.

Naturally a person's performance and how quickly she completes her work is based on her abilities. I have done this experiment hundreds of times on different continents with different people. Regardless of where or with whom the experiment is done (with the exception of the occasional extreme case, good or bad), the throughput is always between five and six ships per minute - much more or much less is simply not possible. Fascinating, isn't it? The result that the ship goes slower through the system does not lie in the folding skills of the participant with the final task, rather the participant has more work to do than the others, thus our work system is the problem. Not only with the ship experiment, but also in companies with which I work, I see the abilities of individual people have an extremely small effect on the entire output of an organization, unless these skills are part of a particular specialization. Looking more closely, the bigger issues are always with the work process, not with the people doing the work. The goal of Kanban is not the local optimization of individual pieces of a system, rather the improvement of the value stream from the time of commitment (Work Agreement) up through the delivery to the customer.

> **Local optimization**, in most cases, results in a decrease of performance over the entire system. To improve the performance of a system, the focus needs to be on the interactions between the individual parts.

At the end of the ship experiment, before delving deeper into the principles and practices of Kanban, I always ask participants what they can take away from this experience and what conclusions they reached. Following is a sample of the answers I receive:

- One should understand the processes used.
- Throughput is determined by the bottleneck.
- What is really important to the customer?
- Implement WIP limits and observe the effect. Base decision-making on the most suitable WIP.
- Prioritization should occur before work enters the system, not when the work is already in the system.
- Encourage and demand active management.
- Without WIP limits there is no time for improvement.
- With WIP limits, there is reduced stress with equal output/throughput.
- With WIP limits it is possible to adjust to new requirements even at a later time.
- WIP limits results in more predictable and faster cycle times.
- Even priorities need to be limited.
- The focus should be on the entire system, not just pieces of it.

1.2 Kanban: Long Live Evolution!

The goal of the ship experiment is to show the difference between the two work systems. In one system, a consistent and continuous workflow is never achieved because the rhythm is determined by external pressure. The other system achieves equal, if not better, results because it regulates the inflow of work into the system through which a continuous workflow is then established. It is an effective system, although there are many things in a flow-based system that seems counter-intuitive. Some of these we observed in the ship experiment (itself actually a flow experiment):

- We are faster, even if we are not working at full speed.
- We have enough time for work for which we normally never have time.
- We become more predictable when we set limits for ourselves.
- When everything has priority, then nothing has priority.
- The later we start the work, the better it is for the customer.
- Local optimization results in global sub-optimization.

I would like to come back, at this point, to the objection which some participants bring up during the discussion about the flow experiment. When we are talking about the use of Kanban, we are not talking about industrial manufacturing, rather about knowledge work with unforeseeable complexities. The term "Kanban" was made famous by the Taiichi Ohno designed pull system at Toyota Production System and simply means "signal card". During the assembly of an automobile, these signal cards showed that a production step had been completed and the next delivery of parts could be received. Kanban systems, however, are not an invention of the 20th Century. At the imperial garden in Tokyo, the number of visitors allowed into the garden was controlled by the use of tokens which were handed out at the entrance and collected again at the exit (Anderson, 2010). This way, the number of visitors was limited to prevent overcrowding in the garden, thus allowing each visitor the chance for enjoyment and relaxation.

Knowledge work has very little to do with tangible objects: knowledge doesn't lie around in half-finished pieces and we cannot measure the workload based on the number of people hanging out in a room. Obviously, the practices from Toyota cannot be transferred directly into the area of knowledge work, but there are system independent principles behind the practices which are applicable to every work system. Every system has limited capacity, thus limiting the work which gets started makes sense regardless if the system is new software development, manual labor activities, or industrial production. Bottlenecks, as well, exist in every type of system in the world. Whether it's the imperial garden in Tokyo, the production plant at Toyota or Kanban in knowledge work, the crucial point in each system is:

a. creating value for the customer, and
b. the desire to keep the system flexible and look for ways to continuously improve.

Kanban, in knowledge work, offers no rigid schema for process improvement, since a rigid schema is geared towards a particular delivery or output. If this were required, nobody would be successful at implementing Kanban, because no two companies or systems are exactly the same. As you remember, each work process should fulfill the customer's wishes - making each process unique - and cookie-cutter procedures do not work for unique processes. Kanban is not a pre-defined or standardized process. In knowledge work, Kanban is custom tailored to each system, allowing the flexibility to define how it is implemented, without dictating what the end product should look like. It is built upon evolutionary thinking; start with the work you do at the moment, and improve it based on the practices and principles which Kanban offers. In time, a process which is specifically tailored to the needs of the individual company, is formed.

Of course, this is completely opposite of what typically happens in a company. In an artificially initiated process improvement, someone, who often has nothing to do with the daily work processes, attempts to invent an optimal work process to keep the company competitive. As soon as the new policies are installed, process improvement is considered finished.

Principles and Practices

Kanban, however, is a bit more modest. If everything within a company was truly terrible, the company would have already fallen out of the market. As such, Kanban takes what already exists, analyses the current situation, and builds from there, without assuming to know how the employees should be working. Kanban helps discover, in increments, how work processes can be improved. When a company implements Kanban, it should be combined with perpetual reflection: what was impacted by the last improvement? Did it improve anything? If it was an improvement, let's continue with it - if not, let's try something else. Best practices, which are given as one-size-fits-all in many other methods, only occur in Kanban, if at all, in the context of an individual company. The idea of evolutionary improvement in Kanban is based on three **principles**:

1. Start with what you are doing now.
2. Follow evolutionary improvement.
3. Promote leadership at all levels of the organization.

In discussions, I often notice that for many, the term "evolutionary" sounds like a tactic for taking small steps. This is not necessarily the case. Evolutionary doesn't define how large or small the improvements need to be. Evolutionary simply means to analyze the current situation in order to understand what is happening in the system and adjust the desired degree of improvement accordingly. An evolutionary improvement can certainly involve major changes: it is possible, after the first draft of a Kanban system, that a completely unnecessary process step is uncovered and can be immediately eliminated. From the Kanban view, this is an evolutionary improvement because observing the system in its current state provided the insight for the improvement. Nevertheless, this evolutionary improvement is very profound. The introduction of visualization and WIP limits is no small undertaking. It is a significant change which must be clarified with the stakeholders (i.e. those who are directly involved or affected by the process) of the system.

Such evolving and massive improvements need to be differentiated from those which are nothing more than a repackaging of old habits under a new name. Kanban is perceived to be *the* new method to solve all problems. As such, it also is put on the drawing board and conceptualized for a "Big Bang" implementation, just as it was done for other change initiatives which have failed. Management works out a complete Kanban system and declares everything else used till now as unnecessary. They throw the new system in their employees' faces and then demand improvement with this new method. This may be done with good intention, but this is not what is meant by evolutionary improvement. Even well-intended changes, especially within rigid and hierarchical organizations, seem like control and surveillance mechanisms to the employees. Most likely, the initiators of the change are met with passive resistance. The introduction of Kanban requires the agreement of all those affected by its implementation, and is necessary for the diligent preparation of a change initiative. Further details can be found in my first book, written with Siegfried Kaltenecker, *Kanban Change Leadership: Creating a Culture of Continuous Improvement* (Leopold & Kaltenecker 2015). Designing a Kanban system with the cooperation of all participants and their delegates is an essential element of a successful Kanban initiative. Nonetheless, even these systems are not meant to be forever, and are meant only for the current state of affairs in an organization.

If the decision is made to follow evolutionary improvement, the third principle of Kanban is unavoidable: Promote leadership at all levels of the organization. I would like to share my perspectives on this principle:

1. As already mentioned, Kanban can only be successful when those directly affected are included in the initiative, and not simply dictated to. The people who are meant to work with the Kanban system need to be brought on board. This is the point we discuss in Kanban Change Leadership: How do you get those affected involved in order to create broad and stable support for the start of the Kanban initiative?

2. Evolutionary improvement only works with those people who are directly involved with the daily activities. These people know best what does and doesn't work. In some companies, employees may not feel free to speak about their observations and ideas. When Kanban is introduced, the participants need to be encouraged to make recommendations for improvement, and this functions best when there is an honest interest in their views. Otherwise Kanban quickly falls into the old paradigm of a small group of people telling a larger group of people what needs to be done.

Kanban is not a top-down approach in which management knows the best way to make improvements and directs the pertinent measures into the company. Kanban is also not a bottom-up approach. This would be no different than a top-down approach, just in the opposite direction, and this approach often fails because the superiors may tolerate the initiative, but are not necessarily convinced of its usefulness. A bottom-up approach would result in local optimization and nothing more. All levels in the hierarchy of a company should be involved in order to develop the Kanban system to its full potential. As you remember, the point of using Kanban is to bring value to the customer. Preferably, the goal is to have a consistent, flow-based system which generates value. The system should be able to show what can be improved, for the customer, during the process of completing a project, product or service. There are six **practices** in Kanban which facilitate the accomplishment of this goal:

1. Visualizing
2. Limiting work in progress
3. Managing flow
4. Making policies explicit
5. Implementing fast feedback loops
6. Driving improvements based on methods and models

Even if it sounds like a mantra, my experience has shown that the following must be continually emphasized: Kanban is nothing more than the implementation of these three principles and six practices. It is not dictated how they should be implemented - it is not even dictated that these principles and practices need to be implemented. The beauty, and perhaps for many the tricky part, of Kanban is like they say at Burger King: you can have it your way! It puts the system under a magnifying glass and clarifies what is and isn't in the best interest of the company's health. Kanban neither improves nor worsens the situation in a company; rather it, at most, triggers a reaction to something that is suddenly apparent. Whoever hopes for a never-changing and ready-to-use paradigm from Kanban should perhaps look for a different solution. In Kanban, thinking for yourself is emphatically allowed!

Let's take a closer look at the practices that can bring a flow-based approach to knowledge work.

Visualizing

In our flow experiment, when the unfinished ships piled up and the poor guy at the end of the assembly line nearly broke his fingers folding paper, it was quite obvious where the bottleneck in the system was. Problems in the manufacture of physical products manifest themselves in ways that are readily apparent, such as overfilled warehouses, poor quality, or warning signals from the machines. In knowledge work, the object of improvement is concealed in the head of the employee. The usual scenario in knowledge work is someone sitting in front of a computer and typing. What is not obvious, however, is what they are working on, why they are working on it, how long have they been working on it, how the work is going, and whether or not everything is okay. We cannot see where, in our work process, we should apply improvements, and hence, we cannot see if our work system is fulfilling the expectations of the customer. By visualizing the work, relationships in the process can be revealed allowing for better decision making.

Limiting the Work in Progress

The flow experiment vividly shows how a work system can calmly operate when the amount of work started is limited. In the flow experiment, we used a simple method to achieve a WIP limit: each activity was allowed a maximum of one item at a time. This, however, is not the only possible approach and, in many cases, a WIP limit of one may not be feasible. What is the consequence when we work in a WIP limited system? In the case of the Imperial Garden in Tokyo, the visitors were forced to wait at the entrance if all of the entry tokens were in use - the system had reached its WIP limit. A WIP limited work system functions in much the same way: eventually, the point is reached in which no new work can be started until work within the system is completed. Hence, the motto of Kanban is "Stop starting, start finishing!" The simple economic consideration is that one piece of work which is 100% completed brings more value than ten pieces of work which are only 10% completed.

Managing Flow

WIP limits are the key to establishing and controlling workflow in a system. Managing a workflow, however, starts with visualizing the activities that a product (or its parts - such as features, user stories, etc.) or service passes through when generating value. The goal of a workflow is to allow the work items to pass smoothly from one activity to the next. The instruments of flow management include not only setting up WIP limits, but also learning and interpreting the indications of a system suggested by its visualization.

It is often not readily apparent, that the workflow should even be optimized. Many times, working resources to full-capacity, or more specifically working the people in the system to full-capacity, is the objective of an optimization. If we are working under the premise of wanting to generate value for the customer, high workload is not necessarily the most sensible strategy. When all of the employees are always working, work will be completed more slowly. Do you like driving on a highway filled at 100% of its capacity? Or does your computer work best when it is running at 100% capacity? It is usually more important to the customer to receive her product as soon as possible - regardless of what percentage of capacity the employees of a company are working. Running at capacity removes the opportunity for a company to correct the weaknesses in the system and incorporate sustainable improvement. It is exactly these improvements, however, which are needed to generate value for the customer.

Regardless of what you are optimizing, you are sending a signal to the people with whom you work. Giving people space to focus on their work communicates a sense of appreciation and trust. Ordering people to work harder and micromanaging their work gives the subliminal message that those people are not working hard enough for their money. In Kanban, the workload is also considered, but generating value is the primary concern. The focus lies in optimizing the workflow and not in optimizing the people, which is why we say in Kanban: Manage the work, not the workers!

Making Explicit Process Rules

Kanban is not a process itself, but rather it is a set of principles and practices which are applied to an existing process. The target process is exactly what needs to be uncovered and written down, so everyone involved is on the same page and can work together to further improve the system. Be careful: existing work processes are governed by certain rules. Often there are official rules governing a process, but the actual process being used can look very different. The subject matter of Kanban deals with the process that is actually being used, not the desired or prescribed process.

Once the guidelines of the actual work process are uncovered and documented, Kanban–which is normally free from rules–uses the following two:

1. We hold ourselves accountable to these rules.

2. When a rule no longer makes sense, we will change it.

Only when the rules of the actual work process are followed, is it possible to determine where the problems in the actual work process exist. Conversely, it is not possible to improve a work system when the rules and processes are never changed. Making explicit rules also has a positive effect on collaboration. "You said at the time...", "He did that instead of..." - with rules in place, people quit accusing and trying to find fault with each other. Instead, the guidelines become the focus of discussions and the participants concentrate on finding a solution for the problems identified in the work process.

Implementing Feedback Loops

An improvement always implies a change, but not every change is an improvement. In order to determine the effect of a change, quick feedback from the process is essential. When in use, the first three practices of a Kanban system already deliver a large amount of information. However, there are many more possibilities for gaining information from the system. The simplest and most efficient method is dialogue, and I recommend three well-known formats for the periodic exchange of information between participants: standups (at regular intervals), replenishment meetings, and retrospectives. These will be discussed in greater detail in Chapter 2.

Measuring is another objective form of feedback. If the work system should, for example, become faster, the cycle time can be measured. If something is changed with the expectation that the system is accelerated, measuring the cycle time can confirm or falsify this expectation. The crucial point is: measuring delivers quick feedback. In Kanban, we don't speak of "lessons learned" in the classical sense of project management, where these are gathered at the end of the project. Instead, real-time information should be used for immediate changes or adjustments to the system. Feedback provided in short intervals on a regular basis allows the possibility to improve something beforehand, instead of having to repair it afterwards.

Driving Improvements Based on Methods and Models

Kanban is not dogma. There is no ultimate Kanban Bible, whose commandments are to be followed, lest you burn in Kanban hell. Kanban "by the book" would be a contradiction in and of itself (this book being the exception, of course) and, as such, anyone who implements Kanban may use any one of the abundant methods and models which exist for optimizing processes. Original thinking is absolutely allowed! The truth is, Kanban forces us to reflect. Colorful sticky notes on the wall only have a decorative value, unfortunately, if you are hoping for a miracle.

1.3 Generating Value: Thinking About Service

At the beginning of this book, I complained that Kanban is often seen as a method for improving teams. This way of thinking is geared towards optimizing people, and as such, the structure of the company (in the form of teams) becomes the focus of the improvement. Although individual parts of the company may be optimized this is not beneficial to the system as a whole–as the flow experiment in a very elementary way showed us. If Kanban is used as an organizational improvement initiative, the company will only be focusing on itself. This is not the goal - customer satisfaction is the goal. Generating value, and not perfecting the organizational structure of the company, should be the purpose of the optimization.

What do we want to achieve with Kanban? We want the customer to be satisfied. When we consider a company process from the Kanban point of view, we strive to identify the necessary steps to go from customer request to customer satisfaction, i.e., we search for the value stream in our system which provides the connection from request to satisfaction. From the outside, the customer sees the value stream as a *single* effort, or as a *single* service. A company is successful when this service functions well. If we take a closer look at the entire effort, the pieces of the value stream are nothing more than partial services which bring success to the whole system. Having said this, these services do not necessarily correspond to the organizational structure (a service does not implicitly denote a team or a department), because establishing a workflow and defining useful service units may involve several areas across the organization. Services will have different spans within the organization depending on who is receiving the service. For example, software development can provide services internally for sales and marketing. In projects that are for external customers, it may make sense to combine the individual services of analysis, software development, testing, and possibly implementation, into a single service entity in order to optimize value.

Ideally, at the start of a Kanban initiative, thoughtful consideration is given to how value is generated and for which customer, and the *current* reality of the system is explicitly defined on the Kanban board. On the Kanban board, the customer request is designated as a work item, and is followed as it makes its way through the system, in order to see clearly where the work is. The main concern is not whether the system is running at full capacity; rather the focus is on the effectiveness of the flow of the service delivery through the system. The structure of an organization only comes into play in the second step, where consideration is given to who is needed at which step in the value stream. This could be individuals, teams or other organization units. Their interactions are the purpose of the improvements, which should lead to a *workflow*. This means that the company organizes around the work, instead of trying to organize the work itself.

Let's order a few books!

Imagine you are ordering a book from your preferred online bookstore. You simply want a book. From the view of the bookstore, the question arises, how to best fulfill this request:

1. First of all, the bestselling book is procured. It is either taken from the warehouse or is ordered from the publisher.
2. After that, the book goes to the packaging station.
3. In the next step, an invoice is written.
4. Afterwards, the book is ready to be delivered and can be handed over to the delivery service.
5. Once the customer has paid, the process for the seller is complete.

A simplified depiction of these steps as a workflow could look like this:

Procure Book > Pack Book > Write Invoice > Deliver Package > Wait for Payment > Process Complete

The columns (activities) of the first Kanban board could also look like this. What did we do? We left out the organizational structure and concentrated on the flow of the book through the work system and to the customer - in other words, the part which holds value for the customer. You, the customer, just want your book and we simply uncovered and defined how this request can be fulfilled.

David J. Anderson wrote in his blog, *The Kanban Lens*, very aptly, "Looking at a current organization through a service-oriented lens and seeing services where currently people only see functions and specializations is liberating and empowering" (Anderson 2013). Thinking in units of service rather than functions or specializations is somewhat liberating. If you visualize the value stream based on organizational structures, you would quickly lose oversight and the visualization would be more of a hindrance than it would be helpful. When services are not bound to organizational units, or even to individual persons, and instead are based on activities, complexity is removed from the question of how to generate value and the answer is easier to illustrate. In addition to this practical effect, a service-oriented, structure-free view of the organization is unlocked, and leads conversations away from finding fault with one another to a more objective level of communication.

The service-oriented view makes the point quite obvious: Kanban is not a method for optimizing teams, since the term "team" isn't even used in the service-oriented view. A service unit does not necessarily mean a team. Naturally, you have to start somewhere with a Kanban initiative, and starting at the team level is acceptable if it makes sense or if nothing else is possible. When we talk about a service span, it is clear that Kanban can be used on several different levels - for this purpose I have developed a description model for Kanban that I call "Kanban flight levels".

1.4 Layers of Design: Kanban Flight Levels

As you already know, during the initial telephone contact with potential clients, I will often be confronted with the following sentence: "We would like to implement this new agile method, Kanban, in our company and with it improve the performance of our software development teams." At this stage, the inquirer and I are speaking of two very different things. The way I see it,

- Kanban is not an agile method - companies can improve their agility with the help of Kanban.
- Kanban is not a software development method - even though Kanban is often used in software development.

- Kanban does not focus on teams - even when teams can use Kanban for their purposes.

In this first personal discussion, I try to adjust their perspectives. I use the notion of "thinking in services" in order to make the point clear: "Try to see what your company does right now as a set of services that can be improved." Then it becomes clear what you can discover with the help of Kanban, namely,

- how value will be generated,
- how and why work finds its way into the system, and
- how work flows through the service units.

The focus of Kanban is always the overall value creation. The next question usually tied into this is, in which area of the company can Kanban be implemented. The principles and practices of Kanban have a key advantage: They are scalable upon delivery, meaning it doesn't matter at which level of an organization Kanban is implemented - it always delivers the same effect. Since Kanban aspires to optimize the entire value creation process of a company, ultimately leading to satisfied customers, my advice is: **Try to start as broadly as possible with Kanban**!

In these preliminary talks, Kanban flight levels are on one hand an instrument of communication with which I can demonstrate the levels where Kanban can be implemented and what effect is created at that level. At the same time, it also helps when contemplating where the current problems (for which you hope Kanban will be a solution) really lie, and at what level it makes sense, or is even possible, to start with Kanban. If you are a team leader and cannot see a way to start at a higher level, because the cooperation is missing, for instance - absolutely no problem. Just remember with your initiative that Kanban is intended for the entire value creation chain of a company and is not specifically a team method. Feel free to share this information as much as possible!

Important: Kanban flight levels are not a scaling template. Even though there are flight levels 1, 2 and 3, it doesn't mean these are levels built upon one another. The flight levels do not model a development path that an organization must follow, nor are they an instrument to test the difference between "good" and "bad" Kanban. In most companies, there exist several flight levels at the same time, either through a deliberate strategy, or because it just developed over time, which is good for a comprehensive awareness of the reality. I did not randomly choose the label "flight levels". Flight level relates to flight altitude and so it should also be understood in this context: The higher you fly, you have more of an overview with fewer details. The lower you fly, you can see more details but no longer the entire landscape.

> The **Kanban flight levels** are an instrument of communication to clearly identify the implementation possibilities for Kanban, as well as to find out where it's possible, or makes sense, to start an improvement process within an organization.

1.4.1 Flight Level 1: The Operational Level

The first flight level belongs to the team that completes the daily work. Often those who are involved are highly-specialized experts, and I encounter such teams again and again, especially in high-tech environments. These specialists work exclusively in a sub-area of an enormous system, such as the fuel-injection systems for automobiles or the graphical processing of a weather radar for airplanes. Another typical manifestation of entities at flight level 1 are cross-functional teams, such as a designer, developer and tester, who work together on a small product or subsystem. Usually a large piece of work makes its way to a team where it is broken down into workable pieces, and implemented step-by-step. Examining just this situation, Kanban can help the team visualize and continuously improve their work process. When a company consists of many teams, and not just one, the limits of optimization occur at the interface to other units and it can - as we already saw in the flow experiment - even lead to sub-optimization of the entire system. The improvements are limited to within the team, and can lead to difficulties in other teams. The biggest disadvantage is that the customer's wishes are not necessarily better fulfilled, despite the best intentions of the team. To explain this, I am going to use the keyboard as an example (Figure 1.4).

Figure 1.4: Is writing a letter improved by typing the letter A faster?

Let's assume a customer would like a letter written. Let's further assume that each team in the company is responsible for a row on the keyboard. Each team is the master of their row, but there is always room for improvement. For example, Team 3 can optimize themselves to the point of having a new world record for typing A the fastest. Fantastic! However, the customer's letter will not be written any faster because of this. When writing a letter, it isn't going about how fast you can type one single letter of the alphabet. It's more important that the correct letter is typed at the right time, in order to achieve an actual increase in performance. That's why Kanban focuses on the entire organization. The organization should be the one adjusting to the customer with an evolving process: What must be done in order to generate optimal value for the customer? If there is more than one team at the operational level, it is important to coordinate the work. It doesn't matter in which branch or which area: On the road from "concept to cash" there exists, as a rule, dependencies between the teams. Each team, or each unit, completes only one portion of the value creation for the customer. For the coordination to be useful, the value creation chain of the products or projects must first be identified. Whether an organization is agile or not has nothing to do with the number of agile teams within the organization. **The interaction between the teams must be agile**.

1.4.2 Flight Level 2: Coordination

We can look at this in terms of a typical situation in the business world. Figure 1.5 shows a value stream that I often see in some form or another in project companies. Design, development and test are just one part of the entire value stream. In most cases, the customer gets no value when tested code is delivered. The value is achieved once the code is integrated into a larger (live) system within the company. On the other hand, customers rarely specify their wishes so clearly that they can be immediately implemented. In fact, it's quite the opposite. As a rule, there is much to be done before the actual development work can be started. There needs to be leads generated and project teams drafted, the team must understand what the customer wants, contracts must be signed, etc. As soon as you take a look at the other areas, the value stream looks completely different, such as in product maintenance or in product management. Nevertheless, the idea behind it is the same: Creating value for the customer is more important than a hyper-productive team. This is exactly where flight level 2 begins.

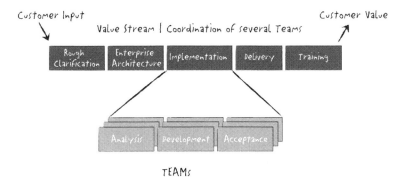

Figure 1.5: **Flight Level 2 - Coordination Level View**

Is that a waterfall?

When you look at this picture, you might have the opinion that flight level 2 is the manifestation of a waterfall-type implementation. What does waterfall development mean? Just because things are worked on sequentially does not mean you are automatically in a waterfall development process (by the way, Winston Royce described the waterfall model as an iterative process - see Royce, 1970). It is, however, a good model - such as programming software functionality before delivering it.

Working literally according the waterfall principle means work items pulled through the work flow are very large, such as a complete project. It is not expedient to first analyze an entire project, the develop it and finally implement it. This is not point I am making. Instead, the work items should be as small as possible, so you can verify the correctness of the approach as quickly as possible. This requires getting feedback as quickly as possible and be able to learn something from it.

At flight level 2, the interaction of the teams is optimized. To stay with the keyboard metaphor, at flight level 2, we ensure the right team is pushing the right key at the right time, i.e. working on the right work at the right time. Therefore, the Kanban board coordinates the work of several teams who together are involved in fulfilling customer wishes, and bring specific services into the value creation chain. The goal is to optimize the work flow beyond the team border. Kanban achieves massive performance improvements primarily for two reasons:

1. The employees work on the right things at the right time because filling the input queues is coordinated.
2. The number of work items is limited throughout, so the work system as a whole can be optimized.

Since the work flow is optimized over the entire value stream, the waiting time at the interfaces is reduced and, most importantly, the bottlenecks become clearly visible. Anyone who has experienced organizations at this flight level can only chuckle when high-performance teams are hyped as the secret to success. The larger the company, the more value creation chains there are within the company. Thus, there are more coordination boards being used.

If we look at flight level 2 from the change management perspective, initiatives at this flight level are sometimes easier than at flight level 1, even if coordinating several hundred people. The decision to work with Kanban across teams falls to higher management. That means management has to set a good example and be the change they want to see. At the same time, Kanban does not necessarily need to be implemented in each individual team at the operational level and nobody must immediately change their way of working. Whether a team uses Kanban or Scrum, or just simply works on their stuff, is completely irrelevant. The only change, if you want to call it that, is that the delegates of the teams coordinate with each other in specific meetings, typically in routine Standups.

1.4.3 Flight Level 3: Strategic Portfolio Management

Normally organizations do not work on just one project or one product. A company's portfolio is comprised of a variety of projects and products, as well as strategic initiatives that keep the company fit for the future. Flight level 3 manages exactly this mix. You want to gain an overview of what takes place in the company. You also want to know which projects and strategic initiatives are having an effect in which way, and how far the implementation has progressed. Can a new project already be started or should you wait until another project is completed? What investments should be made? Should a new market be conquered, or should an existing market share be increased? Which change initiatives are currently running in the company? This last question - what is currently running with which purpose in the company - is especially suited to be visualized on a strategy board. This way, top management can recognize if contradictory orders were given and whether or not the initiatives are obstructing one another. Such contradictions occur primarily when companies want to become agile and several consultants, with their various opinions, are working with the company. On one day, self-organization is promoted, and the next day old-school reporting is requested. At this flight level, it's going about strategic management of the entire organization and not about micro-managing the operational implementation. Large companies with offices around the globe have several strategies due to the various local market requirements, and as such, several strategy boards exist and a coordination board for all locations is at the company headquarters.

Having more demand than you are able to supply is fundamentally a good problem, otherwise a company must reduce its workforce. As a result, there is competition at the portfolio level between the options. This disparity between options and implementation possibilities must be explicitly clear, otherwise there might be an impression that there are unlimited resources available. Since this is not the case, Kanban at flight level 3 deals precisely with this issue: making prudent choices and combination of projects, developing products and strategic initiatives, recognizing dependencies and optimizing the flow through the value creation chain with the currently available resources. At flight level 3, the types of jobs being dealt with are large work items, such as "market entry in Hungary" or "less automotive, more aviation business". At this flight level, these vast functionalities and initiatives compete with one another, so the organization is forced to make a well-considered and deliberate decision about what should be completed next. The focus is no longer the goals of the individual projects, but rather the overall result for the organization. Demand and possibilities must be balanced exactly.

Figure 1.6 summarizes the flight levels at a glance. Flight level 3 is the strategic heart of the organization. The projects and initiatives of the company converge here and strategic management is located here. Flight level 3 is connected with several systems at flight level 2 and flight level 1, where the operational work is managed. The example "market entry in Hungary" at flight level 3 may only contain two tickets, "prepare product group X" and "prepare product group Y", but at flight level 2, these superficial work items will be broken down into smaller workable items and handed on to the teams at flight level 1.

It also happens quite often that work from flight level 3 flows directly to a team at flight level 1. Let's assume that our company is an auto parts supplier and the strategy at flight level 3 states "more aviation business". There is a product that is being developed for the automobile market, but with slight modification, in theory, the product might also interest the aviation market. A team of specialists take care of testing this theory, so the work item flows directly from flight level 3 directly to a specialist team at flight level 1.

As was already mentioned at the beginning of this section, flight levels are not a model for maturity or evaluation. A team problem cannot be resolved with a strategy board, just as a strategy cannot be implemented through a scattered team initiative. Nonetheless, I see similar thought processes with agile initiatives. There is a strategic problem, namely the uncertainty about how the market will develop in the future. And although nobody knows what the future brings, all the teams are made agile as a preventative measure. Agility is a strategic topic and cannot be resolved primarily at the operational level, especially in areas where it is not even necessary. If you want to make improvements in an organization, you must first be clear which level is best suited to achieve them. The flight levels should help identify the appropriate level. Generally, it can be said that the higher the flight level, the greater the leveraging effect. If there is the possibility to start with Kanban at flight level 3, you should do it. The only agile team that is needed at the start of becoming an agile organization is an agile top-management team, which carries out strategic portfolio management. Everything follows from here - lead by example.

FLIGHT LEVELS

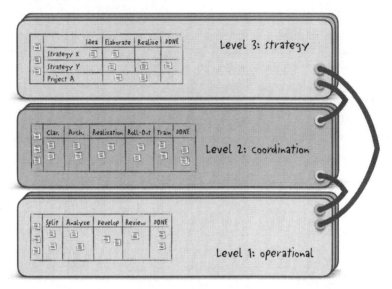

Figure 1.6: Overview of the Flight Levels

The great thing about Kanban is, even though it can be used at several levels, you only need the six recommended practices (see section 1.2) in order to start the process of continuous improvement and create a flow-based work system. Let's take a look at how Kanban systems, based on these practices, function when utilized in a company.

1.5 Summary

If Kanban should be implemented in a company, the first and most important question is: Why do we want to do this and what do we expect to achieve from it? Ideally, the motivation is to create value that is important to the customer, so the real question is: What is important to the customer? The work flow should then be modeled accordingly. If you proceed from this question, you will also see that a successful Kanban system is not built by simply implementing the six practices. Your Kanban will be successful if you have understood the insights, principles and values behind these practices.

Looking at it more closely, certain effects unfold in Kanban by using the six practices that are not always intuitive:

- Just because we work faster does not mean more work will be completed.
- We have enough time for the work we never have time for.
- If everything has priority, then nothing has priority.
- The later we start, the better for the customer.
- Local optimization leads to global sub-optimization.

If you ask yourself what creates value for the customer, you can no longer see the company as simply a conglomeration of individual teams and departments. It makes more sense to think in terms of services or sub-processes - from placing the order to delivering to the customer - that generate a portion of the value for the customer. Services can have different ranges, so it makes sense, at the start of a Kanban initiative, to take a look at which level, or "flight level", you can implement it. In principle, there are three flight levels:

- Flight level 1: The operational level
- Flight level 2: Coordination
- Flight level 3: Strategic portfolio management

The greatest leveraging occurs at flight level 3, because the initiatives at this level are authorized by upper management. The interactions and dependencies between teams and departments can be managed at this level, in order to create a customer oriented value stream. Try to start as broadly as possible with Kanban.

Literature

(Ackoff & Gharajedaghi 1984) Russel Ackoff & Jamshid Gharajedaghi. *Mechanisms, Organisms and Social System*, In Strategic Management Journal, Vol. 5, 289-300 (1984).

(Anderson, 2010) David J. Anderson. *Kanban - Successful evolutionary Change for your technology business*, Blue Hole Press, 2010.

(Anderson 2013) David J. Anderson. *The Kanban Lens*, Blog article, October 18th, 2013, http://www.djaa.com/kanban-lens

(Deming 2000) W. Edwards Deming. *Out of the Crisis*, The MIT Press, 2000.

(Leopold & Kaltenecker 2015) Klaus Leopold & Siegfried Kaltenecker. *Kanban Change Leadership - Creating a Culture of Continuous Improvement*, Wiley 2015

(Ohno & Bodek, 1988) Taiichi Ohno & Norman Bodek. *Toyota Production System - Beyond Large-Scale Production*, Productivity Press, 1988.

(Rother, 2010) Mike Rother. *Toyota Kata - Managing people for improvement, adaptiveness, and superior results*, McGraw-Hill, 2010.

(Royce, 1970) Winston W. Royce. *Managing the development of large software systems*, Proceedings of the IEEE WESCON, p. 1-9, August, 1970.

2. Using and Improving Kanban Systems

2.1 Visualization, WIP Limits and Work Flow

I am fascinated, again and again, by the unbelievable creativity that is put into visualizing work flow on a Kanban board. When people see what and how much they actually do the whole day, and how all tasks are connected to one another and together form a valuable result for the customer, it often sparks an impressive dynamic. Those involved begin to understand, that this board shows a plethora of information about their work system, which they can use to further improve it. Of course, I also see boards that do not fulfill this purpose and are slowly forgotten, because their owner doesn't know what to do with it. Surprisingly, this is rarely the failure of the Kanban board. The owner simply doesn't know how this tool works and what they should pay attention to in order to get useful information from their board. I would like to bring out a few points that often will be misunderstood and weaken the significance of the board.

This question sounds trivial: What do you actually visualize in Kanban? The automatic answer to this question is, "I guess it's the work I do." As such, we find many so-called Kanban boards that look like the one in Figure 2.1.

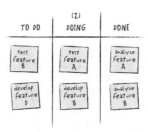

Figure 2.1: How a Kanban Board Should *Not* Look

Why does such a board lead to nowhere, at least when you are pursuing the goal of evolutionary improvement? In the context of Kanban, you could use a board with the columns To-Do, Doing and Done when you only need to retain an overview of your own tasks and wish to see little success stories. This could be called Flight Level 0 or Personal Kanban - Jim Benson and Tonianne DeMaria Barry have written an award-winning book about this (Benson & DeMaria Barry, 2013). From Flight Level 1, such boards are no longer helpful. When the work system of a service should be brought into the flow, the individual activities, through which a value-creating piece of work travels, need to be made visible. These activities can be specifically described. As such, Visualization begins with considering which, and in what order, the activities in a service are carried out in order to create value. Let's label them A, B and C to begin with (see Figure 2.2). The columns of the board are derived from these activities, and in reality, should be labeled with specific activities, such as "Develop", "Deliver", etc. The next thing to consider is: "Which task are we specifically working on at the moment?" This question produces the individual units of work, which are then placed into their respective activities as tickets.

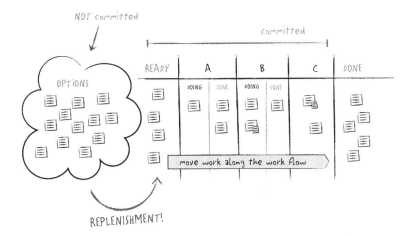

Figure 2.2 Kanban Board Showing Activities that Create Value

At the very left of the board is the *Input Queue*, which is sometimes labeled "Next" or "Ready", depending on your preference. Ideally, the column label states exactly what the item of work is ready for, such as "Ready for Development". In this column, all items of work to be completed next, are gathered. It is the waiting room for items of work that, in the course of a Spice Girls meeting, have already been put into a sequence. All other ideas or wishes, which could be implemented at some point, are initially placed in an Idea or Option Pool, and the Spice Girls decide if and what gets implemented. I deliberately label this collection tank as Option Pool, because they are future opportunities whose pros and cons must be considered before they can definitively be implemented. Only then do they migrate as pieces of work into the Input Queue. This means, all work in the input queue and in the activities, have already received a confirmed commitment. When these committed items of work arrive in the final column, value has been created for the customer. I wouldn't necessarily label this final column as "Done" or "Completed", because the entire value is not automatically created just because a process is (sometimes temporarily) completed. It's better to consider the entire value stream, including customer delivery, and find a label that signals the next step in the process. Additional services can connect to this column and could be labeled "Ready for ...", such as "Ready for Customer Approval", implying the customer could still give feedback.

What else should be visible? In most work systems, problems and obstacles arise, that can slow down the work flow. The activities where these problems occur should be clearly documented. In Figure 2.2, these blockades are illustrated by little stickers on the tickets in columns B and C (these stickers are typically red). In the same way, stickers in a different color can be used to show that work in a particular activity is already completed. Only when that has happened - and this is the important point - can the work be pulled, when resources are available, into the next activity. Remember from the Flow Experiment, raising your hand signaled that work was completed and ready for the next activity. Kanban is a pull, rather than a push, system. Another way to visualize this is to break down the individual columns into "In Progress" and "Completed". Compared to the otherwise completely invisible activities in knowledge work, a small amount of material can already make so much visible. At this point, it can already be seen

- how the work flow looks.
- where the individual pieces of work are currently at, i.e. how far the work has, in total, progressed.
- which work is to be completed next (Next column).
- which ideas and options exist.
- which blockades are present in the work flow.
- what the reason is for these blockades.
- which work has been completed.

2.1.1 Working with WIP Limits

Kanban is not just a pull system, it is a WIP limited pull system. This means, the amount of work in the system is limited. In the ship folding exercise, I placed a WIP limit of 1 for each folding activity (on a board, it would be columns). It is only allowed to have one ship in each activity at a time - regardless if it is being worked on or not. Limiting the amount of work in an activity is one possibility, which I will use in the next pages, to demonstrate the effect of WIP limits. The basic idea of WIP limits applies to the entire work system, which means the number of work items on the board will be limited.

Let's not ask ourselves, yet, how we are going to find the right WIP limit. Let's assume, for demonstration purposes, that we already have found a suitable limit per activity. Above each activity, we write down the corresponding WIP limit (see Figure 2.3). In each column, there should only be as many work items as the WIP allows: two in Activity A, three in Activity B, and two in Activity C. In the input queue, there should also be a limited amount of work items - in the example, the limit is four. What's important here, is that WIP limits apply equally to blocked work items, as well as work items that are waiting in the Finished column of an activity. One of the two work items in the Working On column in Activity A (WIP limit of two) must be either removed or returned to the input queue, because the finished ticket in column A is not a license to pull the next piece of work in to Activity A.

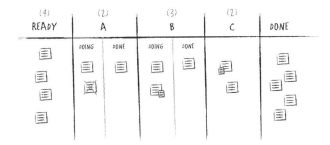

Figure 2.3 WIP Limited Kanban Board

In my day-to-day consulting work, I often see on the Kanban

boards, where the Finished columns in the individual activities are exempted from WIP limits. What happens then? It's simple: In order to enjoy the benefits of WIP limits, the *entire* system must be limited. If you take the Finished column for the individual activities out of the WIP limit, you once again have an unlimited system, and work will begin to back up. This is exactly what happened in the push round of the ship building exercise. Only one ship at a time can be folded in each activity, but there could be an unlimited number of ships piling up. The only thing that remains limited is the degree of multitasking, because there is not an unlimited amount of work allowed in the Working On column. A workflow cannot be accomplished in this way and this cannot be described as a WIP limited system.

How does a WIP limited system work?

I would like you to think about this shortly, before I discuss it further. Here is a little exercise for you. Take a look at the following board:

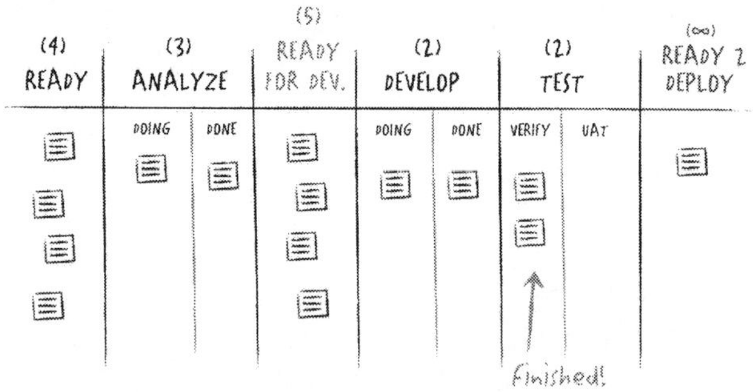

Figure 2.4 How does completed work affect the system?

In Activity C, there is a completed task. This completed work could be moved to the final column. What effect does this have on the rest of the system?

Activity C has a WIP limit of (2). As soon as the completed work in Activity C is moved to the last column, there is space for replenishment. A task can be pulled, since Activity C has a WIP limit of (2) and one item of work is currently blocked. This pulling propagates itself from right-to-left over the entire system (see Figure 2.5):

- The task in the Finished column of Activity B can be pulled into Activity C.
- Activity B, with its WIP limit of (3), has space for the completed work in the Finished column of Activity A.
- Thanks to the space freed-up in the Input Queue, the Spice Girls can get busy again, and decide which item of work gets to be placed in the waiting area.

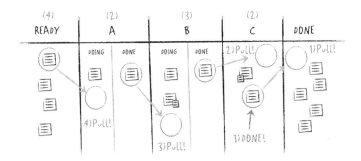

Figure 2.5 Chain Reaction from Pulling Work: Work is Pulled Out of the System

Figuratively speaking, in an unlimited push system, work is pushed into the system from the left. In a WIP limited pull system, by contrast, work is pulled out of the system from the right. For a Kanban system, this means we do not pay attention about the task that could be started on (from the left), rather we concentrate on what we should and could work on (at the right), in order to finish a piece of work. It is only possible to start a new work, when other work has left the system. Stop starting, start finishing!

What can WIP limits offer?

When I work with my customers in a system design workshop, and draft the first Kanban board together, I ask them to place all the tasks, which are currently being worked on, in the individual activity columns. In doing so, a very informative picture of their actual situation is formed. In Figure 2.6, you can see how a Kanban board looked, with a ten-person development team.

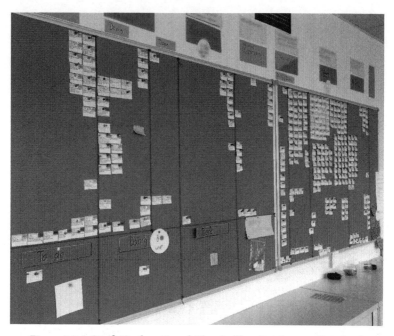

Figure 2.6 A Draft Kanban Board Clearly Showing System Overload

In this picture, you can plainly see what the flow experiment demonstrates so spectacularly time and again. It doesn't matter how much work gets started, because a bottleneck in one of the activities will hold up all of the work. If you don't stop continually starting new work, a wall will gradually be built, that nothing can pass through. This is the advantage of visualization. A slowing down of the system, that is often felt as an uneasy gut-feeling in knowledge work, becomes tangible through visualization. Finally, it is crystal clear where the problems lie. The development team, from this example, no longer needed to discuss or speculate about issues after their work was visualized.

After the initial shock of discovering the presence of such a problem, I turn the discussion towards the topic of WIP limits. Often, the reaction is: "You want us to work less? Sure, tell that to our boss, not to us." That's certainly not necessary. The point of WIP limits is not that you should work less. The point is there should be less work in the system. When a system is so overloaded, even a team of ten people are not capable of working on everything all at once. What this board, and no other board in the world, can illustrate, is that people are not capable of working on many things at the same time. The myth of multitasking has been shattered, and active multitasking does not exist. Can you work on two different computers at the same time, with full concentration and one hand on each computer, and write something useful? What people accomplish, in the best case, is changing continuously between several tasks (task switching). As such, you work first on one task, put it aside, work on a completely different task, put it aside, work further on a third task that has been sitting idle for a few days, put it aside...and rotate perpetually between these pieces of work. If you would like to illustrate this on a Kanban board, the active and inactive work items within each area need to be separated (see Figure 2.7).

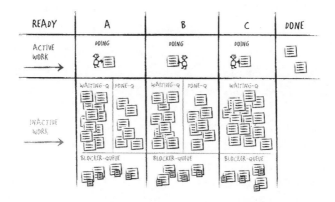

Figure 2.7 Task Switching, as Illustrated on a Kanban Board

In the inactive area, all the pieces of work which are worked on in turn, could be placed in a multitasking queue (MT-Q). Throughout the day, a piece of work is pulled into the active area and worked on, then returned to the MT-Q. The next ticket is pulled into the active swim lane and the process repeats. Naturally, some tasks can't be worked on because they are blocked. These also get parked in the inactive area. Rarely is anything pulled out of the Finished-Q column, because everyone is also multitasking in the next step. It can be a while from here, so there is a lot of inactive work lying in the Finished-Q column. The illustration that you see here is very realistic. A large majority of work in a system is inactive work. Only a fraction is actually being worked on at any given time.

Currently, companies like to measure everything possible. In this context, let's measure the flow efficiency. Flow efficiency is the amount of time a piece of work is in the active area of the board, as part of the entire cycle time (see active work in Figure 2.7). Let's illustrate this with an example.

Take a guess

Assume that it takes ten days for an item of work in the system shown in Figure 2.7 to go from activity A to the last column, Completed.

- What percentage of time is spent in active work?
- What percentage of time is spent in inactive work?

The answer to both of these questions is: It depends. Basically, it depends on how much work is in the system. The more work there is in a system, the larger the divergence between the amount of inactive and active work. The board picture is based on a real-world example, and this team actually measured their flow efficiency. Get ready to be astonished. The amount of active work was 1.4 percent. This means, when a customer waited 100 days for their piece of work to be finished, the team, on average, had worked actively on the task less than 1 ½ days. The rest of the time, the work was somewhere in the system sitting idle.

In most cases, the percentage of active work, as part of the cycle time, amounts to around five percent. If you can manage 15 percent, you are doing really well. In light of these numbers, how much sense does it make to constantly say "Work faster!"? The only thing accomplished by saying this, is using a lot of effort to gain a small percentage in speed. Meanwhile, the real potential lies in a completely different area. Once again, we turn to William Edwards Deming, who emphasized the largest gains in productivity result from improvements to the system. This means working smarter, not harder (Deming, 2000). "Smarter" in this case means, if you want to complete work faster, you must allow less work in the system. Nobody needs to work faster. In Kanban, it isn't going about achieving a high-performance "whatever". Let's free ourselves from the desire to optimize individuals. With Kanban, a system can be built, in which work can be completed quickly. This is completely different than just working faster.

Thanks to John D.C. Little, this can also be mathematically proven. According to Little's Law (which we will see again in Chapter 4), the average cycle time can be calculated by dividing the average work in progress (in a system where work items continuously arrive) by the average throughput.

$$\emptyset CycleTime = \frac{\emptyset WIP}{\emptyset Throughput}$$

Cycle Time
> the amount of time an item of work spends in the system

WIP the number of items of work in the system

Throughput
> the number of completed items of work in a given time frame

Although Little's Law is a formula, it's not rocket science. I like to call Little's Law the Sausage Formula. Imagine you are standing at a Viennese sausage kiosk (Würstelstand) and are looking forward to enjoying a delicious Käsekrainer (cheese-stuffed sausage - that's my favorite anyway). Six people are standing in line in front of you and you see that the charming gentleman running the kiosk serves, on average, two people per minute. When do you get your sausage? You guessed it - in three minutes. If eight people are in line in front of you, it's no surprise, that instead of three minutes, you will need to wait four minutes until you get your sausage. That is Little's Law - healthy common sense.

If we transfer this example into our working world, the following situation could occur. Assume that right now, ten items of work on the board are in progress (WIP = 10). Everyday, five items of work are completed:

$$\frac{10\ items\ of\ work}{5\ items\ of\ work\ per\ day} = 2\ days$$

The average cycle time of ten parallel items of work in the system is two days. When suddenly 20 items of work, instead of ten, are on the board (WIP = 20), the average cycle time increases to four days. If WIP sinks to five, the average cycle time is one day. **Less WIP means shorter cycle time.**

This can also be graphically illustrated, as shown in Figure 2.8. Assuming there are three pieces of work to complete: A, B and C. If you would work on these, one after the other (WIP = 1), task A would be finished after 5 days, task B in 10 and task C after 15 days. This also means you can immediately bill for the work completed. If all three tasks were started at the same time (WIP = 3), this doesn't mean that all three will be worked on. More likely, this will result in task switching. There will be, again and again, a little work done on A, then on B, and finally on C. The consequence of this approach is, that A will be finished after 13 days, B after 14 and C after 15 days. You have a choice: With higher WIP, all work will be finished later, and with lower WIP, only some work will be finished later. WIP limits give an additional decision-making possibility: Which work will be allowed into the system first, and which work later, in order to prevent a bottleneck in the system?

Figure 2.8 also shows that delivery risk is reduced when you work with WIP limits. Let's assume there is a delivery due on day 12. In the second scenario (WIP = 3), on day 10 or 11, there will be a short-term eruption of panic and you will try to work some magic, so at least one piece of work will be finished, even if it is poor quality. In the first scenario (WIP = 1), we already have two pieces of work completed after 10 days.

It should be noted, however, that these considerations are based on the assumption that task switching is free. This is not the case! Continuously switching, from one piece of work to another, means there is time needed getting into the new task. The result is, as in the second scenario (WIP = 3), work will be finished later.

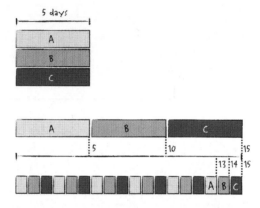

Figure 2.8 Effect of WIP Limits vs. Task Switching

2.1.2 Value and Flow

At the beginning of a Kanban system design, often the most difficult question to answer is: Which activities create value for our customers? If you do not want to avoid this question (and I hope this is the case), then do not simply label your columns "To Do – Doing – Done". In the next step, the question is: Which activities will become the column labels and which work items become tickets in the individual columns? Put another way, what do you want to visualize and what do you want to limit?

Value Stream

In Kanban, we talk about a "sequence of value-adding activities"

- the keyword being "activities". To find the column label for the Kanban board, we must search for the activities performed, one after the other, whose synergy generates value for the customer. These sequences are, of course, different for each company. Value streams are also not limited to just IT and software development areas, rather they can be found in many areas of the company.

Examples of Value Streams in various Areas

Software Development
> Analyze -> Develop -> Integrate -> Test -> Roll Out

Engineering
> Make Hypothesis -> Build Model -> Test -> Evaluate -> Learn

Personnel Department– Filling an Open Position
> Get Approval -> Advertise Position -> Review Applications -> Arrange Interviews -> Decide

---

As can be seen in these examples, individual activities may not be particularly "valuable". For instance, in the scope of the entire hiring process, advertising for an open position does not generate value. However, it is a key element in the process of finding an adequate employee. When looking at it as a whole, it is an essential activity for creating the overall value. It's also important to remember, there are no cookie-cutter solutions to determine these activities. Value streams from different companies could be similar, but they will never be completely identical.

Kanban is focused on activities, and this is reflected in the column labels. It's best to use verbs when modeling the work flow, such as using "Develop Software" instead of "Software Development". This makes it clear, that the columns on the board should not be viewed containers for specific employees or special areas. They represent something that, on the way to the customer, has to be done. This type of thinking is difficult in many companies, because silo structures have been pounded into employees' minds. One of the Kanban principles says, respect the situation which is currently found within the company. Kanban doesn't have an extreme tactic to help people overcome silo thinking. Using verbs is a good start, for gradually freeing yourself from this type of thinking. The phrasing leaves the decision open, about who is involved with the software development - perhaps the assistance of testers or analysts will be needed at some point. The Kanban board manages, in this case, to show the points of teamwork between existing and possible silos.

Creating Value vs. Working on Tasks

If the sequence of activities in a value stream has been identified, the first flow-based system can be depicted on a Kanban board. It could look something like Figure 2.9.

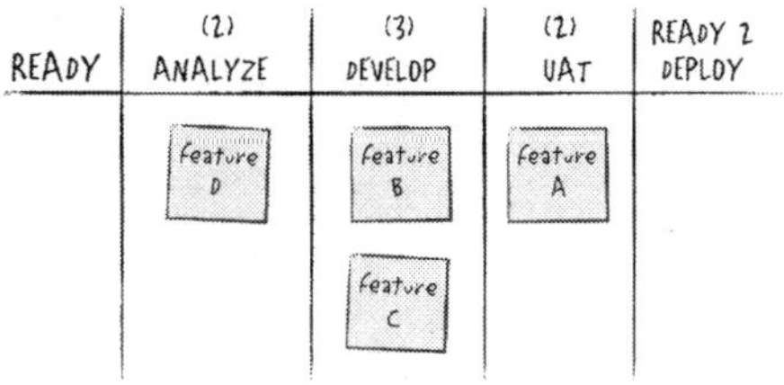

READY	(2) ANALYZE	(3) DEVELOP	(2) UAT	READY 2 DEPLOY
	feature D	feature B	feature A	
		feature C		

Figure 2.9 Value Stream as a Sequence of Activities

Perfect - the columns show actual activities. Features, which are currently being worked on, are hanging as items of work in the columns. As I said at the beginning of this chapter, often Kanban boards look like the one in Figure 2.10.

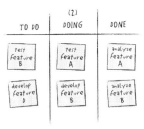

Figure 2.10 This is not a Value Stream!

This is just a to-do list in column form, not Kanban. For organizing your individual work, this description might be sufficient. For larger undertakings, however, it has absolutely no use. What is the essential difference in the effectiveness of these two boards?

Looking at Figure 2.10, we see the board does not focus on the creation of value. It gives the impression, that completely independent activities should be worked on. However, the activities in the value creation process are very connected. The focus on "start finishing" is essentially lost. Value gets created when a feature is completed in its entirety. On this task board, for instance, the To-Do column could contain the task "Analysis for all Features". Wonderful, except there is no value created with this task. The task board doesn't show how far value creation has proceeded. It's entirely different on a "real" Kanban board. The further to the right of the board a feature is found, the closer you are to having created value.

What is written on a ticket?

When the columns of a Kanban board represent the sequence of activities for value creation, it's natural to ask about the tickets traveling through the columns. They are sometimes referred to work items, work objects or simply just work. Previously, I have always referred to them as **work items**, and will keep this convention.

Work items are entities that create value that have gone through all the necessary activities, and are completed or ready to be worked on in a different part of the value stream. In software development, these can be features or user stories for a product. In other areas, it could be a hypothesis in an experiment, or the job advertisement from the personnel department. Work items can also be allocated to specific categories, know as work item types or work types. Computer Scientists would say a work item is the specific instance of a **work type**. For example:

Work Item Type
> Feature

Work Item
> Implement Login

Work Item Type
> User Story

Work Item
> As a user, after starting the application, I would like to see the last files worked on, to save time.

In order to implement a work item, they typically are split into individual tasks, and labelled as such. Let's use a travel website as an example. A feature on this website - a specific usage, which creates value for the customer - could be:

Search for an X-day vacation between Date A and Date B

The tasks needed, in order to implement this feature are:

- Map out the user experience
- Implement the front end
- Implement the back end
- Database

- Security

In this example, none of these individual tasks themselves create something usable for the customer. When all the tasks are completed, though, the feature is complete and the value (or a part of the value) is created. Coming back to the point, this is depicted on a Kanban board when work items are the tickets. In a flow-based system, the number of tasks is not necessarily limited, rather the amount of value-generating work items (the feature, in the case of the travel website) is limited.

2.1.3 Dealing with several Work Types

Depending on the area of responsibility, there can be several work types in a Kanban system. Activities are depicted by columns in the Kanban system, but not every work type necessarily passes through each activity. How can this be illustrated? The simple solution is swim lanes. Figure 2.11 shows such a Kanban system. The work types of Features, Changes and Production Failures (failures that were discovered in an already active system) were assigned their own swim lane.

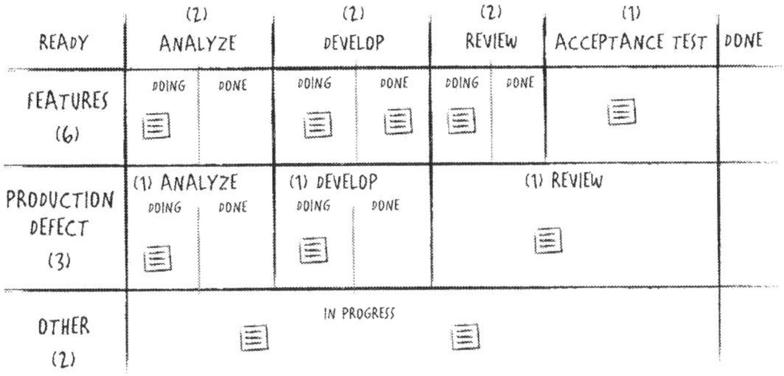

READY	(2) ANALYZE		(2) DEVELOP		(2) REVIEW		(1) ACCEPTANCE TEST	DONE
	DOING	DONE	DOING	DONE	DOING	DONE		
FEATURES (6)	🗐		🗐	🗐	🗐		🗐	
PRODUCTION DEFECT (3)	(1) ANALYZE DOING ¦ DONE 🗐		(1) DEVELOP DOING ¦ DONE 🗐		(1) REVIEW 🗐			
OTHER (2)	IN PROGRESS 🗐				🗐			

Figure 2.11 Kanban Board with Swim Lanes for Different Work Types

Since these work types run through different activities, WIP limits could be given to each swim lane, in order to steer the work flow. Let's try this out with an example. The scenario I imagine, could be about a new product being brought to market. Initially, all planned features will be developed and rolled out in a Beta version. Gradually, user feedback starts coming in. At this point, the work will not be reserved exclusively for features. It also includes changes to the product needing to be integrated, and bug fixes needing to be resolved quickly. To depict our new work situation, we can use WIP limits to steer the work flow. The WIP limit for the Features swim lane will be reduced, while the WIP limits for the Changes and Production Failures swim lanes will be increased.

Looking at it more closely, the Ready column is not yet ideally modeled. In the current illustration, it's not obvious which piece of work will be pulled into the system next, once a piece of work is completed. It would probably depend on what is more important or, at the very least, in the chronological order the tickets entered the Ready column. In this case, you must have very clear and defined rules about which ticket can be pulled and when. There is an easier way, though. To keep an overview, three individual Ready swim lanes can be transformed into a single Ready column for all work types to be gathered (see Figure 2.12). You can define a rule, that says the top ticket must be pulled next.

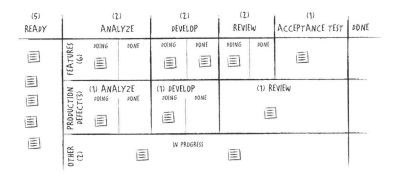

Figure 2.12 A Merged Ready Column

2.1.4 Changes to Work Types over Time

Kanban system operators do not always realize work types can change within the work flow. Most only realize it when a Kanban system is being designed. These changes can be visualized, though, especially on Flight Level 2. For example, when you give a feature to be worked on into the system, it doesn't go through the entire work flow as a feature. It splits itself along the way into other work types.

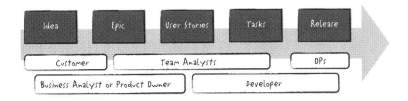

Figure 2.13 Progression of Work Types

Such a change could look like the example above (Figure 2.13):

- A stakeholder has an IDEA.

- The decision is made to implement this idea. It gets transformed into a structured form of the requirements description by business analysts or product owners. Usually this will be one or more EPICS.
- As soon as this epic progresses to development, it will be tailored into USER STORIES from the analysts and worked on piece by piece.
- Development teams split the stories into TASKS, that are worked on the team board.
- When some user stories are completed, they will be built into a RELEASE. If user acceptance tests are done (which are, ideally, not placed at the end of development), they correspond to the release, rather than the individual user stories.

If you think in terms of a Kanban board, there could be columns at the very left labeled "Analyze Idea", then "Develop and Test Epic", and finally "Roll out Release". An individual team, working at Flight Level 1, would not see these work type changes. They work solely on user stories, and at most, split the stories into tasks.

Hierarchical Work Types

As already mentioned, a work item is any entity creating value. For example, in IT or software development, user stories have value. Tasks, on the other hand, do not directly create value for the customer. WIP limits help establish work flow, but what is limited in a Kanban system with various work types?

WIP limits are primarily used on value-generating work items, not on individual tasks. In principle, tasks shouldn't just be completed quickly, rather there should be value creation. Tasks can also be limited - it makes sense to steer work into ordered channels. When tasks are limited, however, we are concerning ourselves with the level of local optimization and personal productivity. WIP limits at the task level should help individuals and small teams to focus, which is a case of Personal Kanban (Benson & DeMaria Barry, 2013). In contrast, if we concern ourselves on the three Kanban flight levels, we are primarily dealing with systems and must be mindful, that work flows as smoothly as possible through the system. Think back to the ship folding experiment. It was clear, in the experiment, that individual performance was not the decisive factor for the flow of work through the system. Limiting tasks for each individual would also not have helped. It's necessary, at the very beginning, to prohibit too much work from entering the system and eventually flooding it. What would a Kanban board with limited hierarchical work types look like?

Theoretically speaking, you should not eat an elephant, but if you would need to eat an elephant, you wouldn't do it with one bite. An elephant is best eaten piece-by-piece, as we can see in Figure 2.14. The first work type to be limited is the elephant itself. There are three swim lanes available, so there could be a maximum of three elephants being worked on at the same time. To digest the elephant more easily, it will be split into pieces. This column has an infinite WIP limit, because it is impossible to know, how many pieces the elephant should be split into. These pieces wander across the board, until they have gone through all necessary activities and are collected in the column "Waiting On", to be consolidated into a complete package "Elephant" again. When the last piece in a swim lane lands in this activity, the ticket "Elephant" will be attached and the complete package is ready for delivery (to a restaurant or refrigerated storage). This is *one* example, how large pieces of work, with the help of a Kanban system, can be implemented. You split the large piece into several small pieces and limit both parts. Another example: Books are comprised of chapters, which are split into sections. Or, for instance, products are made up of features, epics and user stories, and themselves consisting of tasks. Depending on the number of hierarchies, tasks could be stapled to the backside of tickets, or you build an extra task board to track their completion.

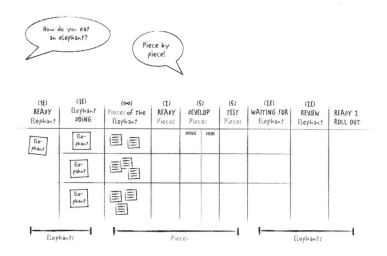

Figure 2.14 Limiting WIP Using Swim Lanes

By the way, the following always applies to a Kanban system:

- There is little effect, when the number of tasks are limited, but not the number of user stories.
- There is little effect, when the number of user stories are limited, but not the number of epics.
- There is little effect, when the number of epics are limited, but not the number of projects.

Generally speaking, the larger the limited item is, the larger the leverage effect. The large items must be cut down as small as possible, in order to receive quick feedback. If the number of user stories is merely limited at the team level, and an endless number of projects are started, the project will not be finished quicker despite the user story limit. This doesn't mean there can't be anything done on the other levels.

2.1.5 Unplanned Work

When developing a new product, everything is wonderful up to the point when it goes live or goes to market. All eventualities cannot be tested ahead of time, and not all failures can be found. After a certain amount of time, failures, suggestions for improvement, or support questions pop up. How can you illustrate these in the Kanban system? These pieces of work, often occurring under time pressure, cannot be planned. Failures do not occur adjacent to planning meetings - they need to be fixed when they come up. The difficulty is when unplanned and planned work collide with one another. The more unplanned work enters the system, the later planned work will be completed.

Unplanned work is not horrible - it is what it is. With all the uncertainties in knowledge work, you will never be able to completely prevent it. Having said this, the existence and amount of unplanned work in the system should be transparent. With this knowledge, the amount of planned work the system can handle can be better quantified. The unforeseeable issues will not cause the system to become turbulent. As with the visualization of various work types, partitioning planned and unplanned work on the Kanban board into swim lanes is also possible (see Figure 2.15).

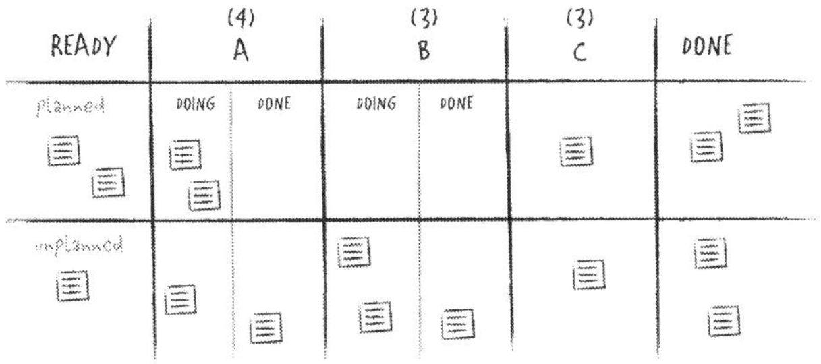

Figure 2.15 Incorporating Unplanned Work on a Kanban Board

With unplanned work being visible, the percentage of unplanned work, as part of the total amount of work in the system, can be measured. Based on this measurement, the amount of planned work can be adjusted. For example, unplanned work is disruptive in settings where work is performed using the principle of time box (such as Scrum teams), because they cannot successfully complete their sprint. Let's assume a Scrum team knows, through past measurements, that they complete ten tickets in a sprint when nothing else comes up. The team then measures the amount of unplanned work over a few weeks and find three to five unplanned pieces of work must be completed in each sprint. At the next planning meeting, the team will simply commit three to five fewer tickets than before.

Is this handling of unplanned work especially Kanban-like? Does it only function with Kanban? From my point of view, it doesn't matter what a method postulates when there is a series of events that can burden a work system, or cause turbulence for a certain time. It's more important to develop a pertinent approach. You can deny reality and claim there can be no failures - then swim lanes are redundant. This is when you go around and look for people to blame. Neither the denial, nor the blame game, will bring improvements. The principles and practices of Kanban simply state: Understand your work by making it explicit.

Making unplanned work visible helps work flow overcome unforeseeable events, and visibility shows when something is not functioning as it should. How you deal with it is completely up to you.

2.1.6 Definition of Done

One question comes up again and again when designing a Kanban system: What determines if an activity should be illustrated as a column on the Kanban board? My answer is: A ticket should spend some amount of time in a column - this is a good indication of it being an activity. If tickets only spend ten minutes in a column each day, this only provides exercise, since you constantly have to run to the board and move tickets around. In the case of visibility, this over-visualization has no advantage, because the column is not strategically relevant. On the other hand, attention should be paid when a ticket stays in an activity for a very long time. If there is no discernable flow, then this indicates this activity on the board needs to be split up.

When you build your Kanban board and simulate real world situations with it, you may also observe shuffling before it is put into operation. Shuffling is when tickets jump back and forth between two steps. When a ticket constantly goes back to the previous activity, it is safe to assume that the process has been defined too specifically (see Figure 2.16).

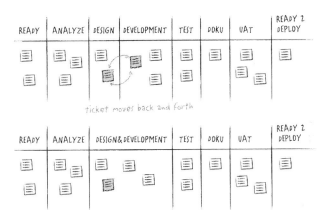

Figure 2.16 Shuffling Tickets

In the top part of the picture, the tickets shuffle between the design and development steps, because the development finds out, over and over, that design work is still needed. Most likely, these were never seen as separate activities before, so they should not be artificially separated on the board. The two activities involved can simply be put together into a single activity.

It's possible you discover an iterative process between several activities. Let's assume in our example, this is the case between design, development, test and documentation. If work is constantly moving between and repeating these four activities (possibly in various sequences), it makes sense to put these four steps into a single activity, "Development", before continuing with the process (see Figure 2.17).

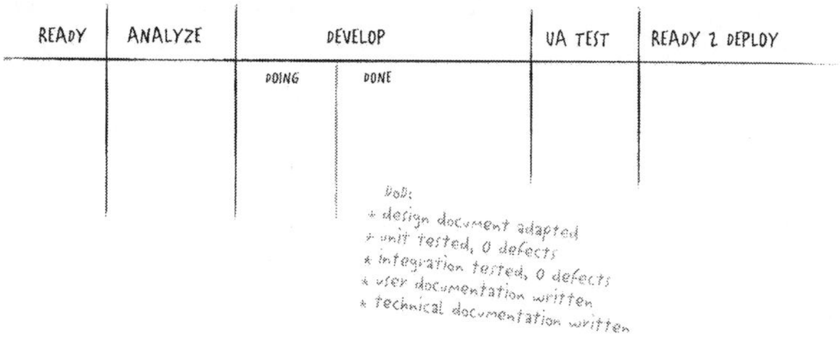

Figure 2.17 Summarization of Iterative Steps

For these considerably extensive activities, a Definition of Done (DoD) should absolutely be defined. The DoD can simply be a checklist which hang above or below the column. In our example, the Definition of Done could be:

- Design document is adapted
- Unit test is completed, 0 failures
- Integration tests completed, 0 failures
- User documentation is written
- Technical documentation is written

The **Definition of Done** describes which result must be delivered by an activity, so a ticket can go from "In Progress" to "Completed". All sub-activities must be completed before the ticket may progress along the board. It is a standard for clarifying the individual parts. You achieve a common understanding about how work in a particular system functions.

Is the Definition of Done unalterable? No. As with any rule formulated and clarified in a Kanban system, the Definition of Done can also change and adapt. According to our exemplary Definition of Done, if the design document was not adapted, there are three possibilities:

1. The document will still be adapted.
2. The rule will be crossed out of our Definition of Done.
3. It's going about an exception.

For a one-time exception, there is nothing more to be done, other than documenting this occurrence to avoid an unresolved conflict with the Definition of Done. It's another case, however, when the exceptions start piling up. It's possible the rules have changed and the Definition of Done should be updated (see the section on Blocker Clustering).

In everyday work, I see the most diverse variations of the Definition of Done. Scrum teams, for instance, decide the specifications for marking a product increment as finished in each sprint. In the same way, every individual process step could have DoD specifications determined. Since Kanban uses input queues (the column "Ready" in Figure 2.17), the opposite variation of DoD - Definition of Ready - is recommended. Definition of Ready describes the prerequisites to be fulfilled, so the Spice Girls can take the next task from the idea pool and hang it in the "Next" column. Is a terse three-liner description enough, or does the task need to be worded as a user story? Do approvals need to be obtained? Is certain equipment needed? The Definition of Ready is not only a checklist, but also a medium for communication between Stakeholders and Performers.

2.1.7 Summary

Visualization is one of the central practices of Kanban, because it makes the value stream, through which work items must travel, visible. That is why a Kanban board does not consist of the three columns "To do – Doing – Done" (this would be a task board), and instead consists of individual activities that show the steps creating value. These activities have specific descriptions, such as "Analyze", "Develop" or "Test".

Within these activities, as well as for the entire Kanban system, capacity limits are determined - the so called **WIP limit**. The quantitative limitation of work allowed to be in the system at any given time, has the effect of work being completed before new work can be started. As a consequence, task switching–the perpetual jumping between tasks - can be avoided. WIP limits do not mean less work should be done. WIP limits mean working in an orderly fashion and preventing an overload in the system ahead of time. The less work actively in the system, the shorter the cycle time.

Single **work items** (tickets) move through the value stream, depicted as individual activities (columns) on the Kanban board. Work items are entities that create value for the customer when they are completed or progress to another part of the value stream. Work items can also be split into categories, known as work types. A value stream is composed of several work types, which could change in the course of creating value. WIP limits, in a flow-based system, will always influence the amount of value-creating work items.

The **Definition of Done** serves as a guideline for completing all necessary work steps within an activity. It describes the result that must be delivered by an activity, in order to consider a work item completed. For those involved, it provides a common understanding about how work in the system functions.

2.2 Dealing with Blockades

2.2.1 Blocker Clustering

What can happen when you work with WIP limits? WIP limits have the pleasant effect of managing, controlling and, above all, improving the workflow. They ensure that there is a controlled inflow of work into the Kanban work system. Once work has entered the system, WIP limits can show where problems within the workflow exist. Let's look at Figure 2.18.

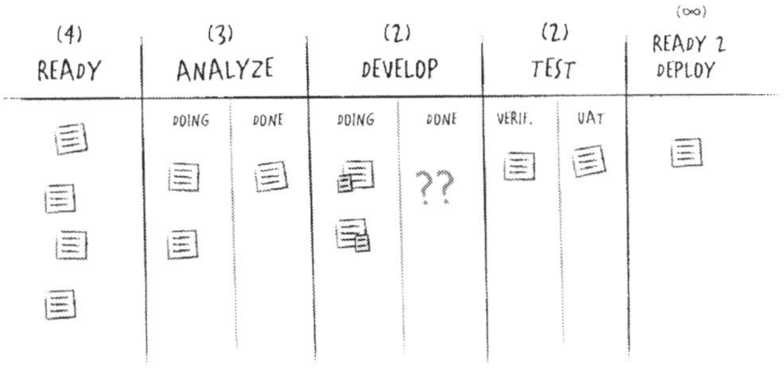

Figure 2.18 Workflow Standstill due to Blockades

In the activity "Developing", two work items are currently being worked on. Or perhaps better said, they are not being worked on, as you can see the blockade stickers on the tickets. The column "Analyzing" has a WIP limit of 3, and has a completed piece of work that could be pulled into the next activity. That is, it could be if there wasn't a blockade in the next activity, and with its WIP limit of 2, already full - a valid state when working with a WIP-limited pull system.

A **blockade** is an unforeseeable occurrence resulting in a piece of work that can no longer move forward in the workflow.

How can you act on this information being sent from the Kanban board? Recognizing the information is the most important part. You can follow any number of strategies - in any system, those involved must find a compatible strategy (Leopold & Magennis, 2015).

- *Increasing WIP limit:* Who says 2 is the correct limit? When the workflow stalls, you can easily set the WIP limit to 3! The finished ticket can be pulled out of "Analyzing" and things are moving again.
- *Ignoring blockades:* Blockades will simply be excluded from the WIP limit. In this case, there are actually two spots available in "Developing".
- *Improving:* We solve the blockade and try to learn something from it.

A thoroughly positive approach is behind the "Increasing" and "Ignoring" strategies: Despite the blockade, you want the employees to be able to work on other things. However, following these solutions is naive precept of hope, i.e. if we look away long enough, maybe the problem will just solve itself. The WIP-limited pull system states very clearly, though: **"You have a problem in your work method. Fix it, before you start new work."**

If you are already working with a Kanban system and have observed, over a longer period of time, blockades emerging, you might have noticed something: It is not dealing with a singular event. Most blockades popping up again and again have the same, or similar, form - they have a systemic cause. **Kanban does not cause these problems, it simply makes them visible.**

Companies that have recognized this, not only resolve the blockades, but also take a closer look at what is behind the blockades. Doing this is quite simple: Instead of throwing away the blockade stickers once the blockade has been cleared, the stickers are collected on a flipchart. Then, in regular intervals, the stickers are analyzed in order to uncover the actual causes of blockades that continually occur. In addition, the activity where the blockade occurred is noted on the sticker, as well as how long the blockade was active and the cause for it. By doing this, the costs of the blockade can be quantified by measuring the cycle time delay (see Chapter 5). It's also important to describe the cause of the blockade in such a way that it can be understood a few weeks later. Personally, I also write down the activity where the blockade emerged (for example, in the activity "Testing").

The crucial point to understand is that you can systematically learn from the blockades. Improvement meetings are an example of how you can get to the bottom of the causes. The blockade stickers collected on the flipchart can be grouped into clusters of related topics. Based on the descriptions, it should be easy to determine the blockades - from an overall perspective - that cause the largest delays (Figure 2.19).

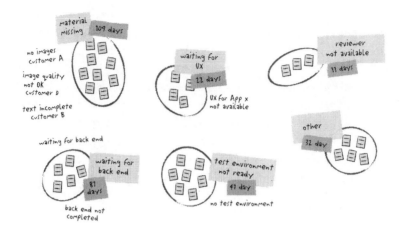

Figure 2.19 Blockade Ticket Clusters

In this example of a web project, the cluster "Missing Material" stands out. The waiting time for photos and text from the customers was 109 days. Instead of jumping straight in to find possible solutions, you can try to understand the problem first. This is best done by asking "Why?" over and over again. The following chain of causation could be revealed:

Q: Why is content constantly missing?

A: Because the customers do not send us the pictures and text.

Q: Why are the customers not sending us the pictures and text in time?

A: Because they often do not know we need them.

Q: Why do the customers not know, what content we need?

A: Because we do not always tell them.

The cause of the blockade becomes clear. What could be an ingenious solution? We always tell the customers beforehand that pictures and text will be needed - a large portion of the 109 days of lost cycle time could already be saved. To be more exact, using this example, the customer discussions in the analysis phase could be expanded to include the point "Material". When taking a closer look, it was determined that the emphasis in the analysis had been placed on technical details. Thus, discussing content with the customers, or reminding them at an earlier time to deliver the content, wasn't even a part of the work process. To make this into a routine, this point was added to the Definition of Done.

Working with WIP limits makes blockades clearly visible. Getting to the bottom of blockades has a desirable effect: Nobody needs to work faster. The reason behind most blockades is actually a problem in the work process, and not a problem with the speed of work. Resolving these systemic causes is more suited to getting work flowing again.

Deliberate Violations of Policy

One of the practices of Kanban state: "Make rules explicit." The Definition of Done or setting WIP limits are examples of such rules or policies. Sometimes, though, the circumstances are such that certain points in the Definition of Done cannot be (or in some cases, must not be) fulfilled or WIP limits will be exceeded. The conscious decision is then made to not follow the rule.

If you want to continue developing your work system, it makes sense to also note these policy violations, and their reason, on the ticket. These can be collected later, along with the blockades and defects, and analyzed. If the same (conscious) policy violations are occurring again and again, it may be time to consider adapting the rule.

When is a blockade a blockade?

If a business analyst needs information from the customer and the customer does not answer their phone, is that already a blockade? From my point of view, such unanswered calls belong to the career risks of business analysts. As such, it would be excessive to count a singular event as a blockade. When waiting on an answer from the customer takes weeks, however, this is definitely a blockade. It's recommended to determine exactly the cause of a blockade.

Influencing blockades - buffer. External blockades are often accompanied by the difficulty of having only a certain degree of influence as to when the blockade is resolved. In some areas, this can be influenced through Service Level Agreements. In many cases, though, another way needs to be found to soften the blow of these external variabilities (irregularities/inconsistencies). It's clear that external blockades would eat up the WIP limits of a Kanban work system. The entire workflow would be blocked if you wait until the external blockade is resolved, because no other tickets could pass the blockade in the meantime. In Kanban systems, you can help yourself in these situations by building parking lots on which the blocked tickets can be temporarily placed. However, these offered spaces should be limited to a realistic size that reflects the amount of variation based on experience. Otherwise the unfinished work would pile up and the parking lots becomes a black hole. Looking at it from a flow perspective, the parking lot is a buffer that absorbs the external variabilities (irregularities/inconsistencies). In an ideal world, the WIP limit of the buffer would never be reached, because you deal with it at a certain point in order that work in the active area does not get jammed up. The goal is not to let blocked tickets completely disappear, rather that you start working in a timely manner to resolve the blockades. In this way, you may increase the overall WIP in the system, but accept this for a smoother workflow.

Blockades from an external workflow. A special form of external blockades is found when work leaves your system as planned and moves to a different location. For example, work is passed on to developers who are located in a different area. Strictly speaking, this is not a blockade, because the cooperation with the developers is part of your workflow. You can also model a buffer for the affected work, although using WIP limits will be more difficult. The work completely leaves your system, because it will be developed further at a different location in a different system. You have absolutely no control over how long it takes for the work to return to your system. The downside is that it is nearly impossible to assure a smooth workflow. Until now, I have been unable to find a satisfactory solution for this all-to-often occurring situation. In this case, the most important thing to do is discuss establishing an overall workflow with your remote colleagues or development partners. We understand this as scaling.

The blockade is a bottleneck. Let's look at the scenario in Figure 2.20. Two tickets can be found in activity B "Done", and in activity A there is one ticket in "Done". Nevertheless, the ticket from A cannot be pulled into activity B, because the column limit would be exceeded. In order to continue working, you could increase the limit in activity B to three. It's worth taking a look at the other activities beforehand, though. In activity C, the work is stagnating. Instead of increasing the pressure by raising the WIP limit in activity B, an improvement for the system would be to assist the colleagues in activity C. When the work in activity C is completed, the work in activity B's "Done" column can be pulled into activity C, and activity B pulls the next piece of work from activity A. Then the work starts flowing again. It could be a one-time occurrence, but it's recommended to keep your eyes open. If completed work repeatedly backs up in an activity, there is a high probability of a bottleneck in the next activity - this is how you recognize bottlenecks in a Kanban system. It's important to pay close attention, however. Perhaps a colleague from activity C is currently on vacation; then this is simply a temporary bottleneck and it doesn't require extraordinary measures.

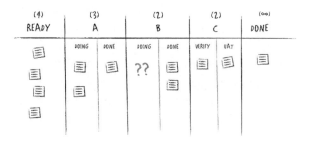

(4) READY	(3) A		(2) B		(2) C		(∞) DONE
	DOING	DONE	DOING	DONE	VERIFY	UAT	
📄							
📄	📄	📄	??	📄	📄	📄	📄
📄				📄			
📄	📄						

Figure 2.20 The blockade is a Bottleneck

2.2.2 Dealing with Backflow and Defects

Imagine yourself sitting in your car in the morning, and puttering slowly along towards work on a completely jammed three-lane interstate. Suddenly, there is honking, blinking and rude gesturing. An accident has occurred in front of you, and at the same time, cars coming from the on-ramp are pushing into traffic without paying attention to what's going on (Figure 2.21).

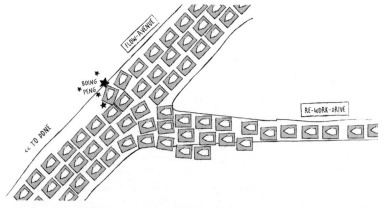

Figure 2.21 Failure - the Wrong-Way Driver in the Work System

Blockades are not the only disturbances that could interfere with the flow in a work system. Failures in the production system (production failures) cause the biggest mess. These are pieces of work that were considered completed and delivered, but then go back to the start and make another round through the system. This naturally slows down the work that should be started, or is currently in the system, and could generate value for the customer, if it would be completed.

At this spontaneously occurring cross-road, where current work and already completed (but defective) work collide, a business decision must be made. Should value for the customer be generated (for example, in the form of a new feature), or should things that have no value for the customer (defects), be worked on? Incidentally, I regularly hear the argument: "But there is enormous value for the customer when a defect is fixed!" I highly doubt that. The customer orders functionality, not defects. At least I've never met a customer that said: "Build me these three features into the software, and add to it these three bugs." By the way, support requests are production defects in most cases. There wouldn't be support requests if previously delivered features weren't defective or unsuitable (because the user interface is not intuitive, for example). The unpleasant message is: **Whoever wants to be faster needs to focus on quality**.

To put it another way, the focus on quality means that the amount of production failures - the reworking of already delivered features - must be reduced. The more production failures present in the system, the longer it takes for actual value-generating work to move forward. In practice, however, the exact opposite strategy is often followed. When the deadline is quickly approaching, but it's looking like there is no chance that the project will be completed soon, they forego testing (which, by the way, is in the wrong place at the end of a project). Foregoing testing in order to be faster makes about as much sense as donating blood in order to lose weight.

When the work system is constantly bombarded with production error issues, it makes more sense to visualize them on the Kanban board accordingly and separate rectifying defects from the actual value-generating work. Figure 2.22 shows such an example: The board is divided into a swim lane for new, value-generating work and a swim lane for production defects. Both swim lanes share, however, a single, limited input queue ("Ready"). Exactly at this point, the Spice Girls must make a conscious business decision about how many new features, as well as how many production defects, move up the input queue. This visibility activates a healthy common sense that often gets lost in knowledge work because of a lack of material tangibility. There needs to be a balance between revisions and new work, otherwise creating value will, sooner or later, come to a standstill. Production defects do not simply wiggle their way through the system without impacting the performance of the system. If you thoroughly document this situation, you again open up the possibility to learn from the situation. So, you collect the production defect tickets in a blocker cluster.

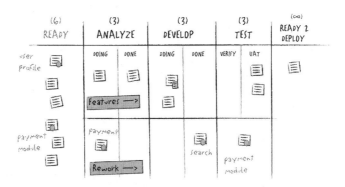

Figure 2.22 Making Production Defects on the Kanban Board Visible

Defects: Rivers do not flow uphill

Let's assume a defect appears in a feature during the "Test" activity. I would designate this case as a production defect, since the feature has not yet been delivered to the customer. Instead, it's dealing with fixing a bug based on test results (I will denote bugs primarily as defects from here on). In my work, I encounter two equally counterproductive reactions:

1. *Suppression:* Testing reveals one defect after the other. After everything has been tested, the ticket, along with its 34 defects, is simply viewed as closed because the testers have completed their work. The 34 defects are subsequently dumped into the input queue of the Kanban system as new work again. I would say to this: Something is only really completed when the customer can use it unrestricted! Cars, for instance, are not delivered without doors and motors.

2. *Deferment:* Depending on where the defect occurs, the ticket is sent back to the respective activity. It seems logical, but it contradicts the idea of workflow. A river does not flow uphill, thus work in a flow-based system can also not move backwards! This spontaneous reaction to defects arise from silo thinking that is deeply anchored in many companies, and it can rarely be overcome right away when you begin working with Kanban.

The following applies for both cases: The Kanban board is a medium for coordinating beyond the silo boundaries. The people who could get the ticket over the finish line meet regularly in front of this board to coordinate the specialist fields, and together create value for the customer. Defects are neither new work, nor do they have a free ticket to go against the direction of the workflow. Instead, the ticket - just like a blockade - is provided with a sticker signaling that a problem must be solved together. Only when the defect is corrected, the ticket can proceed to "Completed" or "Ready for ...".

The occurrence of defects is often documented differently than the occurrence of blockades, but defect tickets could also be collected and clustered, to grasp the root of the problem. Defects are nothing more than blockades. A reliable method is to designate the defects with a different sticker color from the other blockades. Then you have a visual pre-clustering before moving on to a more exact partitioning and analysis of the cause. Just as for the blockades, these stickers should note which defect occurred, when it was identified and when it was fixed. Or, you simply note the corresponding ID from the bug-tracking system.

With this simple method, all phenomena that disrupt the workflow (blockades, production defects and defects) will be visible till the next retrospective (Figure 2.23). In software development, defects are traditionally corrected, but that is also the end of the story. Rarely is the question asked: "What must we do that the defect no longer appears?"

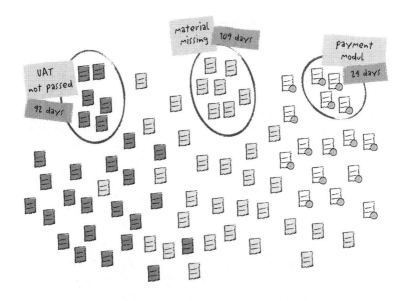

Figure 2.23 Collected and Clustered Production Failures, Blockades and Defect stickers

Just like blocker clustering, a root-cause analysis should also be performed for production failures and defects. Again, it's going about first understanding the problem and doing the preliminary work to discover why the problem occurred, before looking for solutions:

> Q: Why do we fail the user acceptance tests?
>
> A: Because the customers are not satisfied with what we deliver.
>
> Q: Why are the customers not satisfied?
>
> A: Because there is a discrepancy between what they want and what we deliver.
>
> Q: Why is there a discrepancy?
>
> A: Because ...
>
> etc.

Possible solution: After the analysis, conduct another review of the requirements together with the customer, developers and testers.

So, you have collected blockades and defects. You got to the bottom of the problems and have found solutions to them, in order to prevent workflow disturbances in the future. You have a bunch of steps that you could use - which one do you implement first?

2.2.3 Prioritizing Solutions

Naturally, it makes the most sense to deal first with the blockades and defect clusters causing the largest delay. Or perhaps not? Unfortunately, it's not that simple. Some causes are too complex or too expensive to be sorted out quickly. Other blockades could be upstream from a bottleneck - if the blockade is resolved, faster flowing work could possibly exacerbate the bottleneck situation and the flow comes to a standstill more quickly. What seems intuitively useful is quite often anything but useful, because we ignore the long-term and side effects and instead reflexively deal with it:

- People tend to work on those things that are closest to them and can be controlled by them. As an individual or team, you solve your immediate problems, without considering the consequences for others.
- Large, exceptional problems are intuitively perceived to be more important and are quickly resolved, despite this problem not necessarily occurring again in the foreseeable future.
- Endorphins! We love them, and when we solve a problem quickly, we get an endorphin rush. As such, we prefer simple problems because we understand them and can show results more quickly.
- The newest problems always seem to be the most important to us, so we solve them first. Anything that has been sitting around loses its sense of urgency, even when that is factually not the case.
- The costs for resolving issues are either considered equal for all blockades, or just the opposite, that the rectification doesn't cost anything.

Even when certain blockade clusters particularly stand out, you should not let your gut feeling take over, and instead approach it systematically. A system of cluster prioritization helps free you from a biased, gut decision and allows you to find the greater benefit. Your best bet is to sort the clusters in three steps:

1. Work on clusters that obstruct the flow of the system
2. Consider the effort to solve the problem in relation to the value of solving the problem
3. Bring economics into play

Work on clusters that obstruct the flow of the system

In a Kanban system, the following three blockade clusters were identified and the activity where they occurred was determined (Figure 2.24):

- In the analysis phase, the UX results must repeatedly be recorded. In the observation period, it accumulates a total of 22 days.
- In development, the already well-known problem of customers not delivering content, or not delivering on time, arises - this creates 109 days of waiting time.
- As soon as it goes to testing, the test environment is often not yet ready. This causes a delay of 41 days.

Going on first impulse, everyone would want to immediately solve the content problem since waiting more than three months for content really increases the cycle time. But as I like to say: It depends! It depends, looking to the right of the Kanban board, on what effect solving the content blockade would have.

Right now, most of the tickets are sitting at "Finished" in the "Analyzing" and "Developing" activities. Resolving the blockades there first would allow a pile-up to happen more quickly. The work in these activities are finished even faster and increase the pressure on the "Testing" activity. More pressure does not mean the work will be completed more quickly. Since the test environment is not ready at the right time, it leads to congestion at the end of the workflow - this is the point where the workflow is hampered.

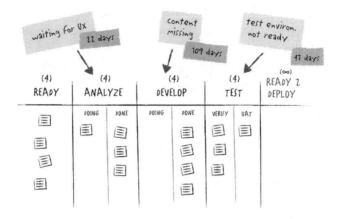

Figure 2.24 Which activity restricts the flow of the system?

Keyword "currently": A Kanban board is always just a snap-shot in time. Observe, over a longer period of time, if an activity continually hampers the system, or if the restrictions are just caused by current conditions. A cumulative flow diagram can help - see Chapter 4 and, foremost, "Actionable Agile Metrics for Predictability" by Daniel S. Vacanti (Vacanti, 2015) - its progression shows if a situation repeatedly occurs based on recurring patterns.

By the way: Giving attention to the flow-constricting points in the work system first does not mean leaving other blockades unresolved! Blockade clusters first occur when blockades are resolved, and blockades must be resolved! A retrospective inspection relates to the accumulation of phenomena that presumably have a specific cause - these causes must be ascertained and resolved, and this is where flow-constricting points have priority.

Consider the effort to solve the problem in relation to the value of solving the problem

Ideally, at the end of the root-cause analysis of blockade clusters, there is a solution for the underlying problem. Some solutions require more time and resources than others, as well as being more difficult to implement. In order to find out what you should start with, based on the available resources, you can compare the individual solutions in a 3x3 matrix. Let's assume, for example, that three blocker clusters are identified and the following solutions have been found:

- For the already familiar problem of missing content, which costs 109 days of cycle time, expand the Definition of Done to solve the problem - the customer would be informed ahead of time that content is required.
- It became apparent that 87 days were spent waiting on the backend. An acceptable solution would be to combine the backend and frontend teams.
- And lastly, the urgently needed Reviewer X is unavailable - 11 idle days is the result. The next step is to arrange a discussion with him on how to change this.

Three problems, three solutions - which is difficult to implement and which is easy to implement? Which brings greater benefit, which a lesser benefit in comparison? In order to get a clear picture, you can form a 3x3 matrix contrasting the difficulty level of the solution (solvability) to the time "costs" caused by these blockade clusters (Figure 2.25). Each company individually defines the meaning of solvability difficulty levels "easy, moderate, difficult" and dimensions "long, medium, short" amount of blocked time.

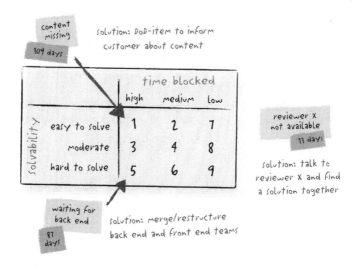

Figure 2.25 3x3 Matrix to Compare Effort and Benefit of a Solution

Which solution should be implemented first? Preferably the solution to the blockade cluster that takes up a lot of time, but whose cause is easily repaired (1). The solution with the lowest priority is the one where the blockade cluster takes up very little time and the cause is difficult to resolve (9).

You might be asking yourself how exact the dimensions of the matrix should be defined. Do you need an exact determination of the day and hour, which is a huge waste of time? No, please! Do not put too much energy into perfection that is not necessary. This matrix is simply a tool with which you and your colleagues could use to develop an understanding of a problem and its solution. The amount of time taken up by blockades can be easily quantified. The difficult part is defining the solvability. A reorganization, like the one needed in the backend team example, cannot be implemented overnight. Having a talk with Reviewer X, in comparison, shouldn't be so difficult, assuming they are not completely anti-social.

Bring economics into play!

We have found the solution to the problem of the failed user acceptance tests using up 92 days (see Figure 2.23). After the analysis, requirements will be reviewed together with the customers, developers and testers. On the Kanban board, this means nothing more than adding a column between "analyzing" and "developing" (see Figure 2.24). Sounds simple and uncomplicated.

Having said this, when we include this review step in the Kanban system, it means the cycle time for all work items increases since all must pass through the review. Higher cycle time means the product reaches the market later - the time-to-market increases, as well as the cost of delay (see Chapter 5). However, the cycle time decreases for each work item that has had to repeat a few laps when failing the "Test" activity. The time-to-market improves for these work items, as does the cost of delay. In addition, there is less expenditure for correcting the defects. On the other hand, there is an increase in expenditure for the reviews in which the developers and testers should take part. The additional review step, from the quality perspective, undoubtedly makes sense. But does it also economically make sense?

The only choice is to quantify the various expenditures with a monetary value - not so easy, since the various dependencies and the related effects from these measures are very complex. In every company, there is information either already available, or can be generated, on which assumptions could be based (see Chapter 5). Again, it's not going about an absolute exact calculation, but using estimates to understand these measures have a cost, and approximately how much. You make decisions that are based on a consideration of economical effects versus being led by impulse. As such, there is no getting around developing models.

With concrete examples, assumptions about the increase in cycle time due to the review step, as well as the cost of delay, can be made. The "baseline" model is the 92 days caused by the failed user acceptance tests. Three simple scenarios can be played through:

What is the effect when 25, 50 or 90 percent of the failures are found in the review step and not sent through testing, but conversely increases effort for developers and testers during the weekly review? Assume weekly throughput of the system is currently ten work items, and the review is scheduled for every Tuesday. Not including the weekend, the cycle time per work item increases, on average, by 3.5 days. At the same time, the developers have freed up resources that were previously needed for rectifying test issues, which can now be invested in actual development. The entire system becomes faster because throughput in development increases. A portion of the developer's available time resources are also committed to the weekly review, depending on how long the review should take. One hour? Then the time expenditure is negligible. Besides the question of how much these specific savings yield, the question of at which point these savings are beneficial arises. Perhaps 25 or 50 percent savings carries no benefit, but 70 percent suddenly brings a lot. Maybe it makes more economic sense to resolve a different blockade cluster, instead of implementing the review step. Doing comparisons is vital.

Just with these deliberations, the complexity of economic considerations becomes clear. When using these considerations, you decide the level of complexity. Even less complex models can give you reference points which help in the decision-making process. It's enough to calculate three models: baseline (the current situation), 50 percent and 100 percent savings. If you want substantially more parameters and dependencies, it is a good idea to use an appropriate software that can simulate and calculate the various scenarios (for example, KanbanSim from Troy Magennis: http://focusedobjective.com/kanbansim_scrumsim). Whether through your own mathematical talents or by using software, all of the players should understand the economic effects in terms of a monetary amount, and that gut feelings and politics are poor advisors for making decisions.

I think it's becoming clear that it pays off to think about everything that goes into a solution. It may also be clear to you, that you should consider whether the three steps of prioritization of the Kanban system are suitable at the team level. The effort for economic considerations at the team level has little value in relation to its benefit. In traditional environments, such decisions are the job of the project leader, i.e. (project) management. Savings of a few days in a small team have almost no impact on the overall picture in a large company. However, if the savings are spread over hundreds of employees at the program level, we are quickly talking about saving a significant amount money per week. Economic considerations at this level could provide powerful leverage.

How often should blockade clusters be evaluated and analyzed? That depends on how many blockades occur. When you analyze the blockades every two weeks, you probably can't form a comprehensive cluster. When you wait too long, many problems have probably resolved themselves, but not always to your advantage. Not to mention, the employees can no longer remember most of the context, even when there is essential information noted on the blockade sticker.

I have had good experience with four to six week cadences. Usually, there have been enough blockade stickers collected in this time frame and the recollection of the causes is still relatively fresh. If too few or too many blockades have accumulated, you can adjust the cadence. Retrospectives are a suitable structure for analyzing blockade clusters. At the team level, all the team members should naturally take part. At higher flight levels of Kanban, or in scaled environments, team representatives, along with program managers and/or project leaders, take part.

2.2.4 Interview with Matthew Philip

Matthew Philip is Director of Agile Coaching at Asynchrony in St. Louis, Missouri.

Klaus: In which context, do you use Blocker Clustering?

Matt: My organization develops customized software for our customers. That is why there are more than 30 small, cross-functional teams for various domains, from health care to retail, products for mobile apps, up to large system integrations.

Klaus: In real-world Kanban systems, there can be different perceptions defining a blockade. How have you defined it in your organization?

Matt: I recommend each team to find the definition which fits for their respective context. But, I also give the team a standard definition, which I borrowed from "Kanban From the Inside" (Burrows, 2014) by Mike Burrows: "A blockade is an abnormal condition, that prevents already committed work from moving forward." This usually requires an answer to the question: "Where does our commitment point lie?" I, for instance, would not consider an item blocked when it is still sitting in backlog. One of the teams I worked with had, when they were just starting, put the stories as blocked each time they went to lunch. I pointed out to the team members, that lunch was not an abnormal condition.

Klaus: When blockade clusters form, which clusters pop-up the most?

Matt: Within the two large categories "internal and external blockades", we often see clusters such as "dependent story", "missing requirements", "environment not available" and "product owner not available". The first attempt from a team to identify the largest cluster had the description "unknown". That was the incentive for the team to be somewhat more exact the next time they were writing down the blockades.

Klaus: Which methods have you embraced to work on the cause of blockades?

Matt: In one case, the cause of the largest blockade-cluster was an internal problem. We used the Fishbone technique to get to the root of the problem and found several possible solutions. In another case, the external cluster was attributed to a customer. The team made the customer aware of the cost of these blockades and asked if this was acceptable to the customer - the team gave the customer the information, so that the customer could make better decisions.

Klaus: What were your insights?

Matt: First and foremost, blocker clustering helps a team, above all else, to think about the ramifications of blockades. Many people see blockades simply as a nuisance, and not as a source for process improvements. Secondly, clustering emphasizes that blockades have a cost. In the case of a customer, whose product owner was never available, it wasn't clear to all those involved that this caused large delays and the team did not repeatedly send reminders just for fun. Quantifying such blockades by number of days quickly creates a greater understanding of the impact to your own company. Many teams occupy themselves extensively with the high-value and large work items, but forget that, in the end, blockades will strongly influence delivery and predictability. Blocker clustering helps them to recognize systemically caused blockades and to take them into account, or completely avoid them, in the future.

Klaus: Which improvements have you observed?

Matt: As with any technique, blocker clustering can only show where the problem lies and help quantify it. It's the team's responsibility to use the information accordingly. One team, for example, was struggling with interdependent story blockades. As a result, the idea to select the work differently emerged, by placing WIP-limited feature swim lanes on the Kanban board. At the organizational level, blockades emerged, which sprawled over several teams involved with the stories, that were not finished for development. So, we started a discussion in management about team structure and whether or not new, or different, roles were needed within some teams. Blocker clustering can trigger improvements on many levels.

2.2.5 Summary

Blockades are unforeseeable phenomena that disrupt, or could disrupt, the flow of creating value. Included are, for example, delays due to dependencies, defects, process violations, support requests or production failures. These blockades are uncertainties that harbor potential risks - these risks are visible through blocker clustering.

Work items that currently cannot be worked on due to a blockade are normally marked with stickers. These stickers can become an important source of information and learning when you record when, why and how long a blockade occurs. The stickers are collected and evaluated at regular intervals. As a first step, similar blockades are collected into clusters. In the second step, you attempt to understand the problem behind the blockades based on a root-cause analysis and then find a solution for it.

Often, several blockade clusters occur. This begs the question about which solution should be implemented first to achieve the best effect for the work system. Since people are biased when prioritizing solutions, it makes sense to implement the prioritization in three steps, based on objective criteria:

1. Work on clusters that obstruct the flow of the system
2. Consider the effort for the solution in relation to the benefit of the solution
3. Bring economics into play

When using these considerations, those who can influence a Kanban system through their decision-making need to have a common understanding about the effects of a solution. These considerations are, especially at the program level, an effective aid for making decisions based on sensible economic viewpoints, thereby optimizing overall value creation.

2.3 Customer Validation

Is work really finished when a ticket passes through the last column of a Kanban board? For the time being, yes. But there is still the customer. As soon as they have evaluated the work results, tested them, implemented them and used them extensively, the response will probably be: "All well and good, but I see the following problem...". A Kanban system is incomplete as long as it only considers the internal view of the work. The order is only truly completed when the customer is satisfied.

For a Kanban system, this means offering a process, or intermediary step, completely dedicated to the customer. This validation step visualizes the fact that there will most likely be feedback from the customer within a given timeframe and, as such, additional work may be needed on the order. What would happen without this intermediary step? If the order would be classified as completed and leaves the Kanban system, the customer's change requests go to the back of the line, because other work has been started in the meantime and is making its way through the system. The customer feedback, which should be an integral part of the order, is made into an exception instead of the rule. As a result, the complexity and cycle time of the work system increases. Handling customer feedback as an exception - through intervention by internal politics or impeding other important work - is also detrimental to good customer relationships. From the customer viewpoint, the promised value has not been completely generated. As long as their product (project, service, order, ...) cannot be used in its entirety, it simply has no value for them. The validation step makes sense for two reasons:

1. Instead of feedback being handled as an exception, it becomes a normal part of the work process. The customer order is fully completed and this supports positive customer relations.

2. The Kanban system retains its predictability, because the potential work in the closing phase of an order is a part of the system (Figure 2.26). Thus, the validation step must be included in all the measurements being used for the Kanban system.

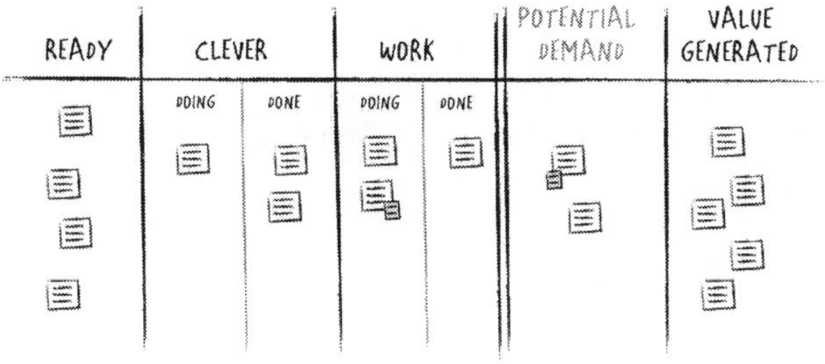

Figure 2.26 Integrating Customer Validation

By the way, "customer" does not exclusively mean external stakeholders. Validation steps also make sense when there are dependencies between teams or organizational units within a project, whose feedback affects the workflow.

There are two models that I have come across in practice for integrating the validation step in a Kanban system:

- There is a very good customer rapport where the customer actively gives feedback and the validation step is explicitly stipulated with the customer. To make a parallel comparison to Scrum, this step comprises the review. Having said this, if a failure is discovered in the review, a new ticket will not be opened, because correcting the failure is part of the process. Naturally, if the customer becomes "smarter" in the meantime and new requirements arise, these will be entered into the system at the beginning as new user stories.

- There is an impersonal customer relationship and you do not expect feedback - this is, for example, the case when products are made for a wide range of users. In this variation, the ticket stays in the validation step for a certain amount of time. During this time, if there are no complaints and no serious problems arise, the ticket eventually moves to the completed column. Should something come up after this waiting period, it will be dealt with as a new request.

How can an optimal waiting time be calculated? It's necessary to have measurements that can indicate how often customer feedback occurs within a given timeframe. For example, it might be observed that, as a rule, 80 percent of the feedback occurs within the first seven days and the remaining 20 percent sometime afterwards. In this case, a waiting period of seven days would make sense.

A Practical Example: Customer Validation in Production Robotics

"We want to improve the time-to-market" was the goal of a mid-sized company developing highly specialized controlling software for production robotics with around 100 employees. The employees are not only experts in their field, but are also driven by a strong sense of innovation. This is necessary in such a cutting-edge field, and it's what separates this company from their competition. They could have just let things continue as they were - the company was, and is, the market leader in their field. With growth increasing, however, it could be seen that implementing innovative ideas into products was taking longer because more and more processes were being established. There were thousands of exceptional ideas in the idea reservoir that couldn't be worked on. Something needed to change so they remain the market leader and profitable.

The transformation began very quietly. Nobody in the company needed to change the manner in which they completed their work. We didn't once use the word "Kanban". The only thing we did was to start with flight level 2 and model the path of the product through the company. In the first step, we built a Kanban board for those involved showing the current value-creation flow. We identified four process steps through which the product passed, from requirements up to customer acceptance. As soon as project management received the contract, the customer-specific development of the product started. Development and testing worked together closely: The customer's production environment was modeled as realistically as possible, in order to put the software into a virtual real-world operation during development. This way, a higher percentage of failures were found before being delivered. Regardless, the installation at the customer site was always the actual litmus test: two specialists were assigned to exclusively observe the production environment for a specific period of time. They reported errors back to development that could have only been recognized once deployed in the actual customer environment. This feedback was seen as a part of the process. Since correcting the errors required the know-how of a specialist, establishing a support-team for the feedback was not an option.

The main problem was uncovered

The error reporting in the installation phase was the biggest concern for development. Each error meant work on other items would be interrupted. Until now, the ticket in the "Installation" activity was simply pushed to "Completed" as soon as the installation specialists packed their bags and left the customer site. However, the customer would report errors a few days later, once the robots had performed all possible operations. The value-generating process was not completely finished with the installation. How could we get a handle on this? The answer was simple: We expanded the company board with a "Validation" column. Beforehand, we spent some time observing how often reports came back from the factory operations and in which time frame this happened. The probability of errors being reported was found to be highest in the first three days after an installation and after five days they bottomed out (see Figure 2.27). With this knowledge, development was committed and available for correcting rollout errors. We introduced a policy during a rollout that the ticket in "Validation" will be moved to "Completed" six days after the software was installed at the customer site. If a report should come after this time frame, it would be dealt with as a normal bug.

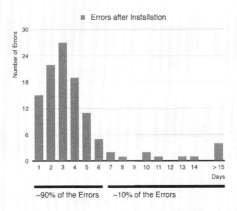

Figure 2.27 **Analysis of Customer Feedback**

What improved?

In a Kanban assessment, we later asked the employees about the effects of introducing Kanban. It was consistently stated that by coordinating the work along the value stream, pressure was noticeably reduced and work had become more structured and enjoyable. Fighting fires was kept to a minimum and everyone recognized the "big picture".

With improved coordination across the value stream of the company, the "better time-to-market" goal was achieved. The cycle time was reduced considerably, while at the same time greatly increasing adherence to delivery schedules. Simply by amending the company boards with a "Validation" column, it could be predicted in which time frame error reports might come from the customers. This also improved the communication with the customers. This phase was mentioned explicitly and the project manager calculated the potential error responses in development when coordinating the appointments. Compared to before, the customer reports, in the phase after installation, were not seen as failures, because they were prepared for them.

It was clear that Kanban did not make the company more successful. Kanban just made the work process visible. The employees correctly drew their own conclusions - they understood their system. Only now they knew how their work affected the entire value stream. With a new understanding for the value creation process, they asked themselves what makes the company fit for business: "What do our customers really want? Do they want a rapid installation in the running operations with the danger of many errors? Or do they want a delivery date with which the product could be 100 percent utilized?"

2.4 Knowledge Transfer

Every work system has its bottlenecks on which the productivity is involuntarily oriented. In knowledge work, bottlenecks are not limited to programmable and adjustable machines, but on individuals with specialized know-how. A few people know a lot and many people want access to their knowledge. If you want to draw a comparison, machines are also "specialized". However, bottlenecks are more stable in a production environment because they are confined and corrected at a particular process phase or at particular machines. In contrast, human knowledge bottlenecks migrate through the system according to their time availability and, as such, determine the throughput. This is why bottleneck theories like the Theory of Constraints are only marginally effective in knowledge work.

The tricky part is to be aware of these bottlenecks created by disparate knowledge, which can never be fully eliminated in knowledge work, but at the same finding a way to work around it. In the section Dealing with Blockades, we observed that solving problems around the bottleneck didn't help, because it increased the flow towards the bottleneck. The throughput of the system is determined by the bottleneck, but there are various types of bottlenecks and there are different solutions for each type. Let's look at this more closely.

2.4.1 Capacity Constrained Resource

By visualizing work on a Kanban board, (potential) bottlenecks can be identified. They can be easily recognized when work is completed and clogs up an activity - because the WIP limit is reached - while tickets in the following activity are still "In Progress" (see Figure 2.28). According to Eliyahu Goldratt, this is an indication of a Capacity Constrained Resource - CCR for short (Goldratt & Cox, 2004). The capacity of the "Development" activity is limited and, therefore, work comes to a standstill.

However, the board only shows the current situation. The situation should continue to be observed for a time before definitively declaring the "Development" activity as a permanent CCR bottleneck. Only when the normal fluctuations such as vacation, sick leave and work variability can be eliminated as the cause, should you then start thinking about taking long-term measures. Naturally, there is a difference between solutions for a short-term capacity correction and those for a permanent modification of the situation.

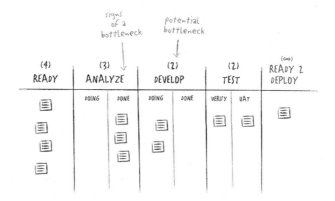

Figure 2.28 Indications of a Capacity Induced Bottleneck

How can you deal with a short-term bottleneck? Simply waiting it out is a perfectly legitimate possibility. The end of the bottleneck can be seen and is often the most economical alternative. You can also try to get additional resources - i.e. employees - from other areas of the company who could even out the missing knowledge for the duration of the bottleneck. When that is not possible, the WIP limit in the "Analyzing" activity can be temporarily increased, in the case where the analysts are going on vacation and the developers shouldn't run out of work in the meantime.

If the "Development" activity is found to have a permanent bottleneck, a different solution makes sense. Since knowledge bottlenecks are inconsistent (there can be at one time too much work at the bottleneck, and then too little), there can be a buffer created between the "Analyzing" and "Development" activities (Figure 2.29). This way, fluctuations can be evened out, since the "Analyzing" activity can also have issues due to employees being unavailable. "Analyzing" could also relatively quickly become a bottleneck - with the buffer, it is assured that the activities that follow have enough work.

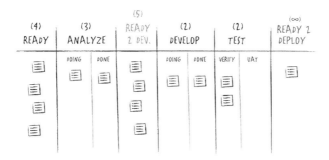

Figure 2.29 Buffer In Front of a Permanent Bottlenec

You have probable already noticed that installing the buffer increases the WIP limit in the system and, with that, the cycle time of a work item increases. This is the trade-off that you must live with in the face of variability in knowledge work: Do you accept the increased cycle time in order to have an uninterrupted work flow and consistent workload?

2.4.2 Specialist Bottleneck (Non-Instant Availability)

In knowledge work, more often you come across a situation like the one shown in Figure 2.30. The analysts have almost completed all of their work and the developers are already idle because one of three possible tickets in "Analyzing" is already completed. At the same time, in "Development" there are two tickets being worked on, but both are blocked because an external specialist is needed. The waiting, not the capacity, is the cause of the bottleneck.

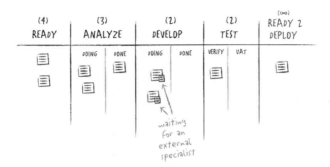

Figure 2.30 External Dependencies Lead to a Bottleneck

Compared to resource induced bottlenecks, there is little you can do to resolve the situation when dealing with external dependencies. Waiting on external preliminary work does not necessarily mean that the entire system is completely blocked and other items cannot be worked on. In this situation, helpful would be a buffer, or better yet a parking space, where you can put the blocked work until it can move forward again (Figure 2.31). This parking space is excluded from the normal WIP limits in the system, but is itself limited. Then the remaining work that is not dependent on external cooperation can keep flowing.

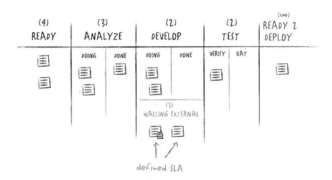

Figure 2.31 Parking Space for Externally Blocked Work Items

If the external dependencies are part of the process, the respective tickets retreat to this parking space and join the normal workflow again after completion. It's self-understood that collaboration with deliverers, partners and customers needs time. Regardless, it makes sense to keep your eye on these parked tickets. If the tickets stay there too long, the external dependency has possibly developed a blockade that you should get to the bottom of. However, it's unrealistic to want to completely eliminate external dependencies. These dependencies always exist within a company, even at the team level, especially when they are built as cross-functional teams.

2.4.3 Specialist vs. Generalist

Let's look at the topic of cross-functionality by using a practical example. An application needs to be programmed for web, iPhone and Android platforms. Since cross-functionality needs to be simple, there are analysts, developers and testers in each of the three application teams that are totally committed to helping one another. Nonetheless, there is immediately a bottleneck - as a matter of fact, several (Figure 2.32). Why?

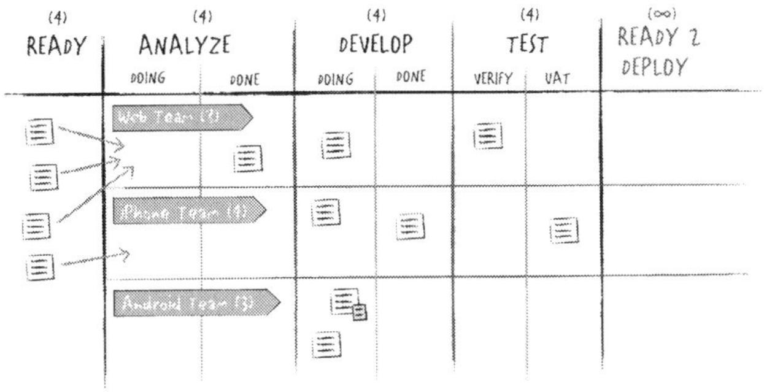

Figure 2.32 Bottleneck Despite Cross-Functionality

The three teams pull their work from a common input queue that has a WIP limit of 4. As you can see in the figure, three of the current work items go to the web team and one goes to the iPhone team, because this is optimal from a business perspective. The Android team, on the other hand, has nothing to do in the "Analyzing" activity. In addition, there is a piece of work from the Android team in development that is blocked because they need the web team. Regardless of how a company sets up teams, whether as silos or with cross-functionality, there will always be a point where specialization occurs and dependencies exist.

The real problem is the assumption about specialists and generalists in the working world. The assumption about specialists is they can complete the tasks within their domain faster and better than a generalist. This is undoubtedly true, but the work must be handed off more often, depending on how many specialists work in a system. The more often work must be handed off, the less efficient the workflow becomes, because the transfer itself is no guarantee that the work will be immediately taken up in the next step (see also Chapter 3). First, the work is tied-up in the next input queue and must wait to be pulled. Naturally, a specialist can use the active working time more effectively, but the total cycle time will increase due to the transfers between specialists. If you use specialists on a large scale, you must be aware that specialists are, by definition, a bottleneck. This is not an argument against using specialists. You should simply understand the effects caused by heavy specialization. Companies do not take this into consideration often enough because they only focus on optimizing active work.

Sigi, the superhero?

There is a superhero on the team: Sigi. Sigi's colleagues are five normal people who do not possess superhero skills, but do good work and are reliable. Even Sigi typically works on completely normal stuff, except for this day when a super difficult superhero tasks finally lands at the team. Sigi puts aside the "normal people" work and disappears for a few days in order to save the world. It takes a long, long, long time for the normal tasks to finally be completed. Too bad, since they could bring in some money.

When you consider this constellation from an economic perspective (for instance, based on cost of delay, see Chapter 5), it is most likely not optimal. Presumably, keeping in mind time-to-market, it would be much less expensive to keep Sigi's resources free so he can immediately take care of superhero tasks in case they arise. A different, permanent solution can be found for completing the tasks in the team's normal workday.

For many companies, however, this is absolutely unthinkable because a full workload for the employee is the highest commandment, not their effectiveness. It is simply not acceptable to pay somebody for waiting and eventually be 110% engaged when the need arises. There are, however, entire occupational groups who are paid for doing nothing - the fire department or emergency response people, for example. At the ship folding experiment (see Chapter 1), I always try to steer the attention of the participants towards the ship - in other words, on the work that flows through the system. Optimally generating value for the customer is the highest priority and a fast time-to-market is a distinct advantage for many companies in today's market conditions. Thus, the focus should be placed first on the workflow and then on the productivity. This absolutely does not mean that workload will be completely ignored. The most important question is whether or not the demands of the customer are being fulfilled with the current setup - only then should the workload be optimized. In reality, the attention is placed on making sure people like Sigi have a full workload, instead of finding ways to more effectively complete the work.

The generalist is the counterpoint: He is well-versed in several disciplines. Perhaps the knowledge is not in-depth, but still good enough to understand the context and be able to complete tasks up to a certain level. This brings greater flexibility to a work system because generalists can be placed in various jobs. Naturally, a generalist works longer on a task than a specialist would since their active working time is higher. There are fewer hand offs, though, which itself improves flow efficiency and reduces cycle time.

In knowledge work, the T-shaped engineer has become the ideal: These employees are specialists in one discipline, but possess knowledge in other disciplines. They have the ability to work in several areas, or work together with representative of various areas. The question is, how do you become a T?

Knowledge Agility

Becoming a T occurs through experience and a personal willingness to learn about knowledge areas that do not always stand in close relation to your own specialization. That doesn't mean a Kanban specialist should learn the undoubtedly fascinating craft of neurosurgery, but perhaps it is good to know how traditional project management or agile approaches work. The same goes for software developers, where knowledge of testing methods would be an advantage in the case that they would need to, in a pinch, do the testing themselves. The software developer should also have knowledge of various technologies and systems. The good news is, it isn't necessary to invest in expensive continuing education programs in order to expand the knowledge of the employees. It's possible to make learning and knowledge transfer an integral part of the work system.

The simplest form of knowledge transfer is pairing. A (future) generalist works on a task together with a specialist. Through the design of the Kanban board and WIP limits, this teamwork can be supported (Figure 2.33).

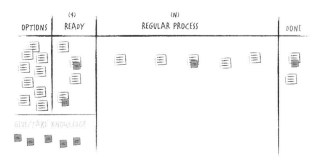

Figure 2.33 Knowledge Transfer Using the Pull Principle - Support Through the Board Design

The easiest way is to split the input queue into two areas: Input Queue and Knowledge Transfer. There are tasks that are better suited for knowledge transfer, others less so. I would not apply knowledge transfer to very complicated tasks. It would take a disproportionate amount of time to convey to the generalist at least a fundamental understanding of the subject matter. At the same time, it also doesn't make sense to only complete extremely simple tasks, because the learning effect is missing. The idea is to identify suitable tasks, based on their level of difficulty, that lend themselves to knowledge transfer and then build specialist-generalist pairs.

Knowledge transfer using the Pull Principle. The board in Figure 2.33 is a real-life example. What I really liked about this case was the "Knowledge Transfer Topics" area. This is, in principle, nothing more than a knowledge marketplace. Employees who want to learn something specific post their requests in this area, and likewise those who can offer knowledge make it public. When a piece of work lands in the input queue and fits to a knowledge offer and request, it is tagged with the corresponding stickers from the marketplace. As soon as the work is pulled, the pair can work on it.

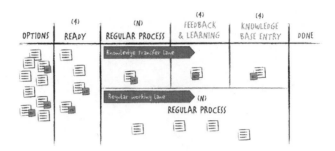

Figure 2.34 Unbundling of Knowledge Transfer and Normal Work Process

Imparting and consolidating knowledge occurs over several steps. The team from which this board originates had a very specific goal in mind: The team members themselves felt like lone fighters and they consciously wanted to overcome this situation. Along with the pairings, they also decided to include reciprocal feedback afterwards. This ability to work in pairs should be continually developed and is depicted on the board with the column "Feedback & Learning". Also, you can either unbundle the knowledge transfer process from the normal work process, or illustrate the columns as part of the normal work process and simply skip over them when the work item is not part of the knowledge transfer (see Figure 2.34).

In a different company, knowledge transfer was used to create a new knowledge database, which I have built into Figure 2.34. Instead of randomly dumping information into the Wiki, the contributions are based on demand. The rule states that when knowledge is requested and is worked on in a pair, one of them writes the entry in the database and the other does a review. Only when this step is completed can the ticket be considered "finished". Does this increase the cycle time? Of course. But at the same time, it is a conscious improvement to prevent longer cycle times in the future. The next time the generalist can complete a similar task by himself instead of having to wait for the specialist.

2.4.4 Summary

Work can only be considered completed when the customer also considers it completed. If this consideration is not taken into account in the Kanban system, the customer feedback (about production failures, for example) will always disrupt the workflow. Thus, it makes sense to integrate customer validation as a process step in the Kanban system. Tentatively completed and delivered work remains in this activity for a certain period of time. This timeframe can be determined by measuring customer feedback after a delivery.

In knowledge work, bottlenecks occur mostly due to strong specialization. Specialists and their knowledge are not always available and, as such, determine the throughput of a system. Even if generalists do not have the same competencies as a specialist, the knowledge transfer between both groups still makes sense. This can be achieved with the pull principle, where stickers and separate swim lanes for pair-work signal who wants to learn what and in which area.

2.5 Coordination

As a consultant, I always prefer to give my customers the fishing rod rather than the fish. It is not my intention to settle in at the customer for years on end and make myself indispensable. Instead, I draft up, as swiftly as possible, any structure that supports my customers' ability to independently work with Kanban. Kanban lives from communication, so I try to quickly establish useful meetings such as replenishment meetings (also Spice Girls meetings), regular standup meetings and retrospectives. When I am invited to a review, I can see that the meetings are working well for the most part - although the retrospectives usually have problems. If the retrospectives are conducted, in many cases they are unsuccessful. In my experience, the retrospectives are essential for the continued development and improvement of the Kanban system - more on this later.

What do I mean by coordination? Until now, we have observed the construction of a Kanban system: Which principles are followed, how are processes made visible, with what means can you create a workflow, etc.? The result is nothing more than a Kanban board with columns, swim lanes and a few numbers that reflects the current situation as much as possible. The point is, the board itself does nothing. When you do Kanban, you have to really use it. The core of Kanban is the company - the way the people utilize the information on the Kanban board, how they interpret it and improve themselves based on these findings. Let's look at the meetings which are useful (but not required) for a company using Kanban, based on the illustration in Figure 2.35.

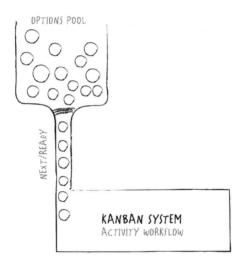

Figure 2.35 The Path from Option Pool to the Kanban System

2.5.1 From Idea to Coordinated Input - Replenishment Meeting

A company should never be sheepish about new ideas and options. These ideas and options are not only generated internally, but are often brought to the company's attention by external stakeholders. They have an interest in the output of the work system (not particularly of Kanban), but themselves are not necessarily a part of the Kanban system. This can be illustrated as a funnel in which external input is collected. It is a pool of options that could be implemented, but the decision makers have not yet made a firm commitment.

What will actually be implemented is actively discussed in a replenishment meeting with the working internal stakeholders of the Kanban system. Anyone who is interested that the work moves forward takes part in the meeting. This can include customers, sales people, technical experts as well as management representatives for an overall team and department point of view. In practice, other names for these meetings have been established: queue replenishment meeting, input coordination and my preferred variation, Spice Girls meeting. The refrain of the Spice Girls hit "Wanna Be" accurately describes the path of the options from the idea pool into the Kanban system: We ask the stakeholders "Tell me what you want" and they fill the funnel with ideas. The next question, "what you really, really want", selects the options that will be coordinated and supplied to the WIP limited Kanban system. Only the items that will be worked on next by someone in the Kanban system are collected in the input queue.

The internal stakeholders should agree that the Kanban system will only be filled by the coordination in the Spice Girls meeting, and a moderator is recommended. In order for every stakeholder to get a chance, the Spice Girls meeting should be held in repeated/regular cadence to determine the length of the input queue and the throughput of the system. How much work can be completed in a specific timeframe must also be measured. A simple example: The employees in a Kanban system complete between eight and eleven tickets each week. If a weekly Spice Girls meeting is planned, the size of the input queue can be set at eleven, so it doesn't prematurely run empty. If the interval changes and the meeting is held every two weeks, there should be a maximum of 24 tickets.

The size of the input queue influences the agility of the Kanban system. A smaller input queue leaves open the possibility to be able to respond promptly, or at least more quickly, to options when they present themselves. By the way, the items making it into the input queue should not be based on a game of power politics. These decisions ideally come from economic considerations, which we will discuss in Chapter 5.

2.5.2 From the Input Queue into the Kanban System - Regular Standup Meeting

The colleagues in the Kanban system pull their work from the coordinated and regularly populated input queue. The internal stakeholders focus on throughput and improvements to the Kanban system, which is why they hold regular strategy meetings. I specifically chose the word "regular" because these meetings should have a cadence, but the intervals can be flexible. The cadence for this meeting depends on the flight level of the Kanban system. At the team level, daily standup meetings are a good idea. At flight level 2 (several teams) and flight level 3 (portfolio level), there should be an overview of the epics or sagas, and standup meetings once or twice a week are usually enough.

Usually the standup meeting is held in front of the Kanban board. It is a meeting with strategic character and not a meeting where technical questions should be resolved. The board is a reflection of the current reality: problems, dependencies, bottlenecks, delays - everything is visible. For me, the most important question in a standup meeting is: "This is the situation. What do we do with it?" The point here is coordination versus just a discussion of what is on the board. For example, what has to be done to resolve a blockade that is caused by an external supplier dependency? A ticket in the express lane needs to be brought quickly through the system - who can help work on it? Three people are on vacation or sick in team X, which delays work A on which work B depends - what do we do? For such coordination topics, the standup meeting is the appropriate and necessary forum. Naturally, I witness discussions in the standup meetings, that I follow up at the review visits, but they are usually content and technical discussions. The participants get lost in the details of their current work instead of dealing with the problems of the system. Yes, content discussions are important - but to fully use the potential of the regular standup meetings, they should be held at a different time in a different forum. Personally, I make a note of the content questions that come up during the meetings and at the end of the meeting read aloud who needs to get into contact with whom about which topic.

> In my trainings, I like to use the getKanban game from Russel Healy (www.getKanban.com). The participants play through different situations on the Kanban board. The fascinating part is, they don't discuss for even a second the content of the individual pieces of work. They don't even know what kind of company it is. This is exactly the point of regular standup meetings: The system and strategic topics should be discussed, not the individual work to be completed.

Who facilitates?

The regular standup meeting should absolutely be moderated. The idea of a moderation is to keep the meetings between five and 15 minutes in length in order to prevent the discussion from sliding into a content discussion. Not to mention that the working world does not suffer from a lack of meetings. From a lean perspective, longer meetings do not generate value for the customer - actually quite the opposite. So, the regular standup meeting in its moderated and focused form is one of the most valuable meetings overall.

Secondly, moderating is the ideal opportunity to put into practice the principle of encouraging leadership at all levels. There are no defined rolls in Kanban about who is responsible for the moderation. Often, I see team or department leaders taking on the role of moderator. This is fundamentally okay, but in my opinion, it's better when this duty rotates between those involved. Each week, a different person involved takes over the moderation of the standup and goes from being a passive participant to having a leading and controlling function. This change requires a completely new skill set - away from a criticizing participant and into a meeting coordinator. This may be too much for some employees, but in practice I see again and again a fantastic approach that makes learning this role easier: double moderation. While one person moderates, a moderation partner follows the flow of the meeting. After the meeting, the observer gives the moderator feedback and step-by-step the moderation abilities of the individuals involved improves.

Asking the three famous questions?

What is a good model for a regular standup meeting? You've probably seen this phenomenon over and over: Participants rarely say anything of their own accord. In the agile community, there are three questions put to the meeting participants and each participant should answer them in the standup meeting. These are: What have I done since the last meeting? What will I do till the next meeting? What hindered me in my work? If at all possible, avoid asking these questions in a regular standup meeting or in any other meeting! A few paragraphs ago, I mentioned that regular standup meetings have a strategic character to them. The only question to be asked is how we are supposed to be dealing with the situation depicted on the Kanban board. These three worn out questions instead steer the attention towards the individual person. No wonder these meetings are nothing more than unpopular status reports. Manage work, not workers!

Don't confine the participants with a list of questions. In the first standup meetings, while work is syncing up with Kanban, individual tickets will naturally be discussed. This cannot be avoided, nor should it be. At some point, the discussions start to concentrate on the issues that standout on the board and obviously need to be resolved. There will be more interest in wanting to understand the current situation. Whoever takes over the moderator role should go through the board from right to left and address abnormalities, ask about the cause and possible ways to deal with it, as well as point out when something has occurred at specific areas. The focus of attention should be the work as it is depicted on the board, and not who, what, when, why or why not something was done.

By the way, here's a little trick for tracking the changes on the board till the next standup meeting. A policy could be to turn the tickets 90 degrees as soon as they go to the next processing step, or a blockade or other problem was resolved. The moderator can immediately see the points where something was done since the last meeting. The ticket is rotated by the person who moves it.

This rule can naturally be varied in many ways. I personally prefer one variation especially well: Tickets rotated 90 degrees will always be discussed, regardless of how it occurred. This means even when an employee has the need to discuss a piece of work or a need for coordination arises, the ticket can be turned - whether their own ticket or a colleague's ticket. It's a simple mechanism that focuses on the essentials during the standup meeting and helps keep the meeting short.

2.5.3 Getting Better - Retrospective

Improvement doesn't simply happen, you have to do something for it. Especially in security critical occupations, it is common practice to conduct regular retrospectives. In this context, it is often referred to as "debriefing". Part of it is for psychological health after stressful situations, and part of it is to objectively review the results and together consider which conclusions and measures could be used in the future. Together you want to find out why something went the way it did, how it went, and from this infer specific steps for improvement.

This is also the goal of a retrospective in the context of Kanban. I often notice that retrospectives are either completely ignored or they are used exclusively as a team event. The retrospective could be any meeting in which a group of people in a safe environment can solely think about themselves. Regardless, I still believe the retrospective is not a team event! I'm in favor of thinking outside the box in the retrospective and regularly including anyone who is connected to your work - whether an external stakeholder or other parallel services or teams where dependencies exist. Precisely in this review, it is useful to take a broader perspective as it offers the chance to learn with and from one another. In "Kanban Change Leadership", we described in great detail how you can and should include stakeholders at the beginning of a Kanban implementation so it is successful, versus being just a flash in the pan (Leopold & Kaltenecker 2015). Through this cooperation, you know which problems need to be solved. However, this is not a one-time deal! For me, never again asking the stakeholder how the solution is working and never again including them in the improvement cycle is a strange way of thinking. A team should want to hear about what can be done better for their stakeholder. In this case, having routine discussions directly with the respective person is hands-down better than speculating. In many companies that are newly agile, I have observed retrospectives at the team level conducted by the book, but the knowledge gained in the individual teams is never linked or, at the very least, connected. The team optimization way of thinking is often still strongly anchored within the company. A project leader at an automobile company described their situation. "Ah, now I understand. We build a lot of Ferraris, but we don't have a road." Thanks to this insight, we found a simple solution for them. In addition to the team retrospectives (the Ferraris), the team representatives met for an overall retrospective (we called it the Ferrari convention) to improve interaction and build a better product together versus optimizing individual pieces. Gradually, a road on which the company could move forward together was created. What you should take away from this is: **Do not limit retrospectives to your immediate Kanban system!**

The Retrospective Object

It is understandable that in the first few months Kanban itself is the center of the considerations during the retrospective. Everyone must get used to the new system. However, after a few retrospectives, the Kanban system itself should no longer be a topic because Kanban is nothing more than means to an end. The work is the object of improvement and that is where the focus of the retrospectives should be placed. So, let's not talk about Kanban retrospectives, but about work retrospectives instead. The Kanban system represents the current work situation, but the work itself will be improved - and it will likely have an impact on the Kanban system.

More abstractly formulated, the purpose of a retrospective is to identify problems and find solutions for them. But, and this is crucial, it isn't about finding the perfect solution. Just as a Kanban system is the latest state of misunderstanding, so too are solutions always having a temporary character. The work afterwards often reveals new facets of the problem that require answers. Thus, the result of the retrospective is always a small step forward. "To do - doing - done" should never be the approach towards improvement. Improvement is cyclical. The Deming-Cycle describes this process simply, but effectively:

- *Plan:* Ideas for improvement have been developed - what should be modified?
- *Do:* The ideas for improvement are implemented.
- *Check:* The improvements are reviewed to determine if they really are improvements. Ideally, metrics are developed over

time that can assist with the estimations, or should be stipu-lated as evaluation criteria in the planning stage.

- *Act:* When the improvement measures were successful, more of it will be done. If not, the cycle starts back at the beginning.

The Retrospective Disposition

Forced to bare your soul or public accusations - neither one nor the other is the purpose of a retrospective. The highest directive in these meetings is that everyone gave their best. In the first run-throughs, it's important to emphasize this so the retrospective does not turn into an arena for personal conflicts and placing blame. At some point, nobody will have the desire to take part if this would happen. At the other extreme - also due to the recommendations of various writers - the retrospectives run under the precept: "What happens in Vegas, stays in Vegas." This means that everything discussed remains within the room and nothing reaches the outside. Granted, this can make the individuals feel more secure at the beginning, especially when a culture of trust is not strongly present within a company.

Regardless, I'm not a fan of it. On one hand, the Vegas rule contra-dicts to a certain degree the highest directive that everyone did their best. It also cements the idea that only a secretive selected group can take part in these meetings and everyone else is excluded, in my opinion. From my point of view, everything which concerns the work itself can be disclosed, regardless if it runs well or not, when the flag of openness is being waved and profound change initiatives have been started. Naturally, it is a question of culture and in many companies approaching openness must be done slowly. In the long term, the goal should be to leave the Vegas rule in Vegas and, with regards to all those involved or affected, to stand for what you've done and allow for external feedback.

The Retrospective Procedure

Let's grab a coffee, gather our chairs into a circle and initiate a discussion about what we can improve. This is perhaps an exaggeration, but a retrospective should not be conducted in this manner. Usually those involved deliver an enormous amount of ideas, but rarely do those involved have a similar, much less same, understanding of the problem. Here is the real challenge: there are solutions like there is sand on a beach, but the problem does not always fit to the solution because the problem was never properly understood. Albert Einstein supposedly said: "When I would have one hour to save the world, I would spend 55 minutes describing the problem and 5 minutes on the solution." Often, though, it goes in the opposite direction: Very little time is spent first trying to understand the problem. A structured procedure that clearly separates understanding the problem from the solution is for me, personally, the prerequisite for a retrospective to yield appropriate improvement measures.

Esther Derby and Diana Larsen wrote the standard reference for agile retrospectives, which is a recommended starting point for anyone who is just getting started with designing their procedure for a retrospective (Derby & Larsen, 2006). Even I run retrospectives according to these original five comprehensive points. However, over time I realized there needed to be another point added - understanding the problem, which I have added as step 3. But more on this later. In principle, every retrospective should have a specific title on which those involved can focus on together. An example might be, "Today is about blockades that occurred" or "We will review the latest release review". Following is an overview of the individual steps, which I will then discuss in detail.

Step 1 and 6: Check-in and Check-out Phase

The participants first arrive and get settled into the meeting to understand the overall atmosphere, and at the end of the meeting the bag of issues is completely closed. This is not only recommended for the retrospective, but for any meeting.

Step 2: Gather Facts

When looking back at what has happened, it's always most difficult to separate facts and opinions. Retrospectives should be based on facts. In the second step, whatever material is available should be gathered without interpretation, such as data, blockade flip charts and objective observations.

Step 3: Defining the Core Problem

Now the facts are looked at and analyzed together. Which problems can be observed? With this, the topic of the retrospective is more exactly defined.

Step 4: Understanding the Problem

It's not possible to prevent the human mind from promptly looking for a solution to a problem. It's tempting to immediately accept the obvious solution because it gives a wonderful feeling of relief. And after a few weeks, the same topic comes up again in the retrospective. That's why it is good to consciously take your foot off the gas and look at the problem from all possible angles in order to understand what the problem is with this problem.

Step 5: Finding Solutions and Determine the Actions to be Taken

When there is an actual understanding of the problem, it's time to start thinking about possible solutions. The most important part of this step is to be really specific: What will be done to implement the solution and who does it? Often there are just tentative statements and nobody feels responsible for the implementation. It is useful to depict the improvement work on the Kanban board so the measures are not just statements of intent, nor too many improvement measures are started. More on this topic in section Making Improvement Work Visible.

Group Size and Group Configuration

At a retrospective, there can be five, sometimes 20 or even 130 participants. In order to get to the solutions, larger groups within the retrospective should be split up - I would even do this by a group size of six people. The partitioning should occur at the latest by step 4 so that research teams can be built, who take on specific problems and define its solutions and measures.

When it's clear that group needs to be split up, I make it clear at the beginning that the presentation of individual solutions during the assembly does not include a general discussion questioning the solutions and overturning them. I want to create an atmosphere that signalizes trust in the work of the small groups. Feedback on the results is desired, but the solution will be implemented. Naturally those involved can decide for themselves on which problem they want to work.

In larger groups, often there are several levels of hierarchy and functions represented, from the CEO to project workers. My golden rule is to build the small groups with members from across the various hierarchy and functions, so the problem can be considered from various points of view. Incidentally, this also supports a mutual understanding of the problem.

2.5.3.1 Check-In

The idea of the check-in is to get the participants tuned-in to the current retrospective. Here the focus is set and the goals are outlined, for example: "Today our topic is blockades. We will analyze blockades from the last two months in order to find measures to reduce the number of blockades in the future." In order that everyone has the procedure of the retrospective clearly in front of them, I write the individual steps as an agenda on a flipchart and leave it standing in the room the entire time. If there isn't much time allocated for the retrospective, I also write down which step at which time should take place. This allows for a good orientation of time and it prevents the meeting from suddenly running an hour longer. By doing this, there is a mutual understanding in the group laid down for the time management. If it would be necessary to exceed the time allocated for the meeting, the decision should be a deliberate decision made by the entire group.

Facilitation. At this point, you can see that retrospectives absolutely must be facilitated. This includes the preparations: The facilitator should estimate ahead of time how much time will be needed for each step and make a time plan accordingly. The facilitator should also have the flexibility to adjust the agenda during the retrospective if necessary. If the meeting takes longer than planned, the participants start to thin out because some need to get to their next appointments. The moderator should be someone with a bit of experience who can deal with the resulting dynamic.

If the retrospective takes place in a larger room with several groups, two moderators or more are recommended for a group of at least 20 participants to lead the meeting. When the moderators are internal employees, I think it's a good idea to have moderators lead groups other than their own. This has two advantages: First, the "external" moderator has a more impartial view. And second, in your own group you are not just moderator, but also a participant, and these two roles are difficult to separate. Taking over the moderation for a different group means you can fully concentrate of the role of moderator. Whenever possible, I recommend finding an external moderator to run the retrospective. This doesn't have to be a paid professional, but perhaps it could be a colleague from a different department with the appropriate experience. I want to give you a bit of insight into my own work as a motivation, not as a detailed moderation guideline.

Mood. I have observed that retrospectives are more successful when the participants are put into the right mood. Small exercises requiring minimal effort are usually enough to help achieve this. I use, for example, a high-speed assessment that exclusively reflects the gut feelings of the participants. On a flip chart, I write down on axes the various topics that correlate to the theme of the retrospective. With smaller groups, I give each participant an appropriate number of stickers as soon as they enter the room and ask them to place the stickers on the pertinent location of the axes according to their assessment. The further out on an axis the sticker is placed, the more positive the assessment. Either at the beginning of the meeting or at some convenient point according to the situation, I calculate for average of the posted stickers for each axis and connect the average points to create an area. By doing this, it becomes very clear how things are currently going: the larger the area, the better. You can see at a glance, how strongly the opinions to a topic deviate from one another. These differences are also good preparation for the second step. I ask the individuals why they placed their stickers on this or that place, and already collect information from this.

HIGH-SPEED-ASSESSMENT

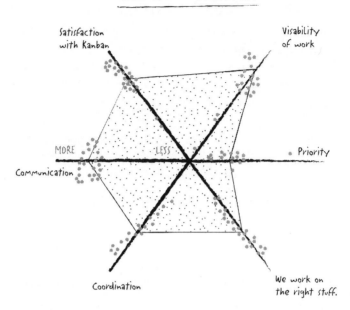

Figure 2.36 High Speed Assessment

A second exercise is the Four-Field-Retro. Again, corresponding to the theme of the retrospective, four quadrants with the subtopics are illustrated. The participants write down keywords that come to mind on post-it notes and stick them in the respective quadrant.

The results of these check-in exercises are quickly addressed and then there is no further discussion about it. In total, the check-in phase should not take longer than ten minutes. By the way, many more check-in exercises for agile retrospectives can be found in "Retromat" from Corinna Baldauf at www.plans-for-retrospectives.com.

2.5.3.2 Gathering Facts

In German, there is a wonderful phrase "laying the facts on the table". For the retrospective, this is an important foundation because often ideas are quickly delivered from a personal perspective. But there is no justification about which problem is being solved when, for instance, a recommendation is that the standup meeting be held one time per week. Measurements deliver unambiguous facts, just like blockade and bug tickets, but also neutral observations, incidents ("Yesterday the cleaning lady vacuumed up our board") and unexplainable facts where a discussion makes no sense ("I cannot explain it, but our throughput is shrinking"). The important thing is that facts are simply collected in this step but not evaluated, and most certainly not provided with a solution! Here's a little example:

- Fact: Our standups take 30 minutes
- Evaluation: Our standups take too long.
- Premature Solution: We want to have only two standups per week!

In order to work goal-oriented, it's important to formulate the facts and neutral and specific as possible. How can facts be collected? To do this, I prefer one of the two following methods:

Method "What pulls, what brakes?"

It seems I have a penchant for ship metaphors. A sailboat can be held in place with an anchor, but it is driven forward by the wind in its sails. So, I draw a ship on the flipchart and ask the participants what prohibited their work in the last week and what drove it forward. I ask for the answers (in groups if applicable) to be written down as detailed as possible on index cards within a fixed time frame. Instead of "Communication isn't functioning", a more concrete formulation might be: "In the last three weeks, we were missing feedback from Mr. X from department Y on subject Z." The group places their cards on the flipchart and quickly comment on the facts they have found.

Method "Timeline"

For a retrospective to cover a longer timeframe, the timeline or time bar is a good instrument for collecting facts. For example, there is a company that indulges in a retrospective for approximately 80 people with Siegfried Kaltenecker and myself to review the last twelve months. In an appropriately large conference room, we place the timeline on the floor and sectioned by month. The individual groups wander through the timeline and lay down cards above the timeline in months where they felt were highlights and below the timeline for the less than favorable happenings. Some groups bring prepared measurements, analyses (of Bugs or Blockades, for example) or other materials that they can place on the timeline accordingly.

When a longer time frame is used for the retrospective, the probability increases that many subjects come up. At some point, you can no longer see the forest through the trees, not to mention the individual facts should also be looked at and read through. Therefore, I set a limit at such retrospectives and ask the groups to choose their top ten events.

2.5.3.3 Defining the Problem

I have added step three for my retrospectives to the outline from Esther Derby and Diana Larsen, where the collected facts are used to deduce the problem. The advantage of a clearly formulated problem is that you can get to the bottom of the cause by asking the question "why?"

Group Facts according to content. First, the feedback from the group(s) must be looked at and collected into meaningful problem areas. We look for similar statements. The challenge is to not choose generalized headings for the individual clusters, because often too many different problems and packed into a single cluster. Under the heading "We do not hold to the rules" for example, you could include retrospective that exceed the time limit as equally as the regularly disregarded Definition of Done. However, these are two completely different problems. The moderator has the duty to pay attention to the binding element. If the statement is "Our standups take 30 minutes instead of 15" and another statement "We always exceed the time limit in the standups", the binding element is not only the rule breaking, but the specific problem that the standup time allowance is often exceeded. You do not want to minimize the possible topics, rather you want to find the overlaps in the feedback.

Define the core problem. If everyone is in agreement that the standups often exceed the time limit, you have already found the heading for the cluster and at the same time found the core issue: "Our standups take too long." You should be able to use the question "why?" on the problem statement.

Prioritize problem statements. Once the core issues are defined, they can be prioritized and the order in which they will be dealt with can be set. One prioritization method is the point query: Every participant receives a certain number of stickers and assigns them to the individual problem statements. I personally find the silent prioritization quite charming. On participant after the other goes to the flipchart and places the stickers with the problem statements - without comment - in the order that makes the most sense. Surprisingly, the prioritization emerges very quickly, often in less than a minute (according to the size of the group).

2.5.3.4 Understanding the Problem

Why are things the way they are? Even when it takes a little longer, you should not skip over this step in the retrospective. Otherwise, the same problems will continually pop-up in one form or another. Also, deliberately allow yourself plenty of time to understand the problem - just like Albert Einstein did. It's understandable that this point is gladly cut short at many retrospectives. When you ask the question "why?" often enough, eventually you bump into human behavior and looking closely at this behavior can be uncomfortable. That's why it is important to be aware that "why?" is our friend. It's very helpful to first concentrate fully on finding the root of the problem and first ask what you can do - as a company, department, team, or individual - to understand the problem before shrugging off responsibility and projecting onto others. It's not going about baring your soul and confessing guilt, rather it's going about accepting the circumstances that things can happen due to certain behaviors. Basically, the moderator should be able to gauge how far the drilling should go and it's often a question of time. In purely technical retrospectives, drilling down to the behavioral level is not always necessary.

The methods for finding the root of a problem are basically a variation of the Root Cause Analysis, which asks five "why" questions (Wilson et al., 1993). Sometimes less than five questions are sufficient, sometimes more are necessary to get to the crux of the issue - it varies from case to case. I like to use the method "That is so, because...", which is actually a type of mind map. I simply write the problem statement on a flipchart and underneath the start of the sentence "That is so, because..." and continually ask the question. For example:

> *Problem statement: In the last release, two hotfixes were required.*
>
> That is so, because...
>
> – ... there was a change in the person responsible for the product.
>
> Why was there a change?
>
> – Because he was needed in a different project.
>
> Why was he needed in a different project?

– Because there are too few people in charge of products.

Why are there too few responsible people?

– Because too many projects run at the same time.

Why are too many projects running at the same time?

– Because we start new projects immediately.

Why are we starting new projects immediately?

– Because we have no portfolio management.

The "Problem Free World" goes a different way. Again, the problem statement is written down, but the participants describe what their work would look like without any problems. For example, what does the perfect standup look like? Hence, you deliberately create steps that should actually be taken. Once the ideal situation is drafted, the current situation is placed next to it so the differences are plain to see. Then we ask the question again, why the ideal situation has not been achieved. What is not being done so that we achieve our optimum?

2.5.3.5 Finding Solutions and Determining Measures

After it has become clear why there is a problem, the next step is to find potential solutions. Perhaps it was determined that the standup was not being moderated and thus continually exceeded the time limit. A possible solution is: "We are appointing a moderator to lead our standups." The retrospective is not finished at this point and nobody is allowed to go home yet. Now it's going about specifics:

1. *Responsibility:* Who is doing what till when? Who is going to take care of finding a moderator?
2. *Measuring:* How will we know if the solution was successful? There should be fixed criteria that will determine the success

or failure of the solution. For example: In the next two weeks, we want to complete four out of five standups within ten minutes.

When there are many suggestions for solutions, you should consider the effort and what will be gained before you decide on a specific measure. When something costs more money or time than it brings in results, it's probably not worth the effort. Whether or not a measure makes sense economically and/or has the expected effect can be estimated by the participants by using the point system.

To determine if something is really an improvement, you should follow and actively manage the development - more on this later. In any case, do not let yourself be frightened by the term "measurements". These do not need to be elaborate data collection systems and certainly not a mile-long Excel report - a simple survey of those involved after a specific period of time can be a measurement. Keep it as simple as possible and use a level of detail that is meaningful and it useful for other solutions.

2.5.3.6 Check-out

An orderly end to the retrospective is as important as a structured beginning that gives guidance. The conclusion is at the same time the first step to implementing the solutions, so the results obtained are once again summarized at the end. Since the retrospective can and should also be improved like anything else, I always collect feedback about the meeting itself. For instance, I do this by using the one-word feedback. All participants stand in a circle. I ask them, "Which word describes the retrospective the best?" and give them a minute to think about it. Then, in clockwise order, each person says their word. It's a way to capture the sentiment in a flash.

A second method that I like to use is the trifecta feedback. I illustrate three "accounts": needs improvement, stay as is and good. These three valuations are based on the group and the moderation. I ask the participants to take a few minutes and write down their feedback on post-it notes. When leaving the room, they simply put the post-it on the appropriate account. This feedback is more detailed and especially helps the moderator if they've just started doing retrospectives.

Even though I consider the retrospective to be an essential meeting, there are coaches like Judith Andersen or Ester Derby and Diana Larsen have worked intensively with this subject material and have written valuable books on this topic. I can only point out again that the retrospective should be seen as a tool to improve team work across the value chain for the long term. This is why I challenge you to look beyond the borders of your teams, your departments and your company and invite those people you work together with outside of your traditional area.

I also know several Kanban systems where the retrospectives exist as a regular meeting, but gets its subject material from the day-to-day happenings. There is a dedicated area on the board where the improvement topics are collected between retrospective meetings, as well as observations, facts or solutions. Before the next retrospective, the notes are collected and gone over. I have observed that by using this method, many discussions about problems and their causes are steered away from the regular standup meetings and into the retrospectives where they are better taken care of. You can - and in my opinion should - go a step further and make the improvement work itself visible in the daily routine.

2.5.3.7 Making Improvement Work Visible

Between two retrospectives always lies the daily routine. The danger of the daily routine is that the most wonderful decisions for improvement threaten to sink like quicksand when you think of improvements as something not related to the daily routine. Kickstarting improvements in a two-week rhythm may clear your conscience for a time, but the real question is: What was implemented and what did these measures bring? It should be monitored whether or not the solution has worked in order to learn something for the future. Currently, I very rarely see consistent tracking being used. It's unclear which improvement plans are active within the company and - analogous to the work flow - how the improvement flow looks. In addition, there are too many improvement measures launched at the same time, starting at the team level and stretching to C-Level. When the concept of the J-curve of changes states that the performance during changes first sinks before increasing thanks to the changes, the opposite is true with too many simultaneous improvement initiatives. You never come out of the performance hole because the next initiative begins before you have completed the first one. With too much improvement and change enthusiasm, the performance can never recover. Even though it is positive when the ideas spring forth during the retrospective, it makes more sense to focus and limit the number of solutions that will be implemented at the same time.

Improvements are a type of work - improvement work. As we now know, the principle which applies to work in a system is: Stop starting, start finishing! That's why it's important to integrate improvement measures, just like all other work, on the Kanban board and deal with them on a daily basis.

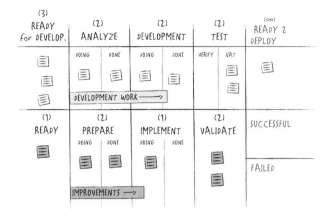

Figure 2.37 Integrating Improvement Work on the Kanban board

This functions relatively easy when a swim lane for improvements is added (Figure 2.37). This swim lane reflects the steps a measure must pass through before you can assess if it was useful or not. Naturally, there should also be WIP limits set for improvement work because the goal is to implement and complete them before starting the next one. In the "Validation" step, the criteria that were defined in the retrospective for measuring success come into effect. Ideally, the board will always be included in the retrospective in order to determine in which stage of implementation a measure can be found. You look at the board from right to left and ask by every measure if the criteria for success have already been achieved. When yes, the measure is "done". If not, what still has to be done to fulfill the success criteria? Does it just need more time or do the measures and/or criteria need to be sharpened? Together with the WIP limits, it will be clear at this point if you can start with the next improvement or if the implementation needs to wait on more ideas. This way, the improvement system regulates itself and you don't run into the danger of being overwhelmed with your own enthusiasm for improvements.

2.5.4 Summary

Kanban lives from communication and the resulting **coordination** - the manner in which those involved use the information they receive through visualizing processes. This communication is supported by three meeting formats: replenishment meeting, regular standup meeting and the retrospective.

In the **replenishment meeting**, the decision about which task will be worked on next is made by someone who actively works with the Kanban system or by an internal stakeholder who is interested in its output. The order is best decided using economical criteria. The replenishment meetings follow an individual rhythm in each company.

In the **regular standup meeting**, which should only last between five and maximum 15 minutes, the work is coordinated by the colleagues who perform the work. It's best when these meetings take place in front of the Kanban board. However, the point is not to ask questions related to the content of individual work items, but to have a strategic view. Where are there problems, dependencies, bottlenecks or delays? Any need for subject matter clarification is noted and can be dealt with between those involved after the standup. The regular standup meeting should be moderated, ideally using a rotation principle.

The **retrospective** serves the continuous improvement processes and methods. It deals with identifying problems and finding solutions for them (for example, based on a blockade cluster). The five recommended steps from Esther Derby and Diana Larsen, plus the additional step from Klaus Leopold, are a suitable method for conducting a retrospective:

1. Step 1 and Step 6: Check-in and Check-out phase
2. Step 2: Collecting Facts
3. Step 3: Defining the Core Problem

4. Step 4: Understanding the Problem
5. Step 5: Finding the Solution and Determining Measures

It's important to not just decide on measures, but also to define criteria to determine whether or not a solution was successful. In addition, who takes care of what must also be stipulated. This improvement work can also be depicted on the Kanban board through the use of a separate swim lane.

Literature

(Benson & DeMaria Barry, 2013) Jim Benson & Tonianne DeMaria Barry. *Personal Kanban: Mapping Work | Navigating Life*, Createspace, 2011.

(Burrows, 2014) Mike Burrows. *Kanban from the Inside: Understand the Kanban Method, connect it to what you already know, introduce it with impact*, Blue Hole Press, 2014.

(Deming, 2000) W. Edwards Deming. *Out of the Crisis*, The MIT Press, 2000.

(Derby & Larsen, 2006) Esther Derby & Diana Larsen. *Agile Retrospectives: Making Good Teams Great*, O'Reilly 2006.

(Goldratt, 1997) Eliyahu M. Goldratt. *Critical Chain*, Gower Publishing 1997.

(Goldratt & Cox, 2004) Eliyahu M. Goldratt & Jeff Cox. *The Goal*, North River Press 2004.

(Leopold & Kaltenecker, 2015) Klaus Leopold & Siegfried Kaltenecker. *Kanban Change Leadership: Creating a Culture of Continuous Improvement*, John Wiley & Sons Inc, 2015.

(Leopold & Magennis, 2015) Klaus Leopold & Troy Magennis. *Using Blocker Clustering, Defect Clustering, and Prioritization for Process Improvment*, Artikel auf InfoQ, June 2015. http://bit.ly/29gGOYM.

(Vacanti, 2015) Daniel S. Vacanti. *Actionable Agile Metrics for Predictability: An Introduction*, Actionable Agile Press, 2015.

(Wilson et al., 1993) Paul F. Wilson & Larry D. Dell & Gaylord F. Anderson. *Root Cause Analysis: A Tool for Total Quality Management*, American Society for Quality, 1993.

3. Large-Scale Kanban

Several years ago, I was asked to implement Kanban at a company for 80 teams. Scaling par excellence. The calculations started running through my head—80 trainings, afterwards a little coaching here and there—I was going to make gazillions! Deep down, though, I knew it was a bad idea. These teams needed to develop a product together. Each team depended on at least five other teams, and up to 20 in the worst case. Optimizing 80 teams would scarcely make a difference in the output of the entire system and, in fact, would have damaged it. As we saw in Chapter 1, local optimization leads to global sub-optimization. I was very close to succumbing to the same false assumptions with which I am continually confronted. Despite what is often claimed, Kanban is not a team method.

The goal of Kanban is not to optimize individual teams, rather it is to optimize value creation within a company. This overall view of the system applies to every level where value for the customer is generated. With so many dependencies, the value is obviously not created at the team level. The motto "Manage the work, not the worker" functions for five employees the same as it does for 500. We are going to go directly to Flight Level 2 in this chapter: How can you keep an overview with large Kanban projects?

Kanban is not not scalable

Whoever assumes that agility can be achieved by deploying some method across the company is suffering from a delusion. Scaling is not achieved by simply following a particular method. There are plenty of convenience products propagated under the catch phrase "agile scaling" that fulfill a company's desire for blueprint copy and paste solutions. These might provide wonderful inspiration, but nothing more. Such templates focus too much on the practices rather than on the underlying thought process. The organization is misled and pressed into a pre-defined mold, instead of giving thought to the current state of the organization and how it can evolve. In "Alice in Wonderland", the queen says at one point: "...here we must run as fast as we can, just to stay in place." This describes today's business reality quite well—a company must continuously adapt in their own fashion. If you don't adopt the appropriate mindset, even the best methods are ineffective. The best practices are always those that you have developed within your own context. Unfortunately, I am not clever enough to find the one sure formula that guarantees success for every company on this planet. However, those that use someone else's solution for their problem shouldn't be surprised when their problem doesn't get solved. I am thoroughly convinced that every organization must find their own approach for success with regards to scaling.

Where does Kanban fit in the question of scaling? In principle, nowhere, because Kanban is simply Kanban. The method itself is nothing more than the established three principles and six practices (see Chapter 1) that should be considered in order to establish a flow-based work system—the rest is simply independent thinking. The cool thing is, these principles and practices do not need to be modified to suit various sizes. Since Kanban focuses on improved value creation, scaling considerations are already included, because the entire value chain is the goal of improvement. However, Kanban does not have a specific target, nor does it give a specific formula for achieving a specific target. Kanban is much more about evolving your thinking: Start with what you are doing right now, and improve it based on what is revealed by applying the principles and practices.

If several teams must work with one another, the focus should first be placed on the *dependencies* existing between the teams. This is often ignored in classical project management, until the failures pile up at the end of the project. The more dependencies there are in a project, the more likely there will be problems in the final phases. The reason for this can be seen by using an example from a completely different field. A statistic from the U.S. Bureau of Transportation states that in the course of a day, until 6 PM, the probability of a flight delay of more than 20 minutes continuously increases. The reason: A plane flies to several destinations. On each route, there can be delays that accumulate over the entire day Decision Science News, 2014).

This cumulative effect also occurs with the sequential processing of work in a project. For instance, tests are often performed at the end of development. Since it is rare that the development is 100% free of errors on the first attempt, the late quality feedback is an unpredictable factor that can ruin a budget and timeframe. Assume four teams must deliver a product at the same time (for example, apps for various platforms). Then Apple launches an iOS update and the Apple application team needs to adapt the software and cannot keep the deadline accordingly. Due to the dependencies, the work from the other teams is also delayed. Four teams mean 16 possible delay scenarios, and only one in which all the teams deliver on time—i.e. only 6.25% of the time everything runs according to plan. With seven teams, there are 128 possible scenarios, with only 0.8% of all scenarios leading to an on-time delivery from all teams. That's why all sources of delay in a project should be uncovered and dealt with as soon as possible. You certainly want to eliminate all dependencies, but this doesn't always work. Thus, managing the dependencies should have priority before team optimization. This functions better from a level across all teams, versus the teams trying to deal with it themselves.

Cycle time is primarily waiting time

When a customer places an order, they do not care which team is responsible, what dependencies exist between the individual teams involved, or which team in the system has a problem at the moment—the customer just wants their product delivered. From this perspective, mere team optimizations are senseless and even counterproductive, because optimizing individual units of a system can lead to sub-optimization of the entire system. Why is that?

Let's assume there is a project with four teams involved (Figure 3.1). In order to fulfill the customer requests (say, for a feature), the teams need to coordinate with one another. The order of work is that Team 1 works first on the order, gives it to Team 3, who in turn passes along their output to Team 4 who again passes the work to Team 2. Finally, Team 2 completes the feature.

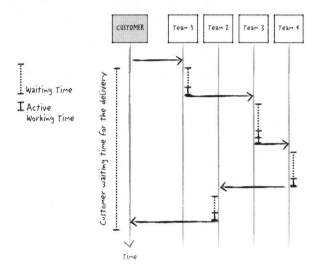

Figure 3.1: Waiting Time vs. Working Time in a Project

In reality, there is seldom a smooth handover when work is transferred from one team to the next. Often, the work is simply thrown over the fence and the teams do not communicate with each other. As such, the next team could be currently working on something else. These handovers produce delays because the next team does not begin working on the order immediately. When you take a look at the cycle time, a notable imbalance can be seen. The active work is a very small part of the entire cycle time, whereas the majority of time is spent waiting.

In order to shorten the cycle time for large projects or other large undertakings, many companies look for agile developments as a solution, and mistakenly think that all teams in an agile company work with agile methods. The assumption is that a simple multiplication of the method over the entire system—perhaps one project with several teams—will make them faster. However, an organization is not simply a container for individual teams. What happens when individual teams optimize their process?

Every project is constructed of dependencies. Through local optimization of the individual teams, what happens is exactly what I wrote about in Chapter 1 by means of the keyboard example: The individual team improves itself and saves working time. However, the entire cycle time of the project is not shortened, because there are bottlenecks in the work system whose units are dependent on one another. The bottlenecks are not necessarily due to poor work: Experts are not always available, intermediate products are handed over to contractors, employees go on vacation, etc. Bottlenecks will always be present in a system and it is not the goal of Kanban to completely remove these bottlenecks. This also means the entire project receives little benefit when individual teams celebrate local productivity successes. In order to minimize the risk, it makes sense to cut the project into smaller pieces. Nevertheless, regardless how small you cut the pieces, it will not be possible to avoid dependencies and handovers.

An agile company is a company where dependencies exist. Even an agile implemented project is a project where dependencies exist. Agility is not the result of adding up agile teams, but the result of agile interactions between those involved. The goal should be improved value creation. From the Kanban perspective, it's going about two things:

1. Coordination: The focus is placed on improving interactions. The right things should be worked on at the right times. This

means minimizing delays at the handover by managing the entire value creation.

2. Customer: To be exact, the organization is the focus of local optimization, not the customer. The question is though: What must be done to improve the service for the customer and to really generate value for them?

Therefore, those responsible need an overview of the relationships between the teams. The methods the teams work with—Scrum, Kanban, voodoo or whatever—is completely beside the point. What's important is a work environment that optimizes the path of value creation, rather than the organizational structures. I would like to show you this by using an example from my work with customers.

3.1 A Practical Example: A Sales Platform with more than 200 Project Employees

It was not possible to see the forest through the trees—that was my experience the first time I visited this company. More than 200 people were working on a project to replace software for all shopping applications with a functionally-rich sales platform. At the end of the project, the Android and iPhone apps, the web shop, as well as the sales software for the stores, should all run on this platform. Due to the high amount, and partially unclear, dependencies between the teams, nobody really knew what the current state of the project was, and whether or not they would make their deadline. The coordination had become a major problem. The backend team was especially under pressure in this situation, because the requirements came in without coordination. This is how the project was structured:

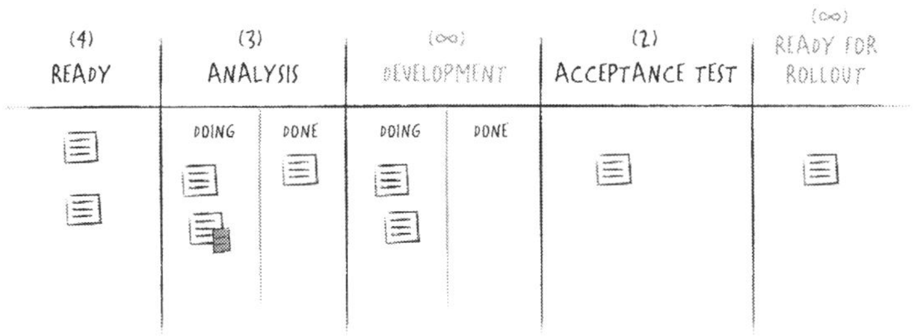

(4) READY	(3) ANALYSIS		[∞] DEVELOPMENT		(2) ACCEPTANCE TEST	[∞] READY FOR ROLLOUT
	DOING	DONE	DOING	DONE		

Figure 3.5: Where is the useful step for scaling hiding?

I often encounter similarly built boards at business analysts or product managers. After the analysis, the work falls into a black hole, i.e. an unlimited step called "Development". This black hole can include any number of systems and steps. For example, the development is done in a different country, and development works with subcontractors there. Only at the point of the acceptance test does the work show up again in the analyst's process, and then disappears again in an unlimited step "Rollout". The two unlimited buffers signal that we are dealing with dependencies that we have no influence over. However, this brings with it the disadvantage that the predictability in the system is hardly factual, because measurements in an unstable system are only marginally useful.

For the scaling (improvement) in this case, I would begin with the handover to development. In terms of predictability and reasonable management of the work, the leveraging effect is much better at this step. First off, the black hole in the process should be removed by assigning a WIP limit to the "Development" activity. That way, activities occurring outside of the system are made a part of the system—that is the idea behind scaling. Scaling Kanban means nothing more than improving the coordination and looking for ways to more efficiently collaborate in terms of value creation. Put another way, good experiences will be carried further. That doesn't mean the neighboring team must absolutely use Kanban. It is an invitation to look at the dependencies together because, with the exception of perhaps a small startup company, no team can fulfill the customer's wishes alone.

Linking Kanban systems is a way to optimize the interactions between units and, as such, value creation. In my work, I primarily come across two types of linking: consolidating services and connecting services.

3.2.1 Consolidating Services

There is a pattern I often see: service A is permanently dependent on service B. For example, a Kanban system exists for the frontend development, but must always wait because backend development is lagging behind (see Figure 3.6). Only when the necessary work in the backend is completed, can the frontend process continue and be completed.

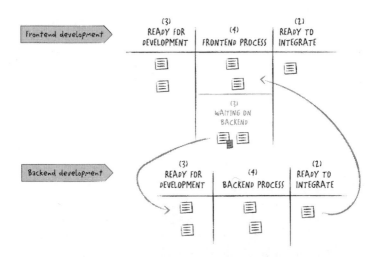

Figure 3.6: Dependencies Between Frontend and Backend Development

Since this is a known problem, the employees in the frontend services have setup a parking space (buffer) in their Kanban system where the affected tickets wait. This waiting time is not immediately designated as a blockade, as long as it remains within a certain time frame—it belongs to the flow of the development process. The parked ticket in the frontend development Kanban system arrives as input in the backend development Kanban system, and returns to the frontend process once it has completed the backend process.

Even if these are known waiting phases, these dependencies increase the cycle time. When such a parking space pattern shows up, a good solution is to consolidate the services and make the workflow more continuous and improving coordination (Figure 3.7). By doing this, the entire system can flow better. Consolidation means, in this case, that both services are collected into a single service, such as "Front- and Backend Development". The WIP limit must be adjusted to the new working reality, but there is no general rule that can be applied. The WIP limit must be decided by those involved, according to their context.

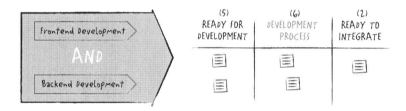

Figure 3.7: Consolidation of Frontend and Backend Development

Practically speaking, this means the involved teams combine into one large team. Usually, this happens quite subtly through the constant, necessary coordination. In time, it becomes clear that this separation does not make sense. Naturally, consolidating teams only functions up to a certain size and I usually see this variation in smaller structures. More often, I observe that the organizational structure remains untouched. The individual interdependent teams or services decide that they should coordinate with one another more carefully, and improve this coordination by using a mutual Kanban board.

3.2.2 Connecting Services

Again, we can look at two interdependent services, but this time the input for service B is the output from service A. The simplest example of this: Integrating a piece of work can happen only when the development is completed and ready for integration (Figure 3.8). This point makes it again clear, why the term "done" or "finished" should not show up as the last step of a Kanban board, because the work continues after this step. I only use "Done" when the criteria for completion are explicitly defined. If feedback from the customer is expected, the column could be called "Ready for Customer Feedback". In the example depicted, it continues with the integration, so it's called "Ready to Integrate". Conversely, the actual continuation of value creation should be reflected in the first step of the following process. The first step of the integration is ideally not called "Input Queue", "Next" or something similar, rather it also includes a clear description like "Ready to Integrate".

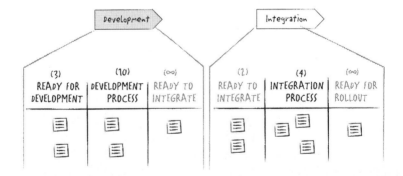

Figure 3.8: Processes Building on One Another: Development and Integration

The final step is an unlimited buffer for services that are not

connected with one another. The step "Ready to Integrate" in
the integration process Kanban system is naturally WIP limited,
because the employees in the integration process want to keep a
smooth workflow. This is the classic "over the fence" tactic. From
development's point of view, the work is completed and, as such,
out of sight, out of mind. From the customer's perspective, there
is still a bunch of work to do because the developed features need
to be integrated into the system and then rolled out. If we look at
these two separate services from the service-oriented perspective of
the customer, these services should be connected into one overall
process. This can easily be done by connecting the last step of
development with the first step of integration (see Figure 3.9).

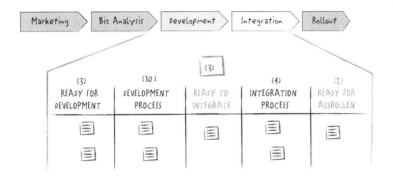

Figure 3.9: Connecting Services by limiting WIP

The point is, by connecting the services, the predictability of the
system improves because the unlimited buffer is replaced by a
mutual, WIP-limited step between development and integration.
At first, this will cause a backup of work that must be taken into
account, because an unlimited buffer collides with a limited process
step. Due to the WIP limiting, this backlog will be resolved in time
since there will not be, in the long run, more developed than what
can be integrated. If it becomes apparent that the integration is a
bottleneck, you have the possibility to take appropriate actions, such

as automatic integration.

What's important is that you have now constructed a continuous system. When it makes sense, the value chain can be scaled further by connecting additional services on the horizontal level. For instance, the interfaces between integration and rollout could be looked at more closely, or the boundary point between business analysis and development. You can call this scaling, but for me these are simply system improvements.

3.2.3 Shared Services

Shared services are those services which are available to the value streams of several projects or product development, such as marketing, integration or rollout (Figure 3.10).

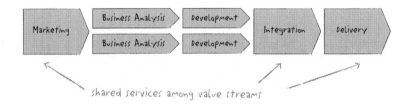

Figure 3.10: Shared Services are Available to Several Value Streams

If we depict the value streams separate from one another on the Kanban board, the separated integration service for could be depicted like situation seen in Figure 3.11. Two different development processes unload their completed work into an unlimited "Ready to Integrate" step, while at the same time the first step of the integration service "Ready to Integrate" is, of course, limited.

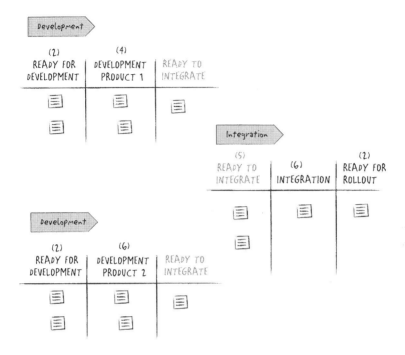

Figure 3.11: Unlimited Replenishment from Two Development Processes

Even with this initial situation, I see a possibility that the services can be connected. The developed features from both development processes land in a mutual, WIP-limited step "Ready to Integrate", on which the integration process is joined. (Figure 3.12). The WIP limit in the original first step of the integration process tell us that there must have been some form of coordination between those responsible for integration and the stakeholders of both development processes. By connecting both product services with the shared service "Integration", a mutual service emerges and along with it the necessity that those responsible for the development processes coordinate with one another.

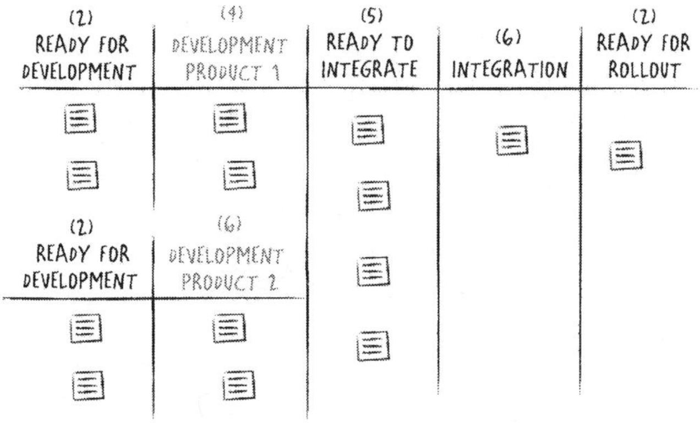

(2) READY FOR DEVELOPMENT	(4) DEVELOPMENT PRODUCT 1	(5) READY TO INTEGRATE	(6) INTEGRATION	(2) READY FOR ROLLOUT
▤	▤	▤	▤	▤
▤	▤	▤		
(2) READY FOR DEVELOPMENT	(6) DEVELOPMENT PRODUCT 2	▤		
▤	▤	▤		
▤	▤			

Figure 3.12: Consolidation to a Mutual Handover Step

Another useful improvement would be to go a few steps to the left and coordinate the entire development better. This means you could also consolidate the two separate "Ready for Development" steps into a single step (Figure 3.13). As a result, the entire value creation process gets closer to the business. A mutual, limited input queue for two development processes requires that the stakeholders involved must make economically sound decisions beforehand. We can see this in Figure 3.13 for instance, where the relationship of the epics in the input queue changed when compared to the board in Figure 3.12. Apparently, it makes sense economically to progress with the work on Product 1. By making such deliberate decisions, the inflow of work into the integration will gradually be regulated.

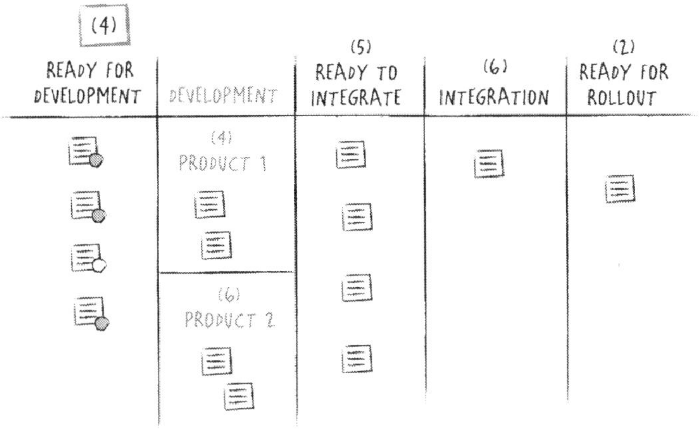

Figure 3.13: Improved Coordination of Development and Economic Decision-Making by Using a Mutual Input Queue

"Scaling to the Left" is one of the most important scaling decisions, because the (technical) implementation and the economical viewpoint coalesce. These two worlds cannot be separated in today's world, which is why it's important for the people responsible for these areas to work together. We will see in Chapter 5 how we can make economically sound decisions with this collaboration.

3.3 Large-Scale Kanban at Bosch Automotive Electronics

Bosch Automotive Electronics, with their headquarters in Reutlingen, Germany, is worldwide one of the most important suppliers and development partners for the automobile industry, but also for other fields of application. The microelectronic products like semiconductors and sensors are used in braking systems, as well as in consumer products like electronic bicycles. Starting with Germany, Bosch Automotive Electronics, with the support of Kanban, wants to become a learning organization, encompassing their locations in China, the USA, India and Hungary. I conducted a written interview with the project leaders Hans-Oliver Ruoß and Andreas Haugeneder about the challenges of this project and how we dealt with them.

Dr.-Ing. Hans-Oliver Ruoß has been working since 1989 in various positions of responsibility for the Robert Bosch GmbH company. From 2001 till 2006, he was in the Research and Advance Development area as manager of "High-frequency technology, EMV and EMVU", from 2006 till 2007 as group manager in Gasoline Systems/Motor Control, and 2007 till 2013 as Department Manager of Automotive Electronics, in addition to being head of the Bosch Center of Excellence for "Electromagnetic Tolerance". Since 2014, he has led the project "Engineering Efficiency at Automotive Electronics".

Dr. Andreas Haugeneder has more than 15 years of practical experience in the development of automobile electronics. After various management positions in development and purchasing, he has devoted himself in the past several years to the advancement of worldwide distributed and networked teams, especially with the principles of Kanban for knowledge work.

Klaus: Some time ago, Bosch Automotive Electronics (AE) started the program "Engineering Efficiency @ AE 2.0" (EE@AE 2.0). What is it going about, what is the goal of this program?

Andreas/Oliver: After a very successful three-year classical efficiency program, just like our mission statement says, "We push the limits!", we wanted to push our boundaries further. We wanted to be continuously better—with what we do and how we do it. The goal is to be a learning organization. The growing complexity and fast pace of the markets require continuous learning at all level. Our customers are very clearly our focus.

Klaus: This program was first limited to Germany. How many employees were included in the transformation to learning organization?

Andreas/Oliver: For this transformation, we first invited all the development managers and employees in Germany. This included around 2,000 developers, who started down the path at an appropriate pace for each of their areas. We wanted to take everyone with us. Nobody should be left behind.

Klaus: We came into contact because I initiated Kanban in a different area of Bosch. You were interested in this and found Kanban a suitable approach for Bosch AE to become a learning organization. What exactly about Kanban interested you as EE@AE 2.0 team and seemed appropriate for achieving your goals?

Andreas/Oliver: In terms of the transformation: Using Kanban for development, especially the Kanban boards, is one tool moving us towards becoming a learning organization. We place great value on transparency at all levels. In the first step, it was going about visualizing what is otherwise invisible in knowledge work. Linked Kanban boards were the second step for transparency in the decision-making process and steered us towards what was most important: The customer is our focus and our effectivity increased. Using Kanban, a sustainable increase in efficiency can be achieved without additional effort from each individual. Quite the opposite, in fact: Part of the goal is to reduce local overloads. Continuous improvement is a part of the method.

Klaus: In our preliminary discussions, we came to the conclusion that you cannot implement a push-principle on a pull-principle based method like Kanban. That meant, however, that you first needed to learn the method of how to be able to use the Kanban method, correct? Does the EE@AE 2.0 team also work with Kanban?

Andreas/Oliver: Yes, it was very important to us to not turn the Kanban implementation into a circus. Instead, we wanted to invite everyone to join in on the transformation. Implementing the method with a method similar to what we were used to seemed to be the best concept for success. Following our motto that "everyone learns", the EE@AE 2.0 team also joined the transformation and didn't shy away from making small course corrections when it was necessary. In this sense, our approach is iterative and adaptive— not a classical roll-out. Our own Kanban board made the next steps transparent and the retrospectives helped us to stay on the right path.

Klaus: Now all of the employees in Germany, as we said around 2,000, are involved in the Kanban initiative and you pursued the conversion to the pull-principle. How did the conversion occur, how did you proceed?

Andreas/Oliver: With the help of Early Adopters, we demonstrated the usefulness and the advantages of the approach. In addition, we offered support to the team, in the form of coaching, to help with their unique challenges. In this sense, the employees and management are our customers. We must offer a good product, otherwise nobody will "buy" it. Specifically, this meant that we, together with you, in the Trainings-Module 1 very clearly demonstrated opportunities provided by Kanban. In Module 2, the Kanban boards to the individual requirements of the teams were created. The teams were coached intensively from the EE@AE 2.0 team for the preparation and follow-up.

Klaus: Kanban for knowledge work has its roots in software development, but as part of your initiative the engineering teams, most notably, chose Kanban. Do you receive any feedback about what appeals to the engineers about this work method?

Andreas/Oliver: The challenges are similar: constantly changing requirements, many parallel tasks, continuous re-prioritization, resource shortages and the demand for shorter processing times. The engineers want to deliver the customers excellent results despite the challenging circumstances. Just like the motto "stop starting, start finishing" states, it helped to finish work, avoid multitasking, as well as recognize and remedy bottlenecks and blockades.

Klaus: Again and again, I see Kanban initiatives that start off brilliantly and then gradually fizzle out. At Bosch, quite the opposite occurs: The modules you offer are constantly booked out, the number of participants steadily increases and remains high. Why do the employees have a passion for Kanban and how do you as the EE@AE 2.0 Team make sure the processes established in the organization are sustainable?

Andreas/Oliver: The incentives for starting are important. We meet our colleagues in their real working environment and offer solutions for their completely unique challenges. Adapting Kanban principles is completely voluntary, nobody is forced to do it. After a successful start, it's essential to not leave the Kanban newbies alone. We offer support not only through personal coaching, but also through a type of hotline. However, the method is not the priority, rather it's "developers helping developers". This is achieved through technical expertise combined with substantial knowledge of the method. After about six months of operational experience, the teams are further challenged and nurtured in the next training module—the so-called "Large Retrospective"—with your support, Klaus. "We want to continuously improve" is the motto for this step. Additional success factors reside in Leading Change, in the communication, as well as the fact that everyone learns together— over many levels of the hierarchy.

Klaus: In the meantime, I have been able to support you with the extension of the Kanban initiative to China, and locations in the USA, India and Hungary should follow. Completely different cultures are now coming into play. What are you watching out for? Which differences are there between Kanban in Germany and Kanban in China?

Andreas/Oliver: We will also stay true to the pull-principle in the regions you mentioned. It does, however, require adjusting the "advertising strategy" of the method for the respective cultures. The benefit aspect, especially the personal benefit aspect in China, is key. This can be seen as the similarity between cultures. In contrast, transparency, and more precisely the decision-making transparency as I described it for Germany earlier, is not a sales argument for the Kanban method in China. The large authority gap, as well as the associated decision-making authority for management, remains untouched. On the other hand, the willingness to change and the eagerness to experiment is much pronounced that in our cultural sphere.

Klaus: When you look back over the last few months: What effects have established themselves in the organization?

Andreas/Oliver: We have already achieved some of the goals we defined at the beginning. We really learn together at all levels. Also, the decision-making transparency has increased in many areas for every individual employee. The result is that we have increased our cooperation in order to fulfill the customer's needs as best as possible. We have taken the first steps towards becoming a learning organization—for our benefit and for the benefit of our customers.

Literature

(Decision Science News, 2014) Decision Science News. *Every U.S. flight in 2013 analyzed* http://www.decisionsciencenews.com/2014/11/06/flight-delays

(Kotter, 2012) John P. Kotter. *Leading Change*, Harvard Business School Press, 2012.

(Leopold & Kaltenecker, 2015) Klaus Leopold & Siegfried Kaltenecker. *Kanban Change Leadership: Creating a Culture of Continuous Improvement*, John Wiley & Sons Inc, 2015.

4. Forecasting

There is probably no worse question you can ask a knowledge worker than, "When is it finished?" Nevertheless, it is a valid question from a business perspective because it is difficult to manage a company without a time frame for the system output. The critical issue is, with the knowledge you possess today, you want to know what can happen in the future. In knowledge work, particularly, the most-used forecasting approach is estimation. The problem with estimating is that there is a very low degree of accuracy for the amount of time it takes.

For the most part, estimations are inaccurate, and especially inaccurate if the prediction should determine when something will be completed. People have a limited view of the cycle time. As I have stated many times already, the cycle time consists mostly of waiting time for a unit of work (see Chapter 3, Figure 3.1). This is exactly where human capabilities hit a snag. To begin with, only the actual working time is estimated. Another 100 or 200 percent is added to the estimate, because you anticipate something could go wrong in the meantime. If several teams are involved in a project that are dependent on one another, as well as dependent on the external parties involved, these estimates are simply added to it. However, this doesn't mean that the entire estimate is more accurate. Aside from the inability to include waiting times in the estimate, there are thousands additional factors that can interfere on the path to completing the product, which also affect the cycle time: vacation, illness, changes to the team, changes to the process, changes in the law, new management rules, reorganization causing short-term decrease in performance, employees taken for other projects, unstable WIP, more employees, better coffee, etc. This is just a small snippet of the entire spectrum of uncertainties that determine work progress. The world is, and remains, uncertain and we cannot influence every uncertainty. How useful it is, then, to invest so much energy in elaborate estimation methods that cannot even factor in the smallest fraction of uncertainties? All over the globe, whether agile or not, there is unnecessary amounts of brainpower invested in trying to figure out when something will, despite the best intentions, not be finished. From the lean perspective, estimating is wasteful because it provides no additional benefit to the customer. It's natural that management needs reference points in order to chose and start a project, as well as plan the implementation, and estimation is often the only alternative. It may help to understand the scope of individual elements, but it doesn't help correlate them. Estimating is necessary when there is no real data to work with. However, as soon as you have data, you can forego estimating, and make a forecast instead.

What use is a forecast?

It is well known that meteorologists do not estimate the weather for the next few days. Weather is the result of many interacting factors, so meteorologists use observations based on collecting, interpreting and building models from the relationships and effects of past and present phenomena. Meteorology is an empirical science whose rules are dictated by nature, and where very few questions can be answered under laboratory conditions. There is a probability for a certain type of weather condition to occur depending on how pronounced the current measurements are of individual factors like air pressure, cloud density, air currents, etc. If a weather forecast states "with 70 percent chance of rain in the early afternoon", and then it doesn't rain, an analysis is performed to see why it didn't rain, and a learning loop is created. The models are adapted with every observation and the results are continuously updated.

> **Forecasting** is an attempt to use model-based prediction to determine the manifestation of future events. These models

continue to be developed by using the knowledge gained with each real result and are, therefore, never "finished".

A model is a simulation of the real world that allows cost-efficient experiments to be performed. The assumptions found in a forecast are defined through the use of the model - and these assumptions are continuously reviewed.

I use the weather forecasting example to make a point. I hear over and over the argument, "Yes, forecasting works when you work in a factory or you always make the same thing. Knowledge work is highly variable, so forecasting can't work." The weather is one of the most dynamic phenomenon on our planet, where every little fluctuation on one end of the planet influences weather development on the other end of the planet (Butterfly Effect). In the meantime, the weather models have been expanded so much that there is a very high probability that the weather prognosis is correct. If forecasting functions with the weather, why should model-based forecasting not function for knowledge work?

The term "model" is certainly fraught with meaning. It sounds like complicated mathematics and highly scientific observations. Let me put you at ease right now. The models I am talking about are relatively simple. You can begin with these models, and you can continue to refine your models as you gain experience and data, depending on your needs. Even adding together cycle times in order to determine the completion date of a project is a "model" (albeit one that leaves out many, many factors). With the knowledge that the cycle time is comprised of five to 20 percent active working time and 80 percent inactive waiting time, the model can already be refined a bit. If you include the causes of the waiting times, you can already create a simulation. For example, if frequent failures are the cause of the majority of blockades, you can determine how the cycle time would change if the number of bugs would be reduced by half.

Let me put it another way: When you begin with your project (or product, etc.) and you want to make a forecast for it, your model will give you uncertain results at first. With every measurement and every refinement, you will receive more accurate results. By the way, this is not a characteristic that applies exclusively to forecasting. It is also possible to get more and more exact estimates - only this fact is often negated. Instead of adapting the estimate, you frantically hold on to a plan that has long ceased to reflect reality. I hear quite often, "We'll manage it somehow", but a miracle rarely occurs. At the beginning, when there is no data to work with, you need a bit of audacity when considering assumptions, probabilities and ranges. Maybe you already know the proportion of working time and waiting time from your own measurements, or perhaps you must first depend on other's assertions, just as I, or other writers, often do. Whatever the case, make it clear what your assumptions have been based on. It's possible, at the beginning, that you will need to work with estimates, which can then be verified and replaced with real data step-by-step. Or as Nobel prize winner Richard Feynman described the first step to scientific knowledge: "First we guess it." In doing so, you must rely on the knowledge of those who perform the actual work. The goal should be, however, to let these people work as quickly as possible without interruption, rather than be held up by continuous estimations of their work. Whether estimated or based on data, it's crucial that you are working with units found in the real world - Euros, minutes, quantity, etc.

4.1 Forecasting Requirements

Knowledge work is a precarious profession. How and when something will be finished depends on the availability, the behavior and the imperfection of the people in the work system. There are millions of external circumstances, too. These uncertainties can never be completely avoided, regardless how vehemently the customer asks the question, "When will it be finished?" - which they have every right to do. In knowledge work, must we really be so fatalistic about our destiny? As Dan Vacanti, an advocate of Kanban at its inception, so correctly states, knowledge workers are often caught up in their own rules when dealing with uncertainties. Frantically, there is an attempt to bend unsuitable key figures and practices to fit knowledge work. In order to reduce uncertainty, what can be measured in knowledge work, should be measured. Then, in time, many inappropriate rules and behaviors that obstruct the work will become apparent (Vacanti, 2015). Dan is the expert on metrics for flow-based systems, which is why I highly recommend his book to you. Also, I do not want to discuss every possible metric in detail here. In this book, I want to give you an overview of the three most significant metrics with which you can gain continuous feedback about the status of your Kanban system, and make predictions. Most importantly, with the help of these metrics, you can make clear decisions. These metrics predominately give you an indication whether or not the work in your system is really flowing.

Three parameters are particularly interesting in flow-based systems and should also be measured:

1. Work in Progress (WIP): How much work is in the system?
2. Cycle Time: How long does a unit of work need in order to be completed?
3. Throughput: How many units of work are completed in a specific amount of time?

Why am I not talking about story points and velocity?

Agile management frameworks bring their own metrics into play, which they use to take readings on the progress of work, and the productivity of a team. There is nothing fundamentally wrong with story points and velocity when they are used as an internal reference point for the team, in order to identify potential areas of improvement. Story points should echo the extent of a request (a work item), but not in hours as is usually the case (the amount of effort needed), but instead as a description of the complexity. These are all relative magnitudes, meaning user stories can be compared to a reference-user-story, and can be appropriately provided with points from an impure Fibonacci sequence, which can be traced back to Mike Cohn (Cohn, 2005).

Daniel Vacanti raises an interesting point: The Agile manifesto explicitly emphasizes the cooperation with the customers - internal as well as external. At the same time, the customer is forced to make use of metrics, which make calculations in time and Euro (or some other monetary value) that does not even have an equivalent form in the world of a CFO. Too often for my taste, the issue of complexity is used as an argument for agile metrics, and even a specific algebra is developed to get a handle on the complexity. We should really stop using complexity as an excuse for using things we either don't understand, or can't do better. I understand the term Agility to mean, among other things, speaking the language of the customer. Time, number of features in a release, Euro, etc.: These are the measurement numbers we need to make available, because these are numbers that customers can use.

I also recommend these three metrics - Work in Progress, cycle time and throughput - because they create a functional interface to the customer. The whole world should not have to change in order to fit into our metrics. Instead, based on generally accepted units of measurement and value, the metrics should help us get the work flowing and keep it flowing.

Work in Progress

When I have developed a Kanban system with individuals in a company, and subsequently put it into operation, I recommend immediately measuring the Work in Progress - even before we concern ourselves with cycle time or throughput. Why? Work in Progress is the best indicator of the stability of a system. A lack of stability is the most pressing problem in the majority of cases. At the same time, stability is the prerequisite for forecasting. **One of the most important requirements for a stable system is limited Work in Progress.**

The term "Work in Progress" contains two elements that you should take a closer look at, before starting with the measurements.

1. *"Work"*, *or a work item*, is understood to be a unit that creates value for the customer, when it's completed. This implies that the individual tasks (parts of a work item) will not be considered for the measurement.
2. *"In Progress"* means, more or less, "being implemented". Thus, it must be defined when work is being implemented, and that requires the defining the boundaries of the work system (see Leopold & Kaltenecker, 2015). It's also necessary to understand that this clearly defined area is limited from the point of commitment - there can only be a specific amount of work within this area at any given time (see Figure 4.1).

The definitions of "Work" and "In Progress" are not always simple. In Chapters 1 and 2, I wrote that both can change when flowing through the work system. The good news is, however, that measuring Work in Progress is quite trivial. You simply count the number of tickets currently being implemented, which are found in the limited area of the Kanban board.

Cycle Time

Measuring the cycle time is important, in order to be able to answer the question, "When will it be finished?" If the Work in

Progress was well defined (see above), the cycle time is quite easy to measure. The cycle time indicates how long it took a work item to be implemented. This is why it is so important to stipulate the boundaries of the implementation area ahead of time. It isn't going about effort or active working time, but on the total time a work item spent in implementation - regardless if it was being worked on, or blocked, or spent some time on a parking space, if it was sent to India in the meantime, etc. As has been mentioned several times, active working time is but a small portion of the cycle time. There is no correlation between cycle time and effort. Another important point is that cycle time is given in calendar days, and not measured in work days. When you tell a customer on June 1st that the completion of their work takes 30 days, then they expect a delivery on July 1st. Naturally, there are weekends and perhaps even holidays in between, but this is of little interest to the customer.

Throughput

Throughput is the amount of work that exits the limited "in Progress" area within a certain time frame, because the work has been completed. For example, the throughput could be three stories per day, or eight features per week, or four projects per month. The throughput answers the question: "How much will I receive until a specific date or till the next release?" If we look at Figure 4.1, the throughput corresponds to the departure rate, while the arrival rate shows how much work per time unit enters the system. The arrival and departure rate should be equal, because when an imbalance is present, the work is either backing up or the system is running empty.

Figure 4.1: Work in Progress, Cycle Time and Throughput of a Kanban System

These three metrics can be observed on different levels. For example, you can treat the "in Progress" area as a subsystem within the value creation. Similarly, you can also zoom-in and apply the metrics on the individual activities in this area.

Acquiring Measurement Data

Work in Progress, cycle time and throughput are not only the most important metrics in a flow-based system, they are also very easy to measure. The only thing you need to accomplish these measurements are timestamps, and these timestamps are the foundation for visualizing these three metrics.

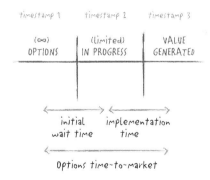

Figure 4.2: Defining Timeframes through Timestamps

Whenever a ticket enters an area, or column, the ticket is marked with a timestamp (i.e. the date). Which timeframes emerge between these timestamps?

The first timestamp is given to a ticket when it is placed in the option pool as an idea (see Figure 4.2). I designate the timeframe between entering the option pool and crossing over into implementation as "initial waiting time"[1]. When work actually begins on a work item and it lands in implementation, it gets the next timestamp. The timeframe between this point and the point where the value has been generated is the "implementation time". Together, these two timeframes yield the time-to-market for an option. When I am working with a company that is at the very beginning of their Kanban implementation, as well as with their measurements, I start with this simplest variation of measuring. My recommendation is that you take it one step at a time. Introducing Kanban is itself a major transition and it takes time to really understand the various tools, such as visualization and WIP limits. Measurements should be brought into play only after the people involved have a gained experience working with the system. Key figures are still seen as surveillance measures by many people, which is why sensitivity towards the change process is needed. Only go into detailed measurements once everyone understands that these measurements are being used primarily as feedback for improving their own workflow. For the sake of completeness, you can see an example of an elaborate Kanban board (from the practical example in Chapter 3), where even more interesting timeframes are revealed.

---

[1]This is only my suggestion. If you find a better definition for your situation, by all means, use it!

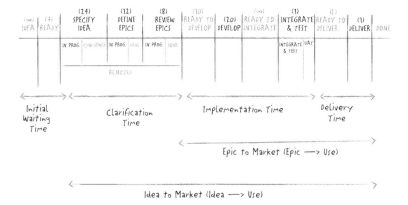

Figure 4.3: Possible Observations within a Kanban System

4.2 Forecast for a Work Unit

Let's look at how the question, "When will *one* piece of work be finished?", can be answered. This question requires creating a forecast for the cycle time of a work unit, so it is recommended to define the measuring points of the cycle time as a first step. The cycle time can be measured as the entire time period between starting a piece of work and its completion. Naturally, the length of time it takes the work item to transfer between two activities must also be denoted as part of the cycle time. I do not try to define cycle time exactly, because every company has a slightly different definition. If you want to go into more depth on this subject, you will certainly be forced into a discussion about lead time and cycle time. My recommendation is to let the others discuss it. Instead, find out what is relevant and makes sense for your situation. For example, do you want to forecast how long is takes until a work item in the option pool is worked on? In this case, the cycle time will include the waiting time between the option pool and the implementation. Before measuring, define how the cycle time in your system is put together, and write down your definition model clearly. Based on the timestamp, the cycle time can be calculated quite simply: Taking the scheme from Figure 4.2 for example, the timespan between timestamp 2 and timestamp 3 yields the cycle time.

Important: The cycle time is calculated for each ticket. When you have specified the starting and stopping points for your individually defined cycle time, the measurement is very simple:

$$CycleTime = Stop - Start + 1$$

The cycle times can be depicted graphically quite well with a scatter plot diagram. Again, "cycle time" is the general term for many types of cycle times, such as the implementation time or the waiting time. Let's look at the example in Figure 4.4. The x-axis is a timeline which is split into appropriate units based on the chosen timeframe, in this case the unit of measure is days. On the y-axis in this example, the calculated cycle time per ticket in days is recorded. How is the scatter plot rendered?

Imagine the following situation on a Kanban board: In the "Done" column (= value created) is a ticket that was placed into the option pool on September 6th, on September 11th pulled into implementation and, on the same day, completed and labeled "Done". Stop date − start date + 1 gives a cycle time of one day. On the timeline, a point with the value of 1 day is placed at September 11th. If you would not add 1 to the calculation, the cycle time would be 0 days, but you are certainly occupied with the item more than 0 days. Using the + 1 convention asserts that all work takes at least one day, or part of one day, to complete. Another ticket was started on September 3rd and completed on September 10th (cycle time: 8 days). A third ticket was started on September 7th and was also completed on September 10th (cycle time: 4 days). For both of these tickets, points are marked on the timeline at September 10th with the values of four days and ten days. And so on for the remaining tickets.

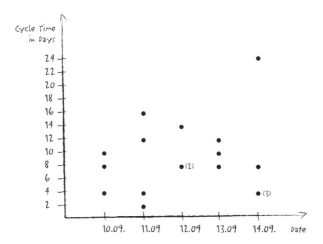

Figure 4.4: Scatterplot for the Implementation Times

Naturally, there can also be the case that several work items are completed on the same days with the same implementation time. In our example, there were two tickets started on September 4th and completed on September 12th. There are two ways to denote this on the scatterplot:

1. On September 12th, the cycle time of eight days is marked with a (2), designating two tickets completed (see Figure 4.4).
2. On the x-axis, September 12th is recorded twice and labeled with the 8-day point on the y-axis. To make it easier to recognize that it is the same day, brackets are placed around these two dates.

When the scatterplot (or the tool that generates the scatterplot, in the case you do not do it manually) is fed data over a longer period of time, the results could look something like the diagram in Figure 4.5.

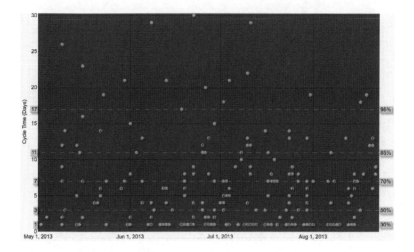

Figure 4.5: Scatterplot for a four-month Time Frame

The scatterplot shows that the cycle times vary greatly: Some work is finished within a day; other work needs 30 days. How can you predict, despite this high variability, when newly started work will be completed? For this purpose, it's necessary to draw the so-called quantile in the scatterplot.

Cumulative Probability of Occurrence: Quantile

The average should never be used for deadline commitments - the definition of average itself is the reason. Whoever uses the average for a forecast (more exactly, the median) will not be able to hold the commitment in one of two cases. You could just toss a coin instead.

If you, in your company, want to have a higher than 50 percent probability of making correct predictions, you should think in terms of the quantile. Quantile are threshold values, meaning a certain amount of the values are smaller than the quantile, the remaining values are larger. If you want to, for example, make a prediction with 80 percent probability of being correct, this would mean that in eight out of ten cases, the deadline will be adhered to.

To determine, for instance, the 85th quantile in a scatterplot, we must find the horizontal line on the x-axis where 85 percent of the measurement points are beneath it. In Figure 4.5, the 85th quantile line is at a cycle time of 11 days, i.e. 85 percents of all cycle times are under 11 days, 15 percent are over.

Quantiles provide outstanding support when communicating with customers. When a customer asks when the work will be completed, you can say with 85 percent certainty, "Within 11 days". When this degree of certainty isn't high enough, and instead a 95 percent certainty is needed, then the 95th quantile must be communicated. In the example from Figure 4.5., the 95th quantile is 17 days. I recommend making the quantile and the cycle time, based on the degree of certainty, visible on the Kanban board. This way, all of the stakeholders can see the current performance of the system. These performance indicators are called Service Level Agreements (SLA). In reality, I often see Service Level Agreements created so: A manager opens a document called SLA.txt and writes down some wishful thinking as to what type of work will be finished when. It should come as no surprise that the SLA cannot be held. A Service Level Agreement must always represent the current performance capability of the system, and not some unrealistic wish. In addition, the progression of the SLA over time is a good feedback mechanism for the Kanban system. Is the system's performance getting better, getting worse, or staying the same?

Interpreting Scatterplots

Depending on the state of the system, various patterns can emerge in a scatterplot, to which you should pay extra attention. It's also important to understand that these situations have already occurred - the scatterplot is not an early warning system:

- If the data distribution forms a *triangle* that opens to the right, the cycle times have increased and most likely the WIP limits - if they still exist - will be permanently damaged.
- Occasionally, *clusters* form - for instance, substantially longer cycle times can be seen at specific times during specific time frames. The cause for this could be unforeseen problems, or larger work items were implemented. You should keep an eye on clusters, because they make the system less predictable.
- A special cluster-form is the horizontal *accumulation of data points* around specific cycle times. For example, there is an accumulation of cycle times between one and seven days, and a second accumulation between 15 and 25 days. There are almost no cycle times between these two accumulations. If you would look more closely at these areas, you would probably find that there are two different types of work being completed. Perhaps the shorter cycle times indicate work that is dealing primarily with fixing bugs, and the longer cycle times with software changes. It would be a good idea to segment the data, take measurements for each type of work and publish a separate SLA corresponding to each.
- Many *outlying* data points are a sign of higher variability, and are a major factor influencing the predictability.

Histograms

Another way to depict the cycle time measurements is through a histogram. In this variation, the frequency of data points is plotted on the y-axis. In our case, this is the frequency of the various cycle times. On the x-axis, the cycle times are represented. The advantage of this diagram is that you can see, at a glance, how the cycle times are distributed (Figure 4.6). Quantiles can also be used with the histogram. Vertical lines show what percentage of the cycle times are smaller than a given value. In Figure 4.6 you can see, for example, that 95 percent of the cycle times are less than 17 days.

Compared to the histogram, the scatterplot has a time axis allowing for trendlines to be illustrated on the diagram. With trendlines you can easily tell if the cycle times are increasing or decreasing - information the histogram doesn't show because of the missing time component. On the other hand, the histogram readily shows how often certain cycle times occur. Thus, these are two different perspectives of the same data.

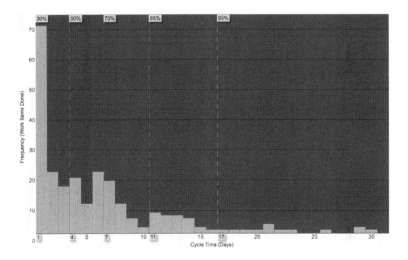

Figure 4.6: Cycle Times Histogram

Generally speaking, measurements are a type of feedback from the system. There is no catalog of standard measurements for certain situations, because a variety of individual variables play a role in each system. The answers are also never as easy as you might prefer them to be. If the measurements show that the cycle times are increasing, the correct answer is not, "The cycle time must be reduced!" The question in the meantime should be, "Why are the cycle times increasing?" Only when you have found the reason behind the changes, will you be able to determine if the increase is good or not so good. For example, the increase might be good because the adherence to delivery dates has also increased in the same time. An increase might be less positive if the reason is too many things were started at the same time. It's important to understand that all the rules used in a system will have an influence on the measurements. Likewise, the measurements also affect the rules. The idea behind metrics is not to set target values to steer your system towards, but instead to understand your own method of operation.

4.3 Forecast for several Work Items without Historical Data

Usually there isn't just one piece of work that enters the system, but several at the same time. Then the question arises, for instance: When will the 20 features be finished, or how many features can you complete in the next five weeks? You might now assume that we can answer this question with the forecast for a work item. If you know with 90 percent certainty that one work item can be finished within ten days, then five work items would be finished within 50 days.

How can we create a forecast for this case? In order to do this, we are going to make a foray into a completely different world.

Every once in a while, I take a break in my native Carinthian Lavanttal Valley, which is known for its apples. For example, the "Lavanttaler Banana" is a unique apple that originated in Massachusetts and, in 1882, made its way over the Atlantic to this sunny valley in southern Austria. The English name for the apple is American Mother. I'm going to explain the basics of forecasting through the role of the apple farmer, who is standing before several tricky tasks.

I am new to the apple juice business and I have received an interesting offer: I could purchase 1,000 crates, each containing 22 apples of various varieties, for € 1,000. The apples have - depending on the variety - different sizes and different amounts of juice. Two questions immediately arise:

1. Should I take this offer and buy the 1,000 boxes of apples for € 1,000, or should I leave it?
2. If I buy the apples, how many bottles do I need in order to bottle the juice?

Independent of my apple business, this is an important moment. At the beginning of every forecast, there is a question for which the forecast should deliver an answer. As such, you always only need enough precision in order to be able to answer the question with an element of risk assessment.

4.3.1 Determining the Minimum and Maximum

What do I need to know in order to answer question number 1? First, I consider approximately how much juice the apples will yield. I know from the neighboring farmer, who comes from a long line of apple juice experts, that I can make € 1 profit from each liter of apple juice I sell. For simplicity, I will forego differentiated cost accounting in this example - € 1 is a convenient number to use for demonstration purposes. If I can determine the number of liters possible from these apples, then I can decide if the 1,000 boxes will pay off. So I ask myself, how many liters of juice will I get from pressing the apples?

The first simple model can be created, where a represents the number of apples, and b represents the amount of juice per apple:

$$Liter = a \times b$$

From the 22,000 apples, I randomly select 19 apples (why 19, I will explain shortly). It's important that the choice is made completely random, because choices that are thought out or made from gut-feelings are always influenced by human preference for certain numbers. A random generator (for example, the random number function in Excel) guarantees an objective choice. My random selection of 19 apples gives the following results:

Apple	Milliliter per Apple
1	58
2	94
3	110
4	103
5	108
6	59
7	107
8	106
9	97
10	108
11	279
12	85
13	123
14	189
15	274
16	196
17	272
18	48
19	236

The highest degree of uncertainty in my forecast can be found by doing a simple min-max calculation. Apple 18, with 48 ml, had the least amount of juice and apple 11, with 279 ml, had the most. The *minimum probable amount* (if all apples only yield 48 ml each) and the *maximum probable amount* (if all apples would have 279 ml each) can be found with a quick multiplication:

$$Minimum : \frac{(48 \times 22,000)}{1,000} = 1,056\ Liter$$

$$Maximum: \frac{(279 \times 22,000)}{1,000} = 6,138 \; Liter$$

In all probability, I will get at least 1,056 Liters of apple juice from each crate, and in the best case 6,138 Liters per crate. How probable is it, though, that the minimum and maximum are correct?

Why 19 apples? Assume there are three measurements A, B and C. A fourth measurement, X, is not yet completed. A and C are the lowest and highest measured values. I want to know how probable it is that the result from X will be between A and C. There are four possibilities for the outcome of the measurement of X (Figure 4.7):

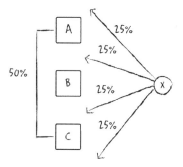

Figure 4.7: **Possible Measurement Results for X**

X could be

- smaller than A
- between A and B
- between B and C
- larger than C.

Every outcome has a probability of 25 percent and the probability that X is between A and C is 50 percent. What's astonishing is that for this determination you only need three measurements. With

19 measurements, the probability is 90 percent that all remaining, or not yet completed, samples are between the minimum and maximum of the samples already measured. This can be represented mathematically:

$$p = 1 - \frac{2}{(n+1)}$$

A graphic depiction of this can be seen in Figure 4.8. The y-axis represents the probability, and the x-axis the number of measurements. Here you can clearly see that a relatively high probability can be quickly attained with very few measurements when minimum and maximum values are present. After a certain point (around 90%), there is much more data needed to gain merely small improvements in accuracy.

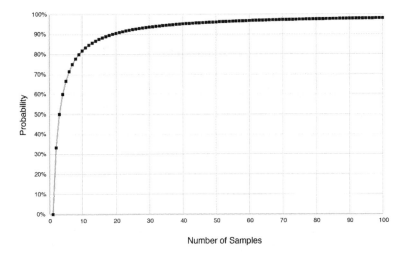

Figure 4.8: Probability that Samples are between the Current Minimum and Maximum

We need to understand this fact, especially in knowledge work and product development. If you do not know anything, you only need a little data and information, relatively speaking, to gain a fairly high amount of knowledge. If you already know a lot, increasing your knowledge can only be achieved with much more information. This is exactly why it makes sense to work with prototypes that are subjected to customer feedback from the beginning of a development project. These small experiments increase your knowledge within a short timeframe.

So, I chose 19 apples because I wanted to be 90 percent sure how much the minimum and maximum amount of juice could be. As soon as I start pressing the apples, I get more measurement data. This data flows into the forecast, which then becomes more precise.

- Minimum: Unlucky for me that all the crates contained apples yielding only 48 ml of juice (the minimum from the random sampling) and the total yield is 1,056 Liters.
- Maximum: Lucky for me that the crates were filled with juicy apples that yielded 279 ml each, making the total amount of juice produced 6,138 Liters.

The degree of uncertainty is quite high: 5,082 Liters. However, I can still make a decision based on this result, whether or not to invest € 1,000 in 1,000 crates of apples. If I bring in one Euro of profit per liter sold - as predicted by my neighbor - my total profit, in the worst case, is € 1,276. This is only a theoretical minimum because I know from the sample juicing that there is more juice in the apples. Thus, I have a very high probability that I will at least be able to cover my investment. It would be more difficult (if not impossible) to make a decision if the minimum and maximum would be 200 and 7,000 respectively. In this case, the risk would be very high that the undertaking would lose money, or only yield a very small profit.

Fortunately, the information I have is enough to make a decision. I used just enough precision in order to be able to answer my question. Thus, my decision is: Yes, I will purchase the 1,000 crates.

If I wouldn't want, or wasn't able, to press the juice from the apples, I could also just estimate how much juice I would get from the apples. The difference with an estimation is, as it is usually done, that I would need to estimate all the apples in the 1,000 crates, i.e. 22,000 apples. This would take a long time. For a high degree of precision (90%), it's enough to choose 19 apples and estimate them - saving a lot of time. The same goes for estimating work items.

Nevertheless, an estimation is still just an estimation, and not based on fact. An estimation is just an alternative when there is no possibility to attain real data.

4.3.2 Monte Carlo Simulation

The second question, "How many bottles should I order?", is a little more difficult to answer. What influences my ordering decision? If I order too few bottles, there will be apple juice leftover that I cannot bottle. If I order too many, I still have to pay for the unused bottles and need enough cash flow to be able to afford it. In addition, the unused bottles have to be stored, which only makes sense if I will be making apple juice again next year. And even if I make apple juice next year, do I have space available to store the bottles? Since it looks like I will produce at least 1,056 liters of apple juice, I could work out a deal for a good price on 1,500 bottles with the bottle supplier, with the option to order additional bottles for immediate delivery, should the apples yield more juice than predicted. I need to ask myself all of these questions when doing risk management for my apple juice production.

As it so happens, I don't have much storage space available. The bottle price is also tightly calculated, so the option of ordering additional bottles isn't feasible. This means, I need to know *more precisely* how much juice I need to bottle. Until now, I have only found out which results are very unlikely - the minimum and the maximum. The reality is, though, that within this range there are results that are *more probable* than others. You can find out these results with the help of a Monte Carlo simulation.

You have a six-sided die in your hand. I think we can agree that every number on the die - as long as it isn't rigged - has a probably of 1:6 of being thrown. If you would roll the die 10,000 times, the result would be an almost even distribution of the numbers 1 to 6, i.e. each number is rolled almost an equal number of times.

Take a second die in your hand. What does the probability distribution look like now? Is it still true that each number has an equal chance to be thrown? With two dice, there is only one possibility to roll a two, just as it is for a 12. The number of chances to roll a four is higher because there are more combinations that result in a four, and the seven has the most combinations possible (Figure 4.9).

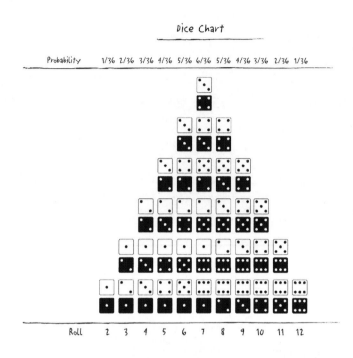

Figure 4.9: Possible Combinations when Rolling Two Dice

There is a total of 36 combinations with two dice, each occurring with varying probabilities. At forecasting workshops, I let the participants reconstruct this themselves, as well as roll the dice if they want to. Roll two dice for two to three minutes and write down the results in a diagram (see Figure 4.10). Stop after the 19th toss and take a look whether or not 90 percent of the values are between the minimum and maximum thrown, then continue rolling the dice. Take a look at your diagram: If you could win € 1,000, which number would you bet on?

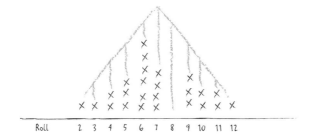

Figure 4.10: Results from Rolling the Dice

The preliminary dice throwing results showed the numbers 6 and 7 to be the favorites, although your diagram may look slightly different. I know, and you probably already know now too, which numbers I would in any case not pick (in my example they are 2, 3 and 12). After several hundred rolls of the dice, the results would form a pyramid, and your choice would be unambiguous.

How does this help my bottle dilemma?

Certain liter amounts between 1,056 and 6,138 occur more frequently than others. In order to find out how this distribution looks in my specific apple case, there must be a 19-sided die for each apple on which the measurement results from Table 4.1 are depicted. That makes 22,000 19-sided die that need to be rolled once and then added up, as we did in Figure 4.10. The rolling of the die needs to be repeated a few thousand times to get the distribution of the values. Naturally, this cannot be done manually, but table calculation programs or special statistical programs make it possible (personally, I like to use "R").

We could build a table with 22,000 rows, where each row represents an apple. Then a random generator will assign a random number to each apple from the range of possible Milliliters (Table 4.1) and finally the sum of all 22,000 is formed. The procedure is repeated several thousand times, and is represented as columns in the table. This is known as a Monto Carlo simulation. Table 4.2 shows a schematic of how such a simulation could be accomplished in a table calculation program.

	Trial 1	Trial 2	...	Trial 10,000
Apple 1	85	108	...	123
Apple 2	103	272	...	58
Apple 3	274	197	...	196
...	...	...	...	...
Apple 22,000	110	196	...	279
Total	3,098	3,103	...	3,032

What is a Monte Carlo Simulation?

A Monte Carlo simulation conducts several simulation trials for a defined model, using random numbers within a predefined possible range of numbers, and calculates the results. With the help of a Monte Carlo simulation, the distribution of possible results and their probability of occurrence can be calculated.

The computer-facilitated Monte Carlo simulation with 10,000 trials results in the distribution of the possible total liters as pictured in Figure 4.11. Through the results of the simulation it becomes very clear that it would have been a poor choice to have based my decision solely on the minimum or maximum values. The minimum of 1,056 Liters, as well as the maximum of 6,138 Liters, are both utterly improbable. According to the Monte Carlo simulation, it is most likely that the juice production will yield between 3,030 and 3,120 Liters. Put another way: With a 90 percent probability, I will not need more than 3,030 bottles for the apple juice. To be on the safe side, I decide to order 3,120 bottles. Finished!

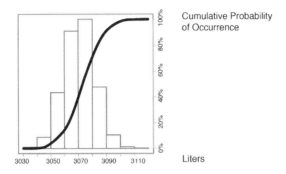

Figure 4.11: Result of the Monte Carlo Simulation: Which Liter Amount is most probable?

4.3.3 Continuous Throughput Forecasting

Estimating is a waste of time because it doesn't add value for the customer. That is why an estimation should only be used at the beginning, provided you cannot yet draw on real data. Even an initial forecast is false. It is with a fairly high probability that, in the end, the product or project will be finished at a different time than was originally calculated. When the estimate is used for a commitment date, everything is done to keep the project moving forward, but shows up in later phases of a project, most often as a boomerang.

As soon as the work is started, real data will be generated and further estimations are unnecessary, because using real data will lead to more precise target dates. When real data flows into continuous forecasting, it will become a tool to accompany the implementation work. The results lead to a fact-based discussion about where you are currently in the process and which actions must be taken. This also means that it will quickly become clear whether or not a project is overreaching its possibilities and must be cancelled.

There were nine Scrum teams in this situation, with 297 stories backlogged as part of a product development. A product that had become outdated was supposed to be replaced with new technology. The product owner had obviously given some thought about how the product was to be implemented. Naturally, he then asked the question, "How long will it take?" Based on the performance data of the team to date, a forecast was made that predicted the 297 stories would be completed in 38 weeks. As we know, forecasting is not a one-time matter, so we set out to make a continuous forecast to accompany the project. If a story wandered out of the Spice Girls option pool into the "Next" column on the team board, it received a start timestamp, and a stop timestamp when it was completed. With both of these timestamps, the weekly throughput of the Kanban system could be calculated.

To measure the **throughput**, we count the number of tickets that leave the "Implementing" area (which we understand to be the entire WIP limited activities - see Figure 4.2) within a specific time frame. The measurement is very easy: Using a weekly cycle for instance, at the end of the week you count the number of work items that were completed within that calendar week. The result is then recorded in a chart where the y-axis represents the number of work items and the x-axis is a timeline. If a project backlog is being worked through, you can also record this on the chart and follow if, and to what extent, the backlog is reduced over time (Burn-up Chart).

In our example, the 297 stories were counted as part of the completed stories in the first week and recorded as a whole in a burn-up chart (see Figure 4.12, the thick black line at the lower left).

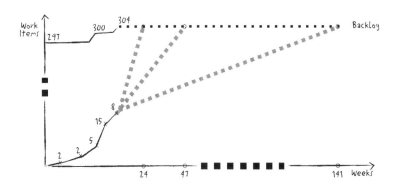

Figure 4.12: Burn-up Chart

At the very top of the burn-up chart, there is a horizontal line that shows the development of the backlog over time. We started with 297 stories and as you can see, nothing changed in the first three weeks. In the fourth week, the backlog all of a sudden jumped to 300 stories, and in the fifth week to 304. It was obvious that new stories were being put into backlog, which meant that the previous forecast was no longer valid. I often see companies with such cases, where the future development of the backlog is simply predicted based on the average throughput, with the assumption that the backlog remains constant. In specific terms, there would be an average of 6.4 stories per week completed and after about 47 weeks, the backlog would be empty. However, the average is only one possible result and there are many other results possible.

Since we already had throughput data from the first five weeks (as drawn in Figure 4.13), we can create a min-max calculation. If the maximum of 15 stories per week could be achieved, the backlog would be cleared by week 24. In comparison, if only two stories per week could be finished, the new system wouldn't be ready until week 141. In this range, there are many combinations and it was very probable that the linear projection of the average would not reflect when the project would actually be finished. That's why it was appropriate, using the real throughput data from the first five weeks, to perform a Monte Carlo simulation (Figure 4.13). Working on the assumption that the backlog from this point on would remain constant[2], the simulation results showed that when considered from the current time, the fastest completion would be 33 weeks, and the slowest variation would take 66 weeks.

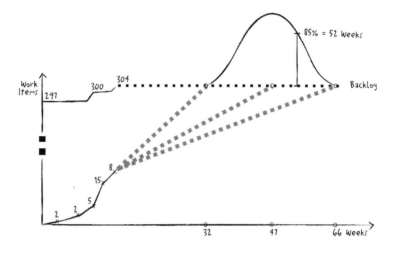

Figure 4.13: Monte Carlo Simulation using the Throughput from Week 1 till Week 5

Taking a quick look at the histogram, it's most likely that completion will take between 45 and 55 weeks. Since we want to know it more precisely, we can use the quantile. In this case, we want to have an 85 percent probability for our forecast, corresponding to around week 52. So, with a probability of 85 percent, the backlog would be cleared after 52 weeks. What could we deduce from this forecast?

With the first forecast, the teams came to the conclusion that they would need 38 weeks to clear out the backlog. There is a fairly large gap between the original forecast and the current performance, and

[2]Please note: Make your assumptions about each forecast clear for all those involved.

more user stories entered the backlog in the meantime (304 instead of 297). These seven additional user stories may not make a huge difference, but the fact was that 84 user stories would be missing at the originally predicted completion date of 38 weeks. The most important step was to discuss this information (without blame) and to interpret and consider which measures should be undertaken:

- Do we stop the project?
- Do we need additional employees?
- Do we just accept it?
- Do we tell the customer?
- This is the current situation, but it can change. The teams have to get warmed up and then increase performance week after week. We will observe the weekly development, and if the forecast doesn't improve in two to three weeks, we must do something.

The forecasts were updated every week with the new data. After three weeks, the trend showed definite improvement, so we continued. After ten weeks, we met again in the larger group to discuss how the situation had developed and whether or not special measures were necessary. The backlog remained constant with 304 user stories and the throughput had increased:

- Week 6: 13
- Week 7: 6
- Week 8: 12
- Week 9: 8
- Week 10: 9

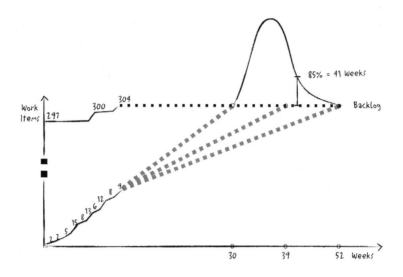

Figure 4.14: **Monte Carlo Simulation after Ten Weeks**

We repeated the Monte Carlo simulation in order to make a decision about possible measures (Figure 4.14). The minimum and maximum were at 30 and 52 weeks respectively. With an 85 percent probability, the project would be completed at week 41. This was a marked improvement compared to the forecast five weeks before. The original had predicted 38 weeks, but that was no reason to get nervous. According to the current measurements, there would only be 26 stories left to complete and that was tolerable. The interpretation this time was very clear: The uncertainty was decreasing and the result more probable - we were coming closer to the goal.

Answering the question, "When will it be finished?" is not a one-time, set in stone prediction, but rather a continuous approximation. When looking to the future, there is always more than one result possible, so it is ridiculous to use averages to predict the future and specify only one result. Naturally, customers are probably surprised if you show them all possible completion dates when answering the question of when it will be finished. That is why it is important, in terms of the forecast, to ask the question, "With which probability can we work with?" Does 85 percent give enough certainty? When yes, then from the current standpoint, we are finished before week 41.

Refining Forecasts

Continuous forecasting is no guarantee that the project progress also continuously improves. How could you progress if there is no significant improvement shown in the burn-up charts after several weeks? How can you get a more precise forecast?

Until now I have only talked about throughput forecasting. The throughput is only one result determined by a multitude of circumstances. A forecast can be refined by not just modeling the system results (throughput), but also the performance of the entire system, which is determined by many more parameters. Questions that arise are:

- How often do blockades occur?
- How long do the blockades last?
- How many defects are there?
- How long does it take to correct defects?
- How many activities (columns on the board) comprise the work system?
- How many queues are there - where does work get held up (for instance, at handover points)?
- How many employees are there for which special areas?
- How many express tasks enter the system unplanned?

Such parameters can be collected and measured (for example, through blocker and defect clustering - see Chapter 2). There is even software that can take the measurement results and expand it to a "what would happen" simulation - one of these is "KanbanSim" from Troy Magennis (Magennis, 2011). Using the example of the 297 user stories, based on the information available from the past five weeks, the situation in the following weeks would get better. If it became apparent after ten weeks that the forecast was still way off from the goal, we would have needed to do something. The software could have helped us simulate various scenarios, with additional parameters to find out which parts of the system needed to be changed, in order to get closer to the goal than was currently the case. Should an additional team be utilized? Or is it better to increase testing capacity by 20 percent? Or is it better to reduce blockage resolution to 6-8 days from the current 10-12 days? Here, you are working in an area of unlimited possibilities (keyword: Monte Carlo simulation), but these questions can be answered with the support of software. However, this is not done by feeding in data. The prerequisite for this type of forecasting is that the company has gotten past the "we must be faster" and "we need more developers" stage, and understands that speed and increasing resources are, in itself, not a solution. Expanded simulations help when you already understand the value of forecasting, and understand its function - and above all, when the work system is understood and stable.

4.3.4 Interview with Troy Magennis

Troy Magennis has been working in software development since 1994. He has held various positions, from Quality Assurance up to Vice President of a multinational company, and several years ago, started his own business, "Focused Objective". Now he concentrates on what really interests him: Forecasting and its applicable simulations - especially Monte Carlo simulations. In this area, he advises companies like Walmart, Microsoft, Skype or Siemens.

Klaus: You use models to simulate different future scenarios. How did you come across this, and what is the best way to use models and simulations?

Troy: I have an electrotechnical education and am familiar with simulating electrical circuits. It felt like a good fit with IT. Simulations - especially Monte Carlo simulations - are used when it is too complex, or impractical from a time perspective, to formulate a mathematical function to solve a problem. Simulations calculate the result quickly and allow for experimentation, based on models, to measure which actions have the largest impact. Typically, Monte Carlo simulations are used when there are many interactive inputs in interrelated processes. Let's take, for example, the weather forecast, which you also mentioned: A small rise in ocean temperature causes changes in temperature that change the probability of rain in an area. These inputs reinforce each other, and some even have repercussions on earlier inputs. It is a complex system. We would never expect perfection from the weather forecast because of these relationships, but for some reason, we expect absolute predictability for IT projects, although they exhibit similar cascading complexity.

Klaus: Why not simply use estimations?

Troy: I established early on that every forecast and estimation are distorted if the effects from events like defect rates, additional requirements or uncertainties in effort are not simulated. Traditional estimations are based on the correlation between effort and time, but in complex systems, the work can also come to a standstill or be blocked for any number of reasons. The effort for a piece of work has absolutely no correlation to the calendar weeks that have passed. It is an unsuitable relation, as if I would say: A flight delay due to a technical defect has something to do with me sitting in the airplane. We always assume that the actual working time denotes a large portion of the delivery time. This is simply not true for most software companies and software development processes, if you also include not only the sheer development time, but also the time for testing, release and waiting time in the backlog. And these times should be taken into account, because from the customer perspective, work is not completed when development is completed, but rather when they can use the product free from failures.

Klaus: Models and simulations - that sounds very complex for many at first. In your view, is this approach even worth it and in which context can it pay off?

Troy: Most of the time it's worth it. You have to do something, though, to achieve the results. If the number of employees is fixed and the current process cannot be changed even a little, it probably doesn't make sense. Whatever the case may be, even simple models can help quantify, in dollars or euros, the effects and benefits of process changes. It was important for me to be able to answer questions and understand the effects when, for example, the defect rate is cut in half. Which employee skills in which situation bring the most benefit? Are defects or missing test environments a bigger problem? Simple models help answer these questions, and that goes beyond traditional estimation. Being able to see the answers in a monetary amount helps the argument as to why an investment in the change is valuable. It helps to make well-informed and carefully considered decisions.

Klaus: What could such a model look like?

Troy: Sometimes a simple spreadsheet can show the effects and benefits before and after a process. Early on, I realized I needed a more detailed analysis to find the answers to my questions. In my case, I wanted to model every step of a work item as it travels through the process of a specific team. So, I developed a simple XML language (SimML), that allows the work and process to be written in text form. It is typically 25 to 50 lines and is a mix of work, historical data and definitions of the team process. When I have a question about the costs of defects, for instance, the model specifies the current defect rate. Then I make a forecast for the delivery date and costs, cut the defects in half and observe the differences in the date and costs. The content of the model and its complexity emerge from the questioning. I cannot emphasize enough how important it is to think about the questions before developing a model. Only when you know the questions, should you then build the simplest model to be able to answer these questions.

4.4 Can You Trust the Forecast?

Now that you are a proper forecasting expert, there is another vital question: Can you trust your forecast? The answer is quite simply yes, if your system is stable - and only when it is stable. To understand a stable system, you must understand the relation between WIP, cycle time and throughput, and this relationship is the basis for "Little's Law".

4.4.1 Relationship between Work in Progress, Cycle Time and Throughput

Little's Law is a fundamental rule of queueing theory and I find it so relatable because John D. C. Little endeavored to explain it using a well-stocked wine cellar as an example (Little & Graves, 2008). The owner of the wine cellar, Caroline, always purchased the newest wine of her favorite vineyards from her preferred wine merchant. The wine rack held 240 bottles and she noticed that it was rarely filled up completely, but after a party it was definitely empty. On average, it seemed to be two-thirds filled, so approximately 160 bottles were stored. Since wine gets better with age, Caroline asked how long her wine, on average, lies in the cellar? Using the invoices from the wine merchant, she determined that she purchased around eight bottles of wine every month - but naturally, she did not know when each wine was consumed. Was it even possible for her to find out how old the wine was, on average, in her cellar?

When I ask such a rhetorical question, the answer is presumably: Yes, you can find it out. Little's Law refers to objects that arrive at a specific rate in a system (Little calls these "Arrivals"). These objects spend some time in this queueing system and then, when the work on these objects are completed, they leave the queueing system ("Departures"). Within this system, the objects are either being worked on, or are in queues. Where the boundaries of this system lie - the arrival and departure points - must be determined for each individual system.

Little's Law implies that under constant conditions, the average number of items (work units) in a queueing system is the product of the average arrival rate multiplied by the average waiting time of an item in the system.

$L = \lambda \times W$

L: The average number of items in progress

λ: The average number of items entering the system

W: The average time an item spends in the system (cycle time)

With an average of 160 bottles in the wine rack and a monthly arrival rate of an average of eight bottles, Little's Law calculates the following average waiting time per bottle:

L (average number of bottles in the rack) = 160

λ (average replenishment per month) = 8

Per year: 8 × 12 = 96

W (average storage time per bottle) = 160 ÷ 96 = 1.67 years

If two parameters are known, the third parameter can be easily calculated. In this context, it is important to note that it is completely irrelevant how large the bottle is (the item – the work unit). A common misunderstanding is that all work items must be the same size for Little's Law to work - this is not the case. The theory does not relate to the individual work item, rather it considers the entire system. That's why Little's Law is not a tool for forecasting. Little's Law helps to interpret past correlations in order to draw possible conclusions about the future, but it is not a forecasting tool per se. With the parameters from the past, you can create "what would happen if" considerations that offer a good foundation for discussions in improvement meetings. For direct future projections, observations based on average values are not appropriate. Unfortunately, I often see Little's Law also being touted as a forecasting tool.

In any case, Little's Law is best suited to get a feeling for the interaction of these three parameters. In the 1980s, Little's Law was a fixed component of operations management and consequently the terms were adapted, which we can apply to our central three metrics. When changed to Work in Progress (WIP), cycle time (CT) and throughput (TH), we get the following formulas:

$$CT = \frac{WIP}{TP}$$

$$TH = \frac{WIP}{CT}$$

$$WIP = CT \times TH$$

Maybe you notice at this point that Little was originally talking about the arrival rate of items in a system, while the throughput was the departure rate. Since flow-based systems are at the same time limited systems, this is irrelevant because the arrival and departure rates are the same in a limited system.

Calculating the cycle time reflects what became clear at the beginning of the chapter with the car washing experiment. Summarized, Little's Law states:

The more items on average being worked on, the longer on average it will take for all items to be completed.

What happens in reality? When things are delivered too slowly, a death cycle is put into motion, to put it bluntly. In nearly 100 percent of the cases, the conclusion is that you simply need to start the work earlier for it to be completed on time. The consequence of starting earlier, however, is that more things will be worked on at the same time. Then what happens? For example, there are three projects being worked on and a fourth already in sight, so management starts to worry about the deadline for the fourth project. Before any of other three projects have been completed, management starts project number four and increases the Work in Progress along with it. Using Little's Law, we know that everything needs longer when more and more things are being worked on at the same time - the system will become slower. The conclusion will again be drawn that the work must simply be started earlier, etc., etc. Little's Law is also so helpful because it simply reinforces what is fundamentally understood with a healthy common sense. However, healthy common sense often fails in knowledge work, because the work cannot be grasped, in the truest sense of the word. It is significantly more difficult to recognize the relationships in knowledge work. Common sense, just like Little's Law, says: If work is being delivered slowly, it is a sign that there is too much work in the system. The correct reaction to this can only be to start less new work! This means, above all, to not start new projects to gain a false sense of security before projects already running are completed.

4.4.2 Measuring the Stability of a System

With the knowledge of Little's Law, we are able to make conclusions about whether or not a system is stable. Stability in this context means that the arrival rate of new work items and the departure rate of completed work items are equal. To stay with the flight analogy, let's imagine an airport is a limited system (which anyone who travels understands when nothing is getting in or out). Compared to knowledge work, it is crystal clear in this context that the amount of arriving and departing airplanes must hold to the available capacity.

Every airplane that lands must also take off again. If the arrival rate is higher than the departure rate, and all gates, runways and taxiways are parked full, the airport is at some point completely incapacitated. When this happens, it will be difficult to get a plane to take off. In knowledge work systems, this logic seems to get lost. You can see this on the vast numbers of projects that are not completed, because new work is continuously pushed into a system that cannot deal with it. When the balance between arrival and departure is damaged, the predictability suffers, and with it the reliability.

Let's look at this in terms of a Kanban system. In its simplest form, a Kanban system can be separated into three areas. The starting point is the unlimited option pool (Options). The committed work passes through various activities in the WIP limited area (Committed) and finally land in the Done area, once the work has generated value for the customer (see Figure 4.15).

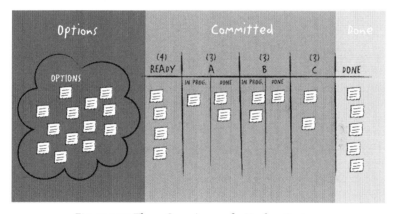

Figure 4.15: Three Core Areas of a Kanban System

From the respective daily conditions of these three areas, measurement data can be drawn by using timestamps which give information about the stability of a system. If you have already worked with metrics, you will recognize the diagrams in the following section as being a Cumulative Flow Diagram (CFD). A CFD is best suited to visualize the arrival and departure rates and measure the flow of

Work in Progress.

Cumulative Flow Diagram (CFD)

A cumulative flow diagram illustrates the flow of work through a process. For a diagram to be considered a cumulative flow diagram, two conditions must be met according to Dan Vacanti (Vacanti, 2015):

1. The top line always represents the cumulative arrivals in a process, while the bottom line depicts the departures from the process.
2. Based on its cumulative nature, no line in a CFD can ever decline.

If you look closely at the diagrams in the next section, you will see that the stability metrics shown do not fulfill all properties of a CFD. In an already stable system, you can gather a lot from a CFD. As long as this condition is not yet met, a real CFD will only be confusing, because it won't be clear whether or not the WIP limits are functioning due to so much additional information. In a "pseudo-CFD", which I use for not yet stable systems, the information is reduced by summarizing the WIP-limited area of a system. In the first step, it's only important to know if the stabilization measures are working.

Every diagram can naturally be refined to the smallest detail. The pseudo-CFD deliberately concentrates on measuring the three core areas "Option, Committed and Done". It may look like too little for some people, but these are the three most important parameters. First and foremost, what you should know about your system: **Is it stable or not?** The degree of stability determines which measures must be taken. With a system like the one you will see in Figure 4.16, it doesn't make any sense to measure more details because the base prerequisite of WIP-limiting is not yet given. When you are just beginning with measurements, start the initial metrics at a broad level to examine the stability of the system. Only afterwards should you go deeper if you need more information.

Let's look at the three most distinctive patterns that can result from the measurements and what they can tell us about the stability of a Kanban system. From the interpretation, it can be deduced where the actual problems lie and which measures should be taken to resolve these issues.

4.4.3 Interpreting Stability Patterns

In the simplest graphical diagram, the stability of a Kanban system is reflected in the interaction of three areas, as can be seen in the example in Figure 4.16. From bottom to top, you can see the progress of the areas Done, Committed and Options.

From the Pieces

Let's begin with the pattern that I see most often when I am called in to help. Figure 4.16 is the textbook example of a completely instable work system. You can interpret the following from this graph: The option pool has a very constant slope, because the Work in Progress area would suggest that work is started very quickly. The discrepancy between the increases of Committed and Done also clearly shows that a lot of work is started, but not completed at the same rate. This work system is not stable and making a prediction about when work will be completed is not really possible. This pattern occurs when a system is not limited and it still caught in the old push principle: Every piece of work is tackled immediately. The goal should be that at least the gradients of Done and Committed run parallel, then the arrival rate (from Option Pool to Committed) and departure rate (from Committed to Done) are more or less equal. That means as soon the line of the Done area begins to move upward, the work is gradually being completed more quickly.

What wouldn't help at this stage would be additional workers. The problem lies solely in the amount of work started and, as such, the most important step is to limit the Work in Progress. New workers are an option only when the system has stabilized.

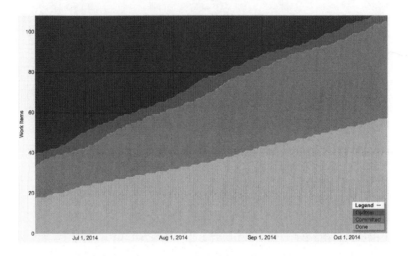

Figure 4.16: Unstable System – WIP limits are not yet Implemented

Let me show you why additional workers in this situation are a bad idea by using a measurement from my consulting work. In Figure 4.17, you can see a highly unstable system. In order to find out where the problem is, I recommended visualizing the number of open orders and also to record the cycle times. The following process was shown: As the number of open orders increased, it was decided that another person would be added. It seems like a good idea, because afterwards the number of open orders reduced to a tolerable amount. However, the number of open orders is only one point. If you look at the progress of cycle time, you can see that the line continued to go up. The people in this system were living in a start culture: As soon as more people were added, it was the signal to start more work. More work started meant higher WIP, and higher WIP meant increasing cycle time.

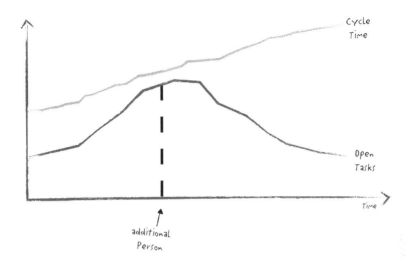

Figure 4.17: Relationship between Additional Workers and Cycle Time

Additional workers putting strain on an unstable system can also be understood with Little's Law (see Formula 4.5). The manpower, i.e. the workers, can be seen as the equivalent of the throughput. Assume that there are twelve work items in a system with four workers available. According to Little's Law, the cycle time for these work items is three days. Let's assume further that the option pool is growing and the system is unstable. If an additional worker is brought in, more work can be started and the work items in the system increases to 18. As a consequence, the cycle time increases to 3.6 days.

In a stable system, the Work in Progress will not be disproportionately increased even with the addition of another worker because the performance of the system is known. With five employees, the WIP limit would increase to a maximum of 15, with the effect that the cycle time remains constant at three days.

You can also go in a completely different direction: If you observe that there is too much work in the system and the employees are working on too many things simultaneously, the WIP limit could be kept at twelve, despite the additional manpower. The cycle time would decrease in this case to 2.4 days. The result: Work is completed faster.

More Options than Manpower Available

The situation in Figure 4.18 is much more desirable. Essentially, we have a luxury problem here: The Work in Progress is stable, which is a good thing. It means that the work can flow through the system in a predictable manner and the implementation time can be easily determined. The catch here is that the option pool is obviously increasing and, because of this, the initial waiting time is also increasing. Ultimately, this means that the time-to-market for these options will also increase. That is no reason to lose your nerve, however. The arrival rate in the option pool is simply higher than the departure rate of the system, but the system itself is stable. Put another way, a growing option pool means there is plenty of work coming in. With this knowledge, you can then make some decisions. For example, resources could be increased to implement the orders. Naturally, the graphs for the Committed and Done activities will not immediately achieve the same increase as that of the option pool. The additional resources, in the form of new workers, cannot immediately bring the same increase in productivity due to frictional losses, but the graphs will slowly approach the same slope.

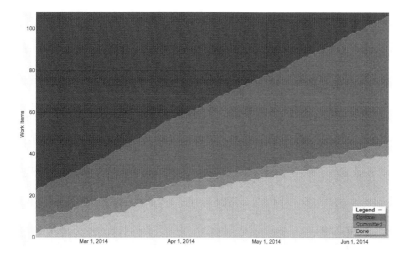

Figure 4.18: Stable Work System, but Increasing Option Pool

Completely Stable

Figure 4.19 shows exactly the state that should be attained with WIP limits: a stable work system. The Work in Progress stays the same, the graph increases - everything easy peasy. If you draw a vertical line in the "Implementing" area, you know how much is currently being worked on. The horizontal reflects the average cycle time.

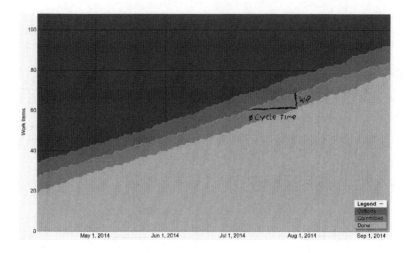

Figure 4.19: A Stable Work System

If there would be a Kanban nirvana, this would be it. Please note that Figure 4.19 is only a schematic representation. Such a perfectly stable system is rarely, if ever, seen in the real world.

What you also unfortunately seldom see is the executive and business decision makers already working together beforehand on a contract to consider which order of execution makes most sense from a business perspective. Prioritizations are often obscure and it can happen that the wrong things are worked on at the wrong time. How you can achieve an economically useful order of execution of work will be discussed in Chapter 5.

4.4.4 Interview with Daniel Vacanti

Just like Troy, Daniel S. Vacanti is a software veteran. He started as a Java Developer/Architect and has worked with Lean and Agile methods for more than 15 years. Dan was completely crucial to the development of Kanban, and implemented the first Kanban project in 2007. With his company "Actionable Agile TM", he has specialized in forecasting tools, and is the undisputed master of flow-based metrics.

Klaus: You are one of the experts for flow-based metrics and you have worked intensively with Little's Law. Why is Little's Law so important?

Dan: The short answer is, it isn't important. Or better said, it is not important in the way most people think it is. Just forget the math. Most of the time, Little's Law is used deterministically. The numbers are assigned and Little's Law spits out the answer. There are two problems with this approach:

1. Little's Law looks at the past, not the future - more on that later.
2. Little's Law is helpful in situations where you can only measure two metrics, because the third metric is too difficult, too expensive or too difficult and too expensive to measure. In our world, it is very easy to measure all three metrics, so Little's Law should never be used for calculations. Accurately measuring the missing flow metric is, in this case, the correct approach.

Regardless, it is important to understand the assumptions that must interact for Little's Law to function. It is not just an equation, it is an equation and a set of assumptions. My recommendation is to forget the equation and focus on the assumptions. These are a guideline for the policies that must first be established for a process to become predictable. Assuming, naturally, that you place a value on predictability.

Klaus: When it's going about metrics, most people want to jump immediately into sexy topics like probabilistic forecasting. In your opinion, is that a good place to start?

Dan: Most often the problem is that, for things like a Monte Carlo simulation, knowledge about the system stability is required. This is where Little's Law shines. If the process follows the assumptions of Little's Law, then the process exhibits a certain stability and you can slowly begin to bring sophisticated techniques, like a Monte Carlo simulation, into play. If the process continuously breaks the assumptions of Little's Law, then the process is, by definition, unstable and every type of forecast - probabilistic or otherwise - is highly questionable. That's why I really like your approach in this book. You first establish a very simple metric to get feedback about the stability of the system.

Klaus: The actual formula for Little's Law is $L = \lambda \times W$, but we use $CT = WIP/TH$ (CT: cycle time, TH: throughput). Wherein lies the difference, and what are the consequences of this?

Dan: Actually, both formulas are legitimate definitions of Little's Law, if you assume that the relationship of average values are observed. The difference lies in the perspective: $L = \lambda \times W$ sees the process from the perspective of arrivals in the system. In contrast, $CT = WIP/TH$ examines the process from the departure perspective. Although both formulas represent Little's Law, the change of perspective makes a huge difference. As I already said, there are two sides: the equation and the assumptions behind the equation. The assumptions behind $CT = WIP/TH$ are different than those behind $L = \lambda \times W$. It is important to realize this, because like I said, you only understand Little's Law when you understand the assumptions behind it. First you must be clear about whether you want to concern yourself more about the arrivals or about the departures, because this perspective influences all the policies used for predictability.

Klaus: How can the readers of this book utilize Little's Law in their daily work with Kanban systems?

Dan: By understanding the assumptions behind it, and establishing policies in their processes through which these assumptions will only minimally be damaged. Like I said, only if predictability should play an important roll.

Klaus: What do these assumptions look like?

Dan: If you use the throughput version of Little's Law, you have the following five assumptions:

1. The average input or arrival rate should be equal to the average output or departure rate.
2. Each piece of work started will be completed at some point and will also leave the system.
3. The Work in Progress should be the same at the beginning and at the end for the calculation of the chosen time interval.
4. The average age of Work in Progress neither increases nor decreases.
5. Cycle time, Work in Progress and throughput must be measured with consistent units. For example, you should not use a day as the unit of measure for the cycle time and a week for the throughput.

It's best if you take a moment and think about your own process. Do you have an eye on the arrival and departure rate of work, or does work enter the system faster than it can be completed? To determine this, you can use the stability metric presented in this book, for instance. Do you pay attention to how old the work items are that are currently being worked on, or does the work remain untouched for an arbitrary amount of time? If you do not pay attention to these things, you are breaking the principles of Little's Law. Every time you act contrary to the fundamental assumptions, the process will be more unstable. The more unstable a process will be, the more difficult it will be to create a precise forecast. In my book "Actionable Agile Metrics for Predictability", it's primarily going about creating stable processes based on Little's Law, in order to be able to make precise forecasts.

Klaus: Why can you not simply use the formula of Little's Law to create forecasts?

Dan: There are two reasons. First, you cannot make forecasts with Little's Law because Dr. Little himself said so: "However, let it be noted that the determinism and exactness are after the fact, i.e., the sample path is known. This is not all bad. It just says that we are in the measurement business, not the forecasting business." Anyone who wants to use Little's Law for forecasting is barking up the wrong tree, because it was specifically developed to use data already gathered as a basis for looking back - not for a forecast where there can be many different results.

Even if you could use Little's Law for forecasting, you wouldn't want to. It is based on the relationship of averages. There is an excellent book that discusses this point in detail: "The Flaw of Averages" (Savage, 2012). The treacherous thing about averages is primarily that plans based on averages will, on average, fail. Even if you could simply put two numbers in the formula so a third number is spit out as a forecast, you should keep in mind that the third value only gives an average - and averages have no value for a forecast.

Klaus: In your book, you write about "flow debt". Can you explain what you mean by this?

Dan: Flow debt simply means that you borrow cycle time from one work item in the work process in order to give it to a different work item in the same work process. In the short term, you can make the process look better because certain work can be pushed quickly through the system. In the long term, this strategy only contributes to making the process less predictable. Express-Tickets are the best example: As soon as teams receive an express request, they typically stop what they are currently working on. Naturally this policy has the advantage that Express-Tickets proceed quicker in the process and the cycle time for these work items looks good. The nice cycle time has a price however: All other work that was stopped for the Express-Ticket has a higher cycle time. At some point this debt must be settled and this occurs in the form of worse cycle times for the delayed work, when it is finally finished. Better cycle times paid for with worse cycle times is what I call "flow debt". Every time you favor certain work items in an already running work process, flow debt occurs. The price that you pay for this is increasing unpredictability of the system.

4.5 Summary

Forecasting is a tool for proactive project management creating predictions based on models that are a mathematical simulation of the real world. Assumptions are made clear for the forecasting and continuously reviewed **based on real measurement data**. Estimations are initially used only when there is no real data available. Compared to traditional estimating, forecasting does not estimate all elements of a basic population (for instance, user stories), rather it uses randomly chosen samples. Depending on how many samples you take, the probability is lower or higher that the minimum and maximum values are included in the sample - with just 19 random samples, the probability lies at 90 percent.

At the beginning of every forecast, there should be a question to be answered. In doing so, it must be clarified how much accuracy is needed to be able to weigh the risks and make a decision. The precision of the prediction can be refined with the help of computer-supported **Monte Carlo simulations**, which calculate the distribution of possible results and their probability of occurrence. Predictions about possible delivery dates with forecasting are not made with the projection of averages, but instead through **choosing quantiles** in the results of the Monte Carlo simulation.

In forecasting, the assumptions made are successively replaced with real measurement values. This way, the predictions will be more reliable and it becomes clear, in the course of the project, if measures must be undertaken to reach the targeted goal. Forecasting does not work under the pretense that estimations are completely unnecessary at the beginning - they are important as long as there is no real data. You cannot expect forecasting at the beginning to deliver 100 percent certainty as to when a project will be completed. But you can achieve more precision with little effort with the help of an ongoing data collection in continuous forecasting. The prerequisite for meaningful forecasts is a stabile system, and that is a system in which the Work in Progress is limited.

Literature

(Cohn, 2005) Mike Cohn. *Agile Estimating and Planning*, Prentice Hall, 2005.

(Leopold & Kaltenecker, 2015) Klaus Leopold & Siegfried Kaltenecker. *Kanban Change Leadership: Creating a Culture of Continuous Improvement*, John Wiley & Sons Inc, 2015.

(Little & Graves, 2008) John D.C. Little & Stephen C. Graves. *Little's Law*, In Dilip Chhajed & Timothy J. Lowe (Eds.), Building Intuition: Insights from Basic Operations Management Models and Principles, pp. 81-100, Springer US, 2008.

(Magennis, 2011) Troy Magennis. *Forecasting and Simulating Software Development Projects: Effective Modeling of Kanban & Scrum Projects using Monte-Carlo Simulation*, FocusedObjective.com, 2011.

(Savage, 2012) Sam L. Savage. *The Flaw of Averages: Why We Underestimate Risk in the Face of Uncertainty*, Wiley, 2012.

(Vacanti, 2015) Daniel S. Vacanti. *Actionable Agile Metrics for Predictability: An Introduction*, Actionable Agile Press, 2015.

5. From Prioritization to Risk Assessment

Prioritizing things is, in principle, a wonderful activity. You bring order to chaos and have the satisfactory feeling of direction. You know which assignment comes next on the list and the level of satisfaction increases as more work on the list is completed. The opposite can also occur, however, especially in companies. In companies, I have witnessed complete prioritization insanity. The problem is that too much work gets started. We even saw it with the ship-folding exercise (see Chapter 1): as more work is pushed into a system, the time pressure is more profound. When everything is being worked on, but nothing is getting finished, the first customers start knocking on the door and asking for the status of their order. The project manager starts to panic, and begins to subvert the carefully constructed prioritization scheme. What was standing at position 3 on the priority list all of a sudden has top priority and the employees leave what they are currently working on in order to appease the customer. Unfortunately, it is rare that just one customer is complaining. Since the completion of other orders gets delayed further, one customer after the other demands their order to be completed - the result is pure chaos. Everything gets constantly reprioritized within the system, where the orders are already being worked on. All of a sudden, work that was less important is now at the top of the priority list and eventually everything has Priority 1 status. Eventually, since nobody is holding on to the prioritization, more overhead is added in order to manage the chaos. I have found a simple indicator that can tell me if chaos is running the system: when nearly half of the people involved in a project are project managers, there are definitely too many things being worked on at the same time.

How can you prevent this disarray and on-going reprioritization of work that is already in the system? After all, most companies (hopefully) are in the lucky position to have more demand than what they can handle. Wouldn't it be enough to simply increase personnel - then all of the customer orders can be dealt with, correct?

Yes, when unlimited resources are available, then there is no need to prioritize. The problem is, however, that the personnel also need to have the appropriate skill set to implement the customer requests. Imagine a company gets an order to build an iPhone App. All of the employees who can complete this order are busy with other work, so only the employees who build Android Apps are available. Technically speaking, there is personnel available, but practically speaking, there is a bottleneck. There isn't a need for just any person to fill an order, rather the right people are needed. This is one of the reasons why prioritization is a good thing, if everyone would keep true to it.

In flow-based systems, you can overcome the weaknesses of conventional prioritization in two ways:

1. Limits: Only a certain number of projects are allowed in the system. Unless the WIP limit permits new work to be introduced, no new work will be started. This prevents too much work from rolling around in the system and competing with one another when all the resources are already assigned. Not to mention that it reduces the overhead, since just one project manager would be needed for the limited number of projects in the system.

2. Traffic Jam Management: Even Kanban, luckily, cannot prevent a company from having more demand than what they are able to fulfill. It is not necessarily a bad thing to have more requests than the available resources to implement it. Achieving total balance is not normally possible, but huge differences between demand and resources should be

avoided. I like to picture a balancing scale to illustrate this. When there is much more demand than resources, the scale can be brought into balance two ways:

- Either you attempt to increase the resources, or
- you pay attention from the start on how to manage the demand reasonably. This doesn't necessarily mean rejecting customer orders; rather, it means doing the right work at the right time.

In Kanban, instead of starting every project immediately, it is deposited in an option pool before it enters the workflow and here prioritization (under different premises) comes into play. The Spice Girls - those colleagues in the company who are responsible for supplying work into the system - asses the options and determine, right at the start, whether or not an option will even be implemented. The Spice Girls serve two roles at the same time. First, they are the bouncers of the system: they determine who is allowed in and who has to stay out. Second, they place the work in a reasonable sequence based on an evaluation of the Cost of Delay.

This requires that the Spice Girls are completely clear about the importance their role plays in the effectiveness of a Kanban work system. Even a Kanban system with all the bells and whistles - WIP limited, visualized and optimized - will break down if the Spice Girls don't understand that work cannot simply be dumped into the system without coordination. Their decision about the order of work to be done (projects, features, etc.) greatly influences the functionality of the entire system. Bonuses for achieving goals are pure poison, because they again reinforce the impulse to act in their own interest rather than in the interest of the company. Agreeing on how future mutual decision-making will be made is part of a sensible change management in a Kanban implementation, as I wrote about in Kanban Change Leadership with Siegfried Kaltenecker (Leopold & Kaltenecker, 2015). Experience has shown me that the economic arguments are eye-opening for many people, especially those in management.

Let's examine the following types of implementations under the assumption that the Spice Girls are aware of their responsibilities.

The Effect of Increasing Resources

In many companies where there is a high demand for their product or service, I often see thinking based strictly on resources. There is so much demand, that the orders cannot be filled with the existing human and material resources. The entire company unit–everything from the structure to the processes is recreated–is built in a new and often cheaper location, but built three times as large as the original. Even if the resources are not increased to these dimensions, the perception is that it works like a faucet - you only need to turn them on or off, and the problems are solved. The business model of some consulting companies and temporary employment agencies are based on this idea. Unfortunately, it is not that easy, especially in the area of knowledge work. The building-up of resources is an absolutely necessary investment in the future, but the positive effects are seen much later. A persistent short-term increase in resources due to bottleneck situations are accompanied by effects which are not intuitive, and thus often ignored. Ad Reinertsen and Smith stated (p. 220, Reinertsen, Smith 1998): "If we add more resources, sooner or later we will be back in the same situation with more projects than we have the resources to handle, and we will be diluting our effort and delaying projects again."

Throughput and Cycle Time

Two measurements are relevant when we are considering how additional resources will affect a work system: throughput and cycle time (see Chapter 4). Throughput is the amount of work which is completed in a given period of time. More throughput in a system means more output will be generated, thus more product that can be sold - throughput is therefore an economic measurement. Cycle time, on the other hand, shows how quickly a unit of work between two measuring points will be completed. The cycle time, when measured from idea to customer deployment, is known as time-to-market. In markets where there is competition from other companies, time-to-market is also an economic measurement which should not be neglected.

What happens then, when the resources in a work system are increased - for example, additional personnel will be hired? In the case of performance, it is probable that two different pictures will form. After an initial decrease in throughput due to additional overhead (see also Little's Law in Chapters 2 and 4), throughput will increase because more employees can work on more orders. However, the Cycle Time also increases. The work system becomes slower and the customer must wait even longer for their product. There are two reasons for this:

1. **Start-up Time:** Every new employee needs a certain amount of time until they are somewhat comfortable with the routines and processes of the company, as well as needing time to get incorporated into a product or project.
2. **Frictional Losses:** When more employees are added to a work system, the complexity also increases since the coordination effort grows. Most of the time, having additional resources leads to stronger specialization, resulting in additional handoffs.

The frictional losses, above all else, affect the cycle time. When building up resources, the company is trying to optimize the active work. I can say, from personal experience, that the amount of active work in the cycle time, though, is between two and 20 percent. You can test this yourself by measuring the flow efficiency of your work system. The cycle time is comprised, for the most part, of waiting time that arises from the handovers between the individual work units involved.

For example, let's assume the cycle time of an activity is 100 days. Let's assume further, that the active working time is around 20 percent. In Figure 5.1, we see in the uppermost bar how the active working time is spread out over the entire cycle time. From time to time, there is a break in the active work because we have to wait for an external contractor, or information is missing, or there is no room in the input queue at the next department, etc. In the bar underneath, the times are sorted together and it becomes clear how low the amount of active work is in the cycle (see also Figure 3.1, Chapter 3).

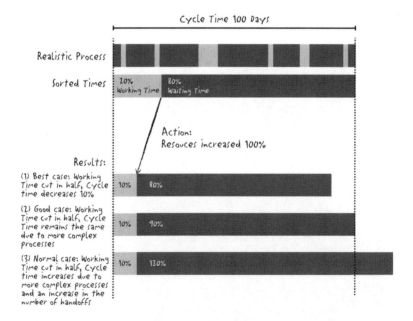

Figure 5.1: Impact of Short-Term Increase of Resources

Naturally, this has to change, so we increase the resources on this project by 100 percent - twice as many employees are now working on it. Even if there are absolutely no frictional losses due to additional complexity and the new employees can begin working immediately with no restrictions, the cycle time will be reduced by a maximum of ten percent, despite the working time being cut in half (1).

The ten percent reduction of working time represents, exactly, something that will never happen: the best-case scenario. We haven't taken into account the fact that additional resources bring more complexity to the system. Let's look at the next to the last bar (2) in Figure 5.1 which shows a more realistic "second best" result. In this case, the working time could be cut in half, but the cycle time remains the same because the process becomes more complex through, for example, additional handovers and increased specialization. This can indeed be seen as something positive. The additional resources purchased didn't make the endeavor slower, rather it supports the current tempo.

The remaining bar (3) represents the normal case. The working time is cut in half, but the cycle time increases since the processes become more complex and the number of handoffs goes up. The only question which remains is, how much the Cycle Time increases.

This game can only be played so long. At some point, due to resources being constantly added, the cycle time increases so much that it takes forever to actually complete the work. There is someone who will not be happy about this, namely the customer. From their perspective, the cycle time is what matters. Large companies who continually add resources are stuck with this dilemma. *More throughput means more revenue, but, at the same time, they lose sight of the cycle time. This is exactly what should not happen, provided they don't want to optimize themselves out of the market.*

In most companies, the problem is that, from the portfolio level down to the team level, what is being worked on is not transparent. Furthermore, the awareness of understanding the difference between active and inactive work is missing. The focus is always on trying to speed up the work, but no one thinks about working on optimizing the waiting time. By using visualization on the Kanban board, it becomes apparent where work is getting backed up, where work is being blocked, where work is being waited on, etc. With color alone, say with red column titles or red "block" stickers, you can illustrate the inactive work (see Chapter 2).

The Economic Perspective on Waiting Time: Cost of Delay

It may be hard to believe, but the fact of the matter is, in most companies, an understanding of the economic impact of long waiting times is missing. It isn't clear to them, when work is not started on time or work not completed on time, that this creates Cost of Delay. All the more satisfying for me then, when a change in their way of thinking occurs. For example, a sporting goods company was losing € 300,000 per year because accounting was not able to recognize deliverer discounts for early payment. By the time invoices were processed through the various departments and finally landed at the person who made the payments, early payment deadlines were long exceeded and the full amount of the invoice needed to be paid. It was a shock to see, when it was finally calculated, how much money could be saved if the early payment discounts were used. The path of an invoice through the company was visualized and it was immediately clear that several handovers were completely redundant. The employees involved were then given more responsibility for decision-making. As such, the "cycle time" of an invoice through the company was decreased from 20 days to three days and every deliverer discount could be recognized. Simply by picturing the process of getting invoices through the company, without hiring new people or needing people to work faster, saved the company approximately € 5,800 per week. That is the economy of waiting time.

As long as a company does not recognize how much money can be lost through waiting time or by a delayed market launch (Cost of Delay), it will again and again fall into a spiral of increasing resources. Time is an economic component, and not only in the form of Time to Market. Time is money, regardless of the context. As Don Reinertsen says (Reinertsen, 2009), "While you may ignore economics, it won't ignore you."

In order to break out of a spiral of increasing resources, and instead find a long-term solution for balancing demand and resources, there should not be more work started than can possibly be finished with the current resources. With Cost of Delay, the Spice Girls have a suitable instrument to help them make effective decisions about work that should be started. By doing this, they can manage the demand.

5.1 Managing Demand with Cost of Delay

In a Kanban system, the full weight of demand and resources is made visible. Demand is mirrored in the options that are decided in the Spice Girls meeting. The WIP limited work system clearly shows how many resources are *actually* available, in order to complete work within an acceptable period of time. What work comes next is decided upon *before* it enters the system - up till now, this was known as prioritization.

Personally, I believe prioritization is a suboptimal concept. There are several typical prioritization methods, for instance

- Dividing into high, medium, and low
- 1, 2, or 3
- MoSCoW – must have, should have, could have and would like but won't get it.

The problem with all of these methods is, eventually everything has the highest priority. When the methods are used over a longer amount of time, and there is enough work which is running concurrently and needs to be prioritized, at some point, all work becomes critical. Let me give you a personal example of this. I am a wine connoisseur, and regularly order wine from my preferred wine store. Somewhere along the line, I started to rate the wine I ordered: four stars being the best, and three stars till one star for the rest. My goal was to expedite my future purchases by seeing which wines were my favorite. At the beginning, my prioritization system functioned quite well. However, the longer I had this system in place, the more four star wines I had in my favorites list and I rarely ordered any wine with three stars or less. If I had kept going with this system, at some point I wouldn't have been able to order all of the four-star wines on my list without it costing around €600. So, I began to rank the wines with four stars as 4++, 4+ and 4-. There could have been endless variations on this. Eventually it dawned on me how ridiculous this system was since it didn't help whatsoever to satisfy my wine passion.

I decided to completely abandon this system of ranking my favorite wines. Now, when I enjoy a wine, I consider how much value this wine has for me. If the wine tastes good to me, I decide how much I would be willing to pay for a bottle. For example, "I would pay €16 for this bottle of Syrah." When my Syrah reserves are getting low, I check online with the wine store to see how much the Syrah costs. If it costs less than €16, then I buy it. I can promptly order this wine, because I know it is in my price range. If I decided a wine is only worth €7 to me, but costs €20 at my preferred wine store, I won't waste my time (or money) ordering it. I removed the prioritization scheme for ordering wine and instead found a system which worked without prioritization. Prioritizing quite simply does not work, because the underlying thinking is based on "containers" - at some point the containers are full and the priorities are no longer useful.

Another problem of classic prioritization is, who decides what is going to be worked on. In many cases, the decision lies with the

HiPPO: Highest Paid Person's Opinion (Arnold, 2015). Another variation is the Eurovision Song Contest procedure. In this case, the highest priority is given to that which we personally prefer or to those who had lobbied the best beforehand. The most common method found in companies, however, is to make someone responsible for the prioritization decisions. In a room full of people who need to come to a decision, there are usually conflicting interests that make it difficult to reach a consensus. "You do it" is the only mutual decision and the responsibility for making the decision is given to a single person by proxy, who in turn carries all the blame when something goes south. That's why the five questions in the root cause analysis of failed projects (see the section on Retrospective) in many companies is "Who?" instead of "Why?". Who is to blame? Afterwards, everyone else can argue that they would have made a completely different decision. It's a shame that decision making is so simplified, since there is plenty of evidence showing groups make better decisions than individuals (Surowiecki, 2005). I don't believe in the Highlander principle of "there can be only one". Proxy solutions do not help us with the issue of how to prioritize.

Cost of Delay for Decision Making

What can we do when classical prioritization only helps as long as it isn't pushed to the limits? The recommended solution is to not use prioritization to begin with, and instead

1. setup **sequences**, instead of priority containers. A sequence means 1, 2, 3, 4, 5, etc. On each position, there is only space for one piece of work.
2. find a **metric** (e.g., money) to compare the tasks at hand in order to make economically sound decisions. Whatever needs to be prioritized also needs to be quantified, so the little games about prioritizing items automatically stop. The danger of the prioritization game is that it is personally motivated rather than being economically rational. The possibility that poor decisions could eventually lead to financial damage often

doesn't matter to the person responsible at the point when the decision is made. Who should make the decisions in prioritization meetings, or in the case of Kanban, Spice Girls meetings? Making a decision should be based on objective measurement which includes economic aspects. Cost of Delay is well-suited for this purpose.

What I hear in the stories and questions of participants in my trainings is that, in many companies, there are indeed the beginnings of an economic approach to task prioritization. These approaches, however, are often not completely thought out. Value, or "business value", is the prioritization tool used in such cases. It's a great idea, but leads me immediately to the question: "How are you using it?" The answer to this question is usually: "Work with the highest value comes first, and those with lower value are implemented later." Sounds logical, doesn't it? Yes, as long as you don't consider the amount of time needed to implement the work. When work X generates high value, and needs four weeks to be completed, while work Y can generate the same value in two weeks, which one gets implemented first? It probably makes more sense to complete work Y first because, stated simply, it brings money in faster than X. When we use value as a prioritization attribute, it should always be considered in relation to the implementation time of the individual work.

Let's go one step further: Is value a static quantity? Chocolate Santa Clauses do not sell well at Easter - in other words, the value of work can change over time. Or it can, subject to seasonal influences, only reach its full-potential at a specific time or within a specific timeframe. The change in value over time should absolutely be taken into account in a prioritization process. Now we have all the ingredients for prioritization based on Cost of Delay:

- How high is the value of the individual work?
- How long does it take to implement the individual work?

- How does the value of the work change over time?

> **Cost of Delay** are those costs, as well as economic effects over time, which occur when the completion of work is delayed or doesn't respond quickly enough to the market. Cost of Delay includes not only actual costs incurred, but also all lost revenues which are incurred, regardless if a project is worked on or not. To be able to work on orders in an economically useful sequence, the Cost of Delay is quantified by visualizing it in concrete monetary amounts.
>
> Cost of Delay is always drawn from the value-generating elements (deliverable units), that give the customer a concrete benefit. It is a function of the value generated by an activity, and its urgency.

I recommend using Cost of Delay *as soon as* the Kanban system design expands. What do I mean by this? The doorkeeper of the system (Spice Girls) do not make decisions based solely on the Costs of Delay. As we will see later, there could and should be other criteria which influence the assessment of the existing options since there are several risks to consider. However, in my opinion, it is a thousand times better, at least at the beginning (as long as no other information or measurements are available) to include Cost of Delay as a basis for making decisions versus falling back into the same old prioritization games. Whoever understands the concept of Cost of Delay also develops a completely different view of work systems:

1) When discussing Cost of Delay, the economic perspective is automatically integrated into the decision-making process. It does not deal with fictional units multiplied by imaginary measurement figures. It deals with values which can be quantified in monetary units and can be compared within the entire company, or even across enterprises.

2) The focus is transferred from costs to **value**. In large companies, the most urgent question asked is always, "What does it cost and when will it be finished?" This is a one-sided consideration, because costs are relative. When something has no value, especially for the customer, then costs of €1000 are already too much. If something has a value of €1,000,000, then costs of €100,000 are acceptable. Without the corresponding value, it is impossible to talk about costs. This reminds me of an example about a bank director of a really small bank in a really small village in Austria. He insisted on getting a report which was technically difficult to generate, and which he would use maybe three times a year. The costs were €60,000. Aside from the director, nobody in the bank even knew this report existed. It was a personal pet issue from the director, and since he was well-connected, the report was compiled.

3) All of a sudden, the economy behind **specialization** and **generalization** is understood. Cross-functional teams aren't put together just because cross-functionality is cool and ideas flow better. Cross-functionality has measurable economic advantages. Specialists are always a bottleneck in a system, which isn't necessarily bad, but it has its own effects. Specialists tend to complete their tasks very quickly. Being a specialist, however, means not always being available, because they are often needed. If a specialist is needed for a particular item, the waiting times, in some circumstances, can be increased. If a generalist takes on the task immediately, he might need five days to complete the same work as the specialist, but he is available now instead of a month from now. Naturally, we assume the specialist and generalist have comparable qualifications. The generalist might need to make himself familiar with the task, but has the fundamental knowledge to be able to complete it (this doesn't mean an accountant would all of a sudden need to program Java). When the generalist does the work, the customer receives their delivery on the sixth day, but if they were to wait on the specialist, they would receive it in 21 days. If you don't realize how much value can be generated in these 15 days, you will always have the tendency to wait for the specialist.

4) In Kanban, we don't work with **WIP limits** just because they are fun (even though they are). Even here, there are specific economic considerations and Cost of Delay helps us to better understand WIP limits. Assuming there are three large work projects to do: A, B and C (see Figure 5.2, a figure we already saw in Chapter 2). If all three work projects were to be started simultaneously, you would, rather quickly, need to start multitasking - work a little bit on A, then on B, then on C. Suppose you would always work one week on each project, and a total of 15 weeks is needed to finish all three projects. In multitasking mode, A will be finished in week 13, B in week 14 and C in week 15.

In contrast to this, a WIP limit of 1 is set. Only one item at a time can be worked on and each item must be fully completed before the next item can be started. Using this method, project A is completed after 5 weeks, project B after ten weeks and project C after 15 weeks.

To look at it a different way, the Cost of Delay with multitasking runs 13 weeks on project A, 14 weeks for project B and 15 weeks for project C. With a WIP limit of 1, value can be generated and money can be made within this time. It makes economic sense to work with WIP limits, because better decisions can be made about the most economical order for work to be completed.

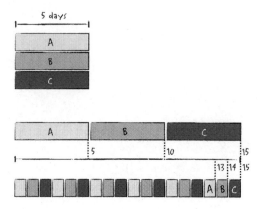

Figure 5.2: Multitasking vs. WIP limit

5) Agile methods essentially differentiate themselves from waterfall methods because the batch size is reduced. Instead of spending a year thinking about what the customer wants, then another year considering how the requirements can be implemented, a further three years programming it, one year for testing and finally delivering the customer something they no longer need, this monster project is broken into many small pieces. The rules of Agile state the customer should receive usable functionality in regular and short intervals. What are the economics behind this? Let's compare the Cost of Delay from a large project with five small projects (Figure 5.3a and Figure 5.3b). In a classical waterfall project, the Cost of Delay builds up over a very long timeframe and suddenly drop off with the completion of the project. Only then is the product put into service, the number of users increases and revenues are generated. Also, this is the first point where the customer can give their feedback. The feedback can also be, however, "I don't like it, I'm not interested, I'm not buying it".

If the project is split into smaller batches, the same Cost of Delay arises at the beginning of the project, just like the large project. Most likely, the total development time remains the same, because small batches are not a guarantee for shorter project times. Nevertheless, the customer receives useful pieces of functionality in a much earlier timeframe. This means Cost of Delay is reduced, because the customer can use the functionality and give feedback. With every additional delivered batch, revenue is generated and quite possibly the number of customers also increases. For this reason, it is so important that value-generating units are delivered.

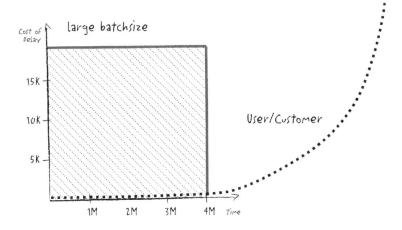

Figure 5.3a: Cost of Delay from Large and Small Batch Size

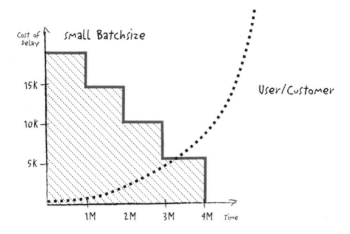

Figure 5.3b: Cost of Delay from Large and Small Batch Size

Quantifying Cost of Delay is overall an effective tool that helps the Spice Girls decide which options, in general, enter the system and what an economically rational sequence of work looks like. The side effect is an intensified understanding of the considerations behind the principles and practices of Kanban.

In order to make strategic decisions, it is especially useful to determine Cost of Delay at the portfolio level for projects. It also pays to use Cost of Delay at the project and product level to quantify value-generating units, i.e. deliverable elements which give the customer concrete functionality. Naturally the next question is, "How is Cost of Delay quantified"?

5.2 Quantifying Cost of Delay

5.2.1 Step 1: Determine the Value

When starting to quantify the Cost of Delay, there is a simple, yes-no decision which needs to be made. Does the feature (or project, story, etc.) have value or not? For the case of simplicity, I will stick to considering features, but this doesn't mean that Cost of Delay is related only to features! Just like Joshua Arnold, I have had positive experiences using the following four categories to simplify the classification of the object of consideration.

1. **Increase revenue**: A feature has value, from a business perspective, when it puts money in the cash register and, as such, increases revenue. For example, the customer wishes to have a particular functionality for their product, and will purchase it as soon as it is available.

2. **Protect revenue**: Revenue could be lost if the feature isn't implemented. A typical situation is when the competition releases a product with new functionality and customers are really excited about the new capabilities. Companies who fail to include these new capabilities in their own products risk losing customers to the competition. It makes sense to offer the new functionality, since this is the only way to preserve future revenues.

3. **Avoid costs**: In the financial branch, this is a classic. When a law requires changes to be implemented by a specific date, not doing so can bring about fines. By not implementing the changes, costs will occur.

4. **Reduce costs**: If the feature is implemented, future costs are expected to be reduced. A good example of this is the automation of process.

If the feature being considered falls into one of these four categories, the next step should be to determine the value of the feature. If the feature cannot be classified into one of these categories, then it does not generate any value and should no longer be considered. On the other hand, a feature could fall into more than one category. For instance, a new law requires the automation of certain processes. The on-time implementation of the automated processes means no fines will be incurred. Additionally, mid- and long-term costs will be reduced.

How is the value of a feature determined? The question of how this should work is one of the biggest questions from participants in my trainings. Before you can put a price tag on a feature, it is necessary to understand its function. As an example, a customer of mine had a huge problem sending invoices. The amounts on the invoices that were sent were different than those in the accounting system. The system generated correct notices for overdue payment, but also generated incorrect notices for the invoices caused by the system failure. The affected customers naturally complained about the incorrect billing, thus the company became aware of the problem in the system. The first measure undertaken was to manually check every single overdue payment notice, in order to see if it was generated by a system failure. This cost a lot of time, and as we are aware, time is money. This problem fell, without question, into the category of preventing costs. The problem could have also fallen into the category of preserve revenue, if customers would have been so angered by the accounting failure that they no longer placed orders with the company. It pays to consider a problem from many different angles - the resulting discussions within the company are valuable for advancing the awareness of the economic impact of work within the company. In any case, correcting the accounting system failure would make the additional costs of manual checking vanish. How much did this failure cost? In order to figure that out, we looked at how many incorrect overdue payment notices were generated by the system and needed to be checked manually in a week. We also knew which employee had to do the manual checks. With this information, we came up with costs of around 15,000 Euros per week that the system failure produced, so the "value" of this failure was €15,000 per week. In the period of a year, there could be costs of approximately one-half million Euros.

The first step is to search for the *total value* that can be obtained. You might be asking yourself, **"Can you really calculate, to the cent, the value of a project or feature?"** The answer is really simple: No, you can't. But the good news is there is absolutely no reason to do so. The point is to make better decisions than those results given by the current decision-making process. In most cases, this is easy to achieve. When establishing Cost of Delay within a company, I try to gather several people together who are responsible for making prioritization decisions. This includes the group of Spice Girls, plus a few representatives from operational areas. For instance, when the software team leader, business representative, developer, designer, tester and project leader come together, each one gets a piece of paper from me on which five features from the Option Pool are listed. I tell the group to secretly write down their "gut feeling" on how much they believe each feature is worth. I collect these estimates and make a list for each feature with the values listed from minimum to maximum. The largest variance I've witnessed was from 1 to 130; represented in Euros, the minimum value was €1,000 and the maximum value was €130,000. Now, imagine that these fundamentally different perspectives are not intentional, but both of these people are decision makers. Conflict is unavoidable, since the decision is based upon completely dissimilar assumptions. The smallest variance I've seen with this exercise is 1 to 10. This is the threshold to beat, and this doesn't even involve precise calculations.

Do not fear a Range of Values!

What do you do when a discussion to determine the value of a feature leads to a large discrepancy? Suppose a Spice Girl believes the option/problem is only worth €1,000, but others in the meeting assign a value of €1,000,000 - there are extreme differences in the valuation. It is highly unlikely, with such a large discrepancy, that the value is exactly €500,000. Simply put, you cannot take the average value in such cases. The better approach is to accept these large differences and try to understand where they come from, since they really mean, "We do not have a common understanding about its worth." It shows that the uncertainty of this option/problem is extremely high and further information is needed, in order to arrive at a common understanding and reduce the value range.

The degree of uncertainty can be simply calculated as:

$$max - min$$

The degree of uncertainty for a range of €1,000 to €1,000,000 is €999,000, which correlates to a factor of 1 to 1,000.

In very few cases, after an informed discussion, would the degree of uncertainty be as extreme as in the case above. If the maximum is €20,000 and the minimum is €10,000, the degree of uncertainty is €10,000 which yields a factor of 1 to 2. This might be acceptable for one person, but for the other still too large a difference. Each company needs to decide for itself, at what degree of uncertainty more information is required. The beauty of this is, when the degree of uncertainty is extremely high, often only a small amount of additional information is needed to reduce the difference. However, much more information is needed to be more precise when the degree of uncertainty is already low (see Chapter 4).

Tip: Do not try to compromise with average values when a high degree of uncertainty arises. Examine the discrepancy and discuss it, and obtain additional information as necessary to reduce the degree of uncertainty. Don't over analyze and remember that the analysis only has to be better than doing no analysis at all. The best "gut feeling" approximation that I have seen was a factor of 1 to 10 and this defines my threshold to be beaten. (Savage, 2012)(Hubbard, 2014)

5.2.2 Step 2: Determine the Cost of Delay

Once the Spice Girls have arrived at a mutual understanding on value, the next step is to consider what Priority Profile exists. Priority is understood to be the development of value for functionality, product, etc., over a period of time. Let me point out, I am not trying to present a complete set of profiles. When working with Priority Profiles, you and your colleagues should develop a feeling of the financial implications when things are, or are not, done at a specific time.

Let's refer back to the example of incorrect invoices. Regardless of the technical glitch responsible for the problem, the "value" of work to manually control the overdue payment notices accrues week after week. In Figure 5.4a and Figure 5.5b, the horizontal line represents the performance, i.e. it shows the maximum value that could be earned if the problem is acted upon in a timely matter.

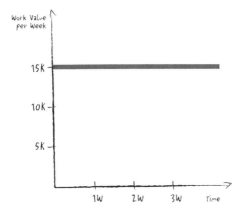

Figure 5.4a: Priority Profile A: The long, continuous peak is unaffected by delay. The Cost of Delay begins immediately.

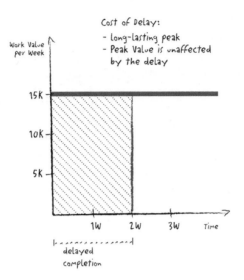

Figure 5.4b: Priority Profile A: The long, continuous peak is unaffected by delay. The Cost of Delay begins immediately.

If the failure in the accounting system could be corrected immediately, €15,000 in value would be attained each week since the costs would never occur. When the problem isn't corrected today, the Cost of Delay starts to grow. Assuming the failure is corrected after two weeks, the accrued Cost of Delay in the meantime is €30,000. What is noticeable on the Priority Profile is that the value of the work in the course of a week doesn't change - we are dealing with a long, continuous peak which is unaffected by delay. Thus, the value to be achieved is the same as the Cost of Delay.

The world, however, is not so simple. In the case of the accounting system failure, the Priority Profile depicted something different. The problem was corrected, but up to that point, there had already been many invoices sent. This meant that the overdue payment notices still needed to be controlled manually, despite the system functioning correctly again. In Priority Profile B (Figure 5.5a and Figure 5.5b), there is a ramping-up phase in which the full value could not yet be recognized. Only after all of the invoices sent before the problem correction were checked, could the full cost-savings be recognized. The Cost of Delay is represented in the shape of a parallelogram and amounts to €45,000.

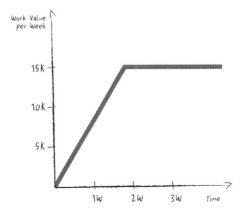

Figure 5.5a: Priority Profile B: The long, continuous peak is unaffected by delay. The Cost of Delay begins immediately, but not to its full extent.

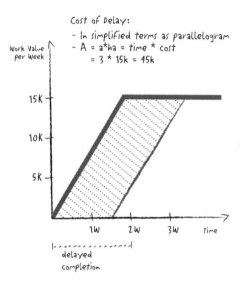

Figure 5.5b: Priority Profile B: The long, continuous peak is unaffected by delay. The Cost of Delay begins immediately, but not to its full extent.

In these two variations, the Cost of Delay begins immediately when you don't react. When dealing with product development, regulatory adaptions, seasonal business, etc., however, the Cost of Delay *will* begin at a specific time in the future. In this case, from an economic perspective, it makes no sense to deliver before this point. It's better to complete other things that could be used before this specific time in the future.

The Priority Profile C in Figure 5.6 corresponds to an unforeseeable change. Assume a store sells a specific brand of jeans. The deliverer changes the interface in the ordering system. This will not lead immediately to economic problems, since the store still has these jeans in stock. As the sizes start to sell out, the Cost of Delay occurs and continues to increase. Once the stock is completely sold out, the total Cost of Delay is recognized.

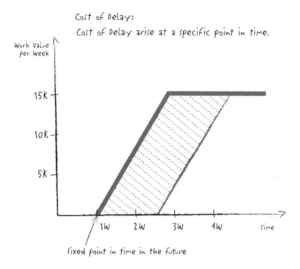

Figure 5.6: Priority Profile C: The long, continuous peak is unaffected by delay. The Cost of Delay begins from a specific point, but not immediately to its full extent.

You probably know such situations, or something similar. For instance, "quick fixes" are slipped into a product. Everything still functions properly, but ignoring the sloppy work long enough could lead to larger problems in the future. The question is, at what point have the technical liabilities been ignored long enough? The Priority Profile might look like the one in Figure 5.7. Currently, there is no Cost of Delay. At some point in the future, though, the costs increase dramatically; we just don't know when exactly. In this case, I recommend quantifying the Cost of Delay from the start and evaluating this work regularly - above all along the time axis.

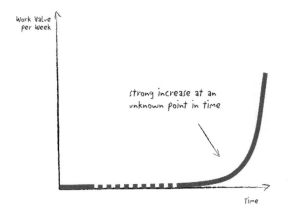

Figure 5.7: Priority Profile D: Exponential growth of the Cost of Delay from a specific point.

For many companies, seasonal business needs to be taken into account (see Priority Profile E in Figure 5.8a and Figure 5.8b). From the beginning of November, the potential revenue continuously increases until reaching its peak during the week of Christmas, then decreases through the end of January. If a company is unable to deliver their product or feature in the "hot" sales weeks before Christmas, it is impossible to earn the entire income (value) within this time frame. The company should consider whether or not it makes sense to concentrate on seasonal business when the delivery would be too late and the peak sales time cannot be taken advantage of. Maybe it is *more* valuable to concentrate on something else and skip the Christmas sales period altogether.

The Cost of Delay for this type of Priority Profile does not need to be calculated on the basis of complicated discussions about the sales curve. The easiest way is to use a table for the pertinent time frame, split into weeks, and assign the allocated values (for example, based on the sales results of the previous year) accordingly.

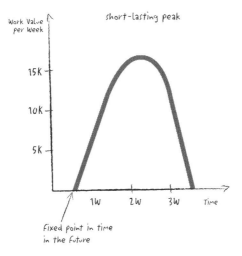

Figure 5.8a: Priority Profile E: The short-term peak is affected by delay. The Cost of Delay begins from a specific point in the future.

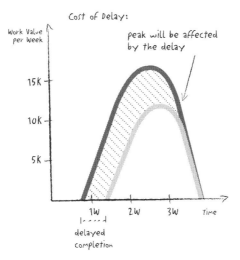

Figure 5.8b: Priority Profile E: The short-term peak is affected by delay. The Cost of Delay begins from a specific point in the future.

Let's recall, once more, the accounting example. As soon as the problem was fixed, it was possible - with a small lag due to the notices already sent before the fix - to save the entire early payment discount losses, the costs of manually checking the overdue payment notices, as well as the costs of fixing the problem. Once the problem was fixed, the company was back on track. Essentially, this worked because the problem was an internal one. If, however, the market comes into play, potential revenues could be lost for a longer period of time, if not forever (see Figure 5.9a and Figure 5.9b). In this case, a delayed entry into the market affects the peak value which could be obtained. In all other Priority Profiles, it was still possible from a specific point to attain almost maximum value. That is not the case here. Such Priority Profiles manifest themselves in already occupied markets. For example, a company wanting to introduce a new soft drink to the market will have a hard time. The peak, which is theoretically possible in the soft drink market, will never be attained. Exactly like it was for Apple, which operated for many years on the smartphone market before they lost market share to the competition. With this Priority Profile, it cannot be predicted if and when the market potential might improve. The consequences of a delayed entry into the market are much more dramatic than, for instance, the seasonal business, which deals with a temporary peak value. The Cost of Delay in Priority Profile F is more difficult to define, because market data is necessary. It is not, however, impossible.

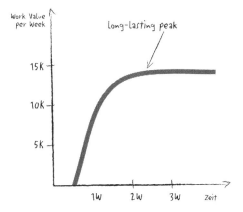

Figure 5.9a: Priority Profile F: The long, continuous peak will be affected by delay. The entry point of the Cost of Delay is at some point in the future, but cannot be predicted exactly.

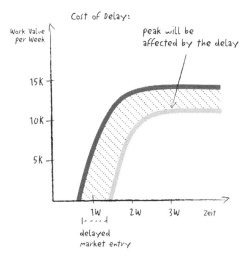

Figure 5.9b: Priority Profile F: The long, continuous peak will be affected by delay. The entry point of the Cost of Delay is at some point in the future, but cannot be predicted exactly.

> ## Summary - The most important Terms
>
> *Priority* denotes the performance over a specific period of time.
>
> *Value* is the monetary amount that can be generated from work when everything is running ideally.
>
> *Cost of Delay* is a function of the performance over a specific period of time, and is best expressed as a monetary unit per week. It depicts how many monetary units per week are either unable to be earned, or arise as additional costs, when a situation is not dealt with in a timely manner.

5.2.3 Step 3: Sequencing

Based on the Priority Profile and the quantified Cost of Delay, which are used to determine individual options, the Spice Girls are able to decide in which order (Sequence) these options can best be implemented. Hence, they fill up the available places in the ready column. The sequence or order does not simply result from sorting the Cost of Delay values. The time needed to complete the work must also be taken into account. This means the time frame from commitment to customer delivery, and is not, in this context, necessarily the Cycle Time. To determine the duration, exact measurements are not absolutely needed (unless you have access to past suitable measurements). Instead, you only need enough accuracy to be able to make a decision. This especially applies to the sequencing of projects. Only when both dimensions - Cost of Delay and completion time - are considered, is it possible to make useful sequencing decisions.

Let's do a thought experiment. We are in a Spice Girls meeting and there are three different features - A, B and C - before us and we should put them into a sequence. For all three features, we have calculated the Cost of Delay and the Cost of Delay begins immediately. When considering how to do the sequence, we must take into account how long it takes to complete the individual features, because time is an economic component. Let's assume we know the completion time for the three features:

- Feature A has a low Cost of Delay at €5,000 per week, but has a long completion time of ten weeks.
- Feature B has a low Cost of Delay at €5,000 per week and has a fairly short completion time of five weeks.
- Feature C is finished fairly quickly in five weeks, but has a very high Cost of Delay at €10,000 per week.

These three features can be illustrated in a diagram as blocks (see Figure 5.10a and Figure 5.10b). Regardless in which order the features would be worked, the total Cost of Delay at the beginning is always CoD(A) + CoD(B) + CoD(C) = €20,000 and must be amortized. The same applies for the duration, as the completion time for all three features is always t(A) + t(B) + t(C) = 20 Weeks. We would like to know which sequence is the best for reducing the total Cost of Delay as quickly as possible.

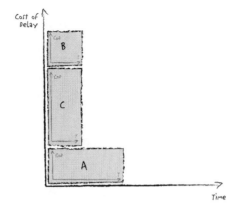

Figure 5.10a: Reducing Cost of Delay

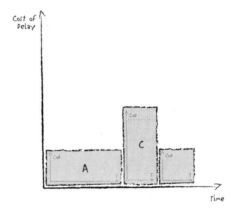

Figure 5.10b: Reducing Cost of Delay

To begin with, let's choose the sequence ABC. When we start with Feature A, the €20,000 Cost of Delay from A, B, and C, remains until the work on Feature A is completed, i.e. ten weeks. The Cost of Delay for Feature A is removed once completed. The Cost of Delay for B and C remain, €15,000 per week, as long as Feature B is being worked on, which is five weeks. After a total of 15 weeks, the Cost of Delay for B can also be removed, and remaining is only the Cost of Delay for C, €5,000 per week, which needs five weeks to be completed. Figures 5.11a and 5.11b illustrate this cost-reduction process. The area created gives us the Cost of Delay, which can be quantified using an area formula for the three rectangles that are formed:

$$(10 \times 20) + (5 \times 15) + (5 \times 10) = 200 + 75 + 50 = €325,000$$

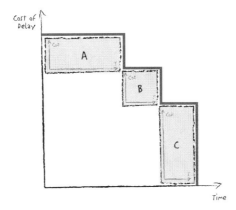

Figure 5.11a: Poor Sequencing with High Cost of Delay

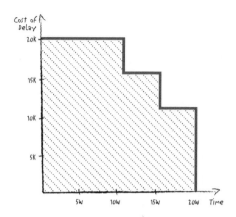

Figure 5.11b: Poor Sequencing with High Cost of Delay

Let's try to minimize the area. It makes the most sense to reduce the highest Cost of Delay as quickly as possible, so we choose sequence CBA. While we are working on C, the total Cost of Delay of €20,000 are present. However, as soon as Feature C is completed, five weeks later, its high Cost of Delay of €10,000 is removed. The remaining Cost of Delay from B and A is relatively low in comparison. Next, we work on Feature B and after five weeks another €5,000 in Cost of Delay is removed. Finally, we dedicate ourselves to Feature A, and after ten weeks, the remaining €5,000 Cost of Delay is removed. As can easily be seen in Figure 5.12a and Figure 5.12b, the area is much smaller than it was for Sequence ABC. Here, too, we can quantify the area:

$$(5 \times 20) + (5 \times 10) + (10 \times 5) = €200,000$$

Sequence CBA saves a total of €125,000 over 20 weeks when compared to Sequence ABC. This is because we thought out the sequencing before starting the work, and decided wisely as to the order of the work. Take a moment to really consider this. Saving €125,000 was achieved simply by changing the order of work - not a single person had to work harder or faster. This is the strength of

Cost of Delay!

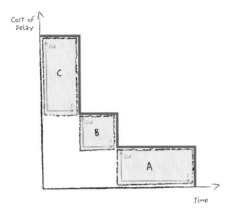

Figure 5.12a: Sequence with Low Cost of Delay

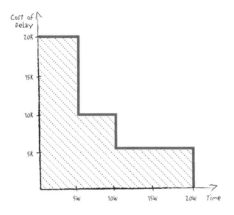

Figure 5.12b: Sequence with Low Cost of Delay

CoD Weight

From this example, the following can be derived: It makes

sense to complete work with the highest Cost of Delay and can be quickly completed first. Work with a longer completion time, but lower Cost of Delay, should be tackled at a later time. There is a relation between Cost of Delay and Time that can be represented by the following division formula:

$$CoDWeight = \frac{CoD}{Duration}$$

The result, CoD Weight, can be used as a guide for determining the order of work.

This formula corresponds to the algorithm "Weighted Shortest Job First", when all Cost of Delay begins at the same time (Reinersten, Smith 1998). This algorithm stems from the beginning of the computer age, at a time when technical resources were scarce and expensive. It was necessary to plan exactly how to use resources optimally. Don Reinersten recommended this algorithm for prioritization decisions in knowledge work. *The higher the CoD Weight is, the earlier the work should be started.* This formula can be helpful for determining sequence when various projects have different Cost of Delay and different completion times. The downside of CoD Weight is that it only produces meaningful results when all elements of the CoD occur at the same time.

Sequence Decisions when Cost of Delay starts at varying times

In the real world, often Cost of Delay for various work begins at different times, and not all at the same time. Each piece of work can have a different Priority Profile. This property must be included because it influences the sequence. The CoD Weight cannot be used as the only ordering attribute. If work has the highest Cost of Delay, but the Cost of Delay doesn't begin for a few years, it makes no sense to put this work ahead of work with lower Cost of Delay that begins earlier. In order to make a final sequence, this fact must be taken into account.

Let's continue with our example about the Features A, B and C. What sequence makes the most economic sense when the Cost of Delay for Feature C begin in 20 weeks instead of immediately? If we would stay with the cost-effective sequence CBA, the Cost of Delay would never come into effect since it is completed within five weeks. However, the Cost of Delay for Features B and A begin immediately. As a result, the Cost of Delay for Feature B are stretched out over ten weeks (five weeks waiting time + five weeks completion time), and those for Feature A over 20 weeks. By working on Feature C first, there will be no Cost of Delay reduction. For this sequence, there is a total Cost of Delay of €150,000.

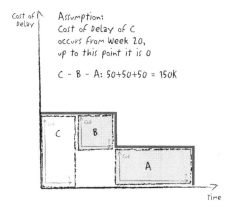

Figure 5.13a: Sequence scenario with varying Cost of Delay start

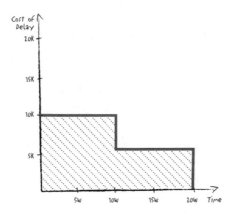

Figure 5.13b: Sequence scenario with varying Cost of Delay start

Features A and B have considerably short completion times and could be finished before the Cost of Delay from Feature C even starts. As such, in a second scenario Feature C is worked on last (see Figure 5.14a and Figure 5.14b). The Cost of Delay for Features B and A remains the same, but Feature B is finished earlier. If we calculate the CoD Weight for this scenario, Feature A has a weight of 500 and Feature B has a weight of 1,000. In this case, it makes sense to start working on Feature B first. Thus, the Sequence BAC has a total Cost of Delay of €100,000. Again here, it's important to point out that we have saved €50,000 just by sequencing the work in a different order.

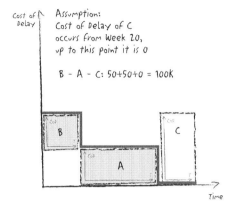

Figure 5.14a: Work with the latest Cost of Delay start will be completed last

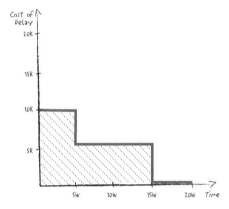

Figure 5.14b: Work with the latest Cost of Delay start will be completed last

Naturally, in the real world there is often work where the Cost of Delay has different starting times and, as such, needs to be ordered. If it is necessary to calculate all ordering permutations manually, the limits of possibility will be reached rather quickly. With three pieces of work, there are a total of six possible combinations. Ten pieces of work look completely different, however, with the possible combinations amounting to 3,628,800. The number of combinations can be calculated using the factorial function, but working with adequate software is recommended (useful material can be found on the website for this book, www.practicalkanban.com). The most important, however, is:

> When deciding about the sequence of work which makes the most economic sense, the starting time for Cost of Delay must be taken into account.

Do you have a 100% guarantee that you will make an absolutely correct sequencing decision when the Cost of Delay has been calculated? Sadly, I must disappoint you. It is not possible to make a final correct decision, rather just a decision that is the least incorrect. To reach a 100% certainty, endless amounts of factors need to be taken into account, and some of these factors cannot be predicted from the present standpoint. The good news is, Cost of Delay helps you to make much more accurate decisions, more so than if you were to ignore the fact that time is money. Even if the calculations are not done to the cent, you still get a realistic picture of the financial possibilities and risks. What's important is that the Spice Girls deliberately consider this and develop a common vision. With Cost of Delay, they have a factual argument, based on objective and economic considerations, that takes the personal vanity and political games within the company out of the decision-making process. As time-to-market becomes more and more critical for many companies, Cost of Delay translates this into a language which, above all, management understands: money.

5.2.4 Determining Cost of Delay in Practice

Determining Cost of Delay is best done at Flight Level 2 and Flight Level 3, if it does *not* involve highly innovative projects or strategic issues which are difficult to quantify. In the case of strategic or innovative issues, there is often too little information and too much uncertainty, especially at Flight Level 3, to be able to determine a reasonable range of values. At Flight Level 1, on the other hand, the work projects are often too small for a Cost of Delay calculation to be useful. Also, it would be nearly impossible to complete, due to the frequency of work at this level.

In order to start the discussion of Cost of Delay in a Spice Girls meeting, there are simple templates which summarize the information needed. One *example* - I highly recommend developing your own templates - can be seen in Figure 5.15. This template is to be filled out for each piece of work to be discussed, and the most important question to be answered is: "*Why* is this work important for our company?" Determining the Cost of Delay is not about putting a monetary value on the work as quickly as possible, rather it is about considering the specific difficulties. Only when the problem and its effects are understood, is it then possible to arrive at a monetary *value* and outline the Priority Profile. Hold on to uncertainties - if there are any - by documenting the range of values which occur.

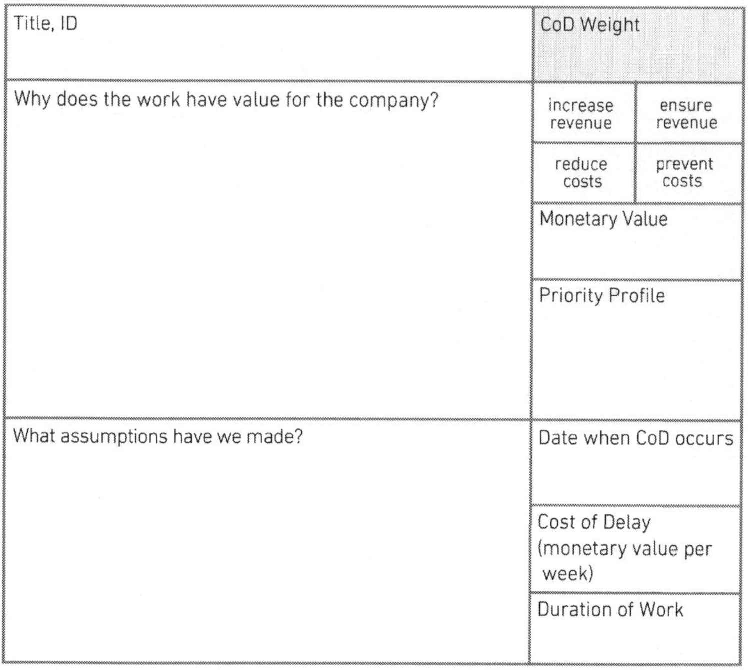

Title, ID	CoD Weight	
Why does the work have value for the company?	increase revenue	ensure revenue
	reduce costs	prevent costs
	Monetary Value	
	Priority Profile	
What assumptions have we made?	Date when CoD occurs	
	Cost of Delay (monetary value per week)	
	Duration of Work	

Figure 5.15: Discussion Template for determining Cost of Delay

When outlining the Priority Profile, the versions depicted can be used for reference, but are not the only possibility - feel free to design your own Priority Profile. What fits to the immediate issues of your company? With every Priority Profile, it is important to consider the point at which Cost of Delay begins. Does Cost of Delay start affecting the project immediately, or does it start at some point in the future? Here, too, we can work with ranges. The *amount of time* to completion can be based on estimations, but you need them to determine sequence in order to weight the Cost of Delay. Please do not forget to document your *assumptions* on which your estimations are based. Only then will you be able to, at a later time, understand how you arrived at your results.

Since we want to say good-bye to the Highlander principle ("There can be only one"), it's necessary for several Spice Girls to come to a mutual decision. In practice, this functions quite well. Each participant fills out the template for each piece of work that is to enter the system. In the meeting, each Spice Girl presents their work while the others ask about their assumptions and calculations. The goal is to achieve a common understanding about the work being discussed. The results are then recorded in the template.

Let's assume that the input queue of our system has a WIP of 6 (Figure 5.16). In the option pool are the projects that the Spice Girls (for our purposes, there are three) have reviewed individually, but have not yet discussed in the group, nor a common understanding achieved. There are four places available in the input queue that could be filled. Ideally, each Spice Girl would only present their most important work to be discussed and evaluated together. After presenting all of the projects, Cost of Delay will be weighted and the projects can be placed into a work sequence.

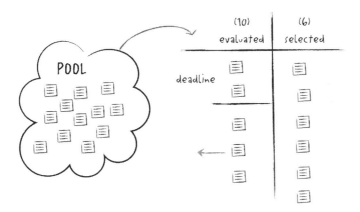

Figure 5.16: Input Queue and Pre-Queue

It can also happen that work has already been evaluated and is still not put in the sequence. For example, the completion of that particular work is not as urgent as it is for other pieces of work.

In such cases, a separate "Evaluated" queue (or Pre-Queue) makes sense, as work can be pulled out of it as resources allow. The Evaluated Queue does normally not belong to the Committed area. In each Spice Girls meeting, this queue will be checked for any changes which may have occurred in the meantime and, when necessary, a new order will be made. The Evaluated Queue should also have a WIP limit. As long as there is evaluated work in the queue, it makes little sense to evaluate new projects.

When you want to make determining Cost of Delay a permanent part of the workflow, it not only can, but *should*, be illustrated on the Kanban board. Look at the example in Figure 5.17, which shows an upstream portion of a Kanban board at the project level, from one of my customers in the banking branch. The upstream includes each activity through which a piece of work must pass in order to be executed. This is the point where Cost of Delay is determined and other risks are evaluated by the Spice Girls. The visual representation of the upstream is, at this customer, normally stretched out to include the finding ideas phase. However, we will start with the Spice Girls' evaluation of ideas.

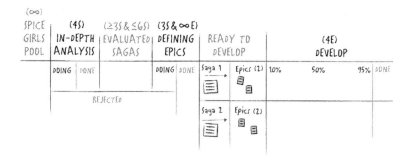

Figure 5.17: Illustration of Upstream Risk Evaluation

On this project level Flight Level 2 board, there are two types of work: Sagas (S) and Epics (E). A project includes several Sagas that are ordered by the Spice Girls based on Cost of Delay. A Saga must have customer value and must be rolled out. From the point of commitment up to delivery, the cycle time of a Saga should be less than six weeks. The developers then take the Sagas and sort them again into Epics. An Epic has customer value, but does not necessarily need to be rolled out. Epics should have a cycle time of less than three weeks.

The developers, which number around 60, are used by several stakeholders, from marketing to diverse business departments, who are responsible for various customer products at this bank. In the column "Spice Girls Pool" are ideas which are waiting to be evaluated. Occasionally, the opinions are very far apart, or there is information missing that is necessary to make a decision. In this case, the Saga must be analyzed in-depth - therefore, the step "In-depth Analysis" is optional. If a Saga doesn't need to be further analyzed, or it has made it through the in-depth analysis without being thrown out (the area designated "rejected"), it moves into the next step, "Evaluated Sagas". The interesting part of this step is the WIP limit. At this step, there should never be less than three, or more than six, Sagas in play. Minimum WIP and Maximum WIP is often seen in upstream, because you want to prevent that ideas run out and development has nothing to work on. The Sagas in this column are ordered based on their weighted Cost of Delay. In this order, the Sagas are also pulled into the next step, "Defining Epics". The business representatives and the development representatives separate the Sagas into appropriate Epics. A maximum of three Sagas should be found here, but naturally, an unlimited number of Epics. This means, quite simply, that at this point it cannot be determined how many Epics comprise a Saga.

The Sagas and their corresponding Epics are together pulled into the next step, "Ready to Develop". In this step, there are a maximum of two Sagas, with their corresponding Epics, allowed. The Epics must also be placed into a useful order, but differently than in the upstream. Instead of being based on Cost of Delay, they could, for instance, be ordered on the basis of technical criteria. Then two Epics at a time can be sent to development.

In my opinion, what's charming about this constellation is that, at this point, there is considerable cooperation between business and development. For instance, the developers support the Spice Girls upstream with their know-how when there is a question about the technical risk. At the In-depth Analysis step, it is possible that a prototype is needed for further decision making. The corresponding ticket (for the prototype development) is not placed in the Develop column. Instead, it stays under In-depth Analysis with a notation that it is being worked on by a developer. In the case of this customer, the ticket will be visibly marked so it is clear for everyone that downstream resources are limited at this time. Thinking about individual interest is prevented since the preparatory work can be viewed as a common task, versus forcing it on development.

On the other hand, developers take over the decision-making downstream and are supported by their business colleagues. With their understanding of market risks, they are able to help the developers put the Epics in a sequence, because it's likely that some functionality is more important than others for the customer or user. You need both points of view - the technical and the business - in order to determine a useful sequence for the Epics.

However, don't fool yourself into thinking the collaboration will function perfectly right from the start. More often, in most companies, it develops gradually over time. Ultimately, these are two very different cultures coming together. On one side is the business group, who can spend weeks discussing unimportant details (from the developer's point of view) such as the shade of color for an application. On the other side are the developers, who sometimes prefer to design and develop applications for themselves rather than focusing on the user. Don't expect a Kanban board to overcome all of the misunderstanding and incomprehension that arises. The consolidation of upstream and downstream requires a high level of maturity within the company and a mutual appreciation for each other's area of expertise (Wardly, 2015).

In Summary: Why Cost of Delay?

There are many criteria that influence the prioritization decision making, such as risk assessment, as we will see in later sections. Please do not view Cost of Delay as a one-size-fits-all solution that is the only tool to reach the correct decision. That being said, understanding Cost of Delay is, in my work with companies, always an ideal starting point for showing those involved that classical prioritization causes more problems than it solves.

Cost of Delay helps steer away from arbitrariness and towards economically rational considerations, thereby focusing on the company goals again. Since Cost of Delay provides a common language - the value of a piece of work estimated in Euro - for the discussions, all alternatives can be compared with a common basis.

For me personally, using Cost of Delay to give a price tag to waiting time is critical, since it is a large portion of the cycle time. The longer the wait during work being completed, the less likely it is for the full value of work to be attained and the more likely it is that additional costs arise. I have seen many of my customers gasp for air after calculating, for the first time, Cost of Delay for their projects and deferred improvements. All of a sudden it becomes clear that the employees do not simply need to work faster in order to save the Time-to-Market. "A bad system will beat a good person every time", W. Edwards Deming said in 1993 at a seminar in Phoenix, and he was absolutely correct. Let's not work on cultivating high-performance workers, rather let's find a way to make the work easier for them. When everyone involved realizes how much handoffs and unnecessary processes cost, discussions about improvements are initiated. This is exactly the idea and purpose behind such considerations.

5.3 Additional Refill Factors: Risk Assessment

Once the idea of Cost of Delay has been established and is well-practiced during the Spice Girls meetings, you can consider other factors for determining sequences or making refill decisions. Strictly speaking, it is going to be about gauging risk when dealing with business decisions. Knowledge work is, by default, uncertain. If you start a piece of work today, it cannot be determined with 100% certainty, when and how the work will be finished. It is difficult to evaluate, or even understand, which problems and unforeseeable circumstances may occur till then. Not to mention, it's impossible to say when you will even have the brilliant idea to begin with.

That being said, some uncertainties will have a larger impact on the business than others. For example, if the forecast says the work will be completed between May 1st and August 1st, the degree of uncertainty - three months - is quite high for the customer. If, however, they want to see the product on November 1st, the uncertainty given by the forecast is irrelevant. This illustrates that it's not necessary to completely eliminate uncertainty. When the forecast has a 90% probability of occurrence, it's enough to reach a decision to accept the contract. We can see here that there is another factor in play: risk.

Risk

First Scenario Two envelopes are lying in front of you. One envelope has 10 Euros. The other is empty. You can choose to do one of the following:

- Pick one of the envelopes, or
- Take none of the envelopes, and instead receive three Euros.

If you choose the first option and take one of the envelopes, you have a 50/50 chance of choosing the envelope with 10 Euros. Thus, the uncertainty of winning something is 50 percent. If you decide for the second option, you have a 100 percent certainty of receiving three Euros. By the way, the majority of people choose the first option in this scenario.

Second Scenario

Let's change the conditions. One envelope contains a check for € 1,000,000 and in the other envelope is a blank sheet of paper. You either pick an envelope, or you forego choosing an envelope and get € 300,000 cash in the hand instead. What do you do?

In both scenarios, the probability - or degree of uncertainty - of choosing the envelope with money in it is exactly the same. Regardless, in the second scenario, many more people choose the sure thing, € 300,000, rather than taking a chance on not picking the € 1,000,000 envelope. In the first scenario, however, it didn't seem to matter if the participant received the 10 Euros or not.

Even when the uncertainty is the same in both scenarios, the risk is not. Whether or not something like risk will be taken into account always lies in the eye of the beholder. For me personally, € 300,000 is a lot of money, and I would take it immediately. Bill Gates, on the other hand, would perhaps choose an envelope since neither of the possible outcomes would affect him financially.

Let's adhere to the following definitions:

Uncertainty is the absence of complete certainty. There isn't a single outcome, but rather several possible outcomes, for a given situation. The measure of uncertainty is **probability**, with each possibility being assigned a probability. An example: There is a 60 percent chance that the market volume will double within five years.

Risk is the individual impact from uncertainty, as relating to

> profit or loss (of money, stuff, life, etc.). Risk is measured by the assigning the possible outcomes *quantified probabilities* and *quantified losses*. An example: There is a 40 percent chance, that we will not find oil at the site suggested, resulting in a loss of 12 million dollars for drilling costs. Risk can also be something positive, however, by getting the chance to gain something that you did not have before (as in the envelope scenario).
>
> The question which needs to be answered by such decisions is: **Which and how much risk is present in the uncertainty?**

There is always uncertainty, but not all uncertainty contains a risk. Before making a decision, there needs to be a differentiation of what is actually a risk, and what isn't. Whether it's going about project or product development, the important thing is to recognize and understand risk. Then, instead of ignoring or deferring risk, you manage or reduce it. This means assessing risk as soon as possible. Forecasting risk is even more important when a product or project must be completed quickly. The responsibility for considering how to reduce risk is prevented from being deferred.

In the real world, exactly the opposite occurs. Deferring risk assessment to sometime in the future is an odd, but strangely enough, popular strategy in knowledge work. Potential customers are only first shown a product when it enters the market. This classical approach actually maximizes market risk. The same game can be observed within the quality control. Testing is pushed out to the very end of a project instead of integrating it as part of the development work. Although experience constantly shows us the opposite, there is a naive trust that the failures accumulated, but ignored, over the months or years of development, can somehow be repaired a month before the official project deadline. If the project is absolutely bound to its deadline, you are operating with your eyes wide open to the highest possible degree of self-produced risk.

This is why I constantly emphasize the importance of end-to-end consideration. Kanban systems illustrate the value stream because the risks of extremely uncertain knowledge should be clearly expressed and be made manageable. Splitting work into smaller pieces is geared towards distributing the risk and reducing it piece by piece.

5.3.1 Types of Risk

Risks in a business context can be separated into main categories: Technical Risk and Market Risk.

Technical Risk is the probability that a technical problem will affect a development effort or the outcome of a project. For example, it becomes apparent that a product cannot be developed with the materials which were originally planned. Or a software-related example: When the display size of the iPhone changes, an application developer must consider the risk associated with this change. Technical risk also arises when a technology doesn't do what it is supposed to do. When this happens, side effects can develop which could not be seen ahead of time, i.e. collateral damage occurs when using the technology.

Market Risk exists when you do not understand or have not adequately involved yourself in the market. In the worst case, your product will be ignored in the market or a customer refuses to accept it because the result is not what he expected. Customer-related market risk can be more readily dealt by including the customer in the development process - which is the approach of agile development frameworks. When the customer does not know, and cannot formulate, what they want or need (and rarely does the customer know what they want). To find this out, it's necessary to have frequent conversations and observe user behavior. Market risk does not always need a customer, however: Even products within a company can compete with one another.

Naturally, there is not exclusively technical risk or market risk, rather both occur simultaneously. In technology-oriented companies, as well as in software development, often the focus is too much on technical risk and market risk is neglected. The reason is partly due to technical risks being concrete and easy to quantify. This is where the danger lies: Focusing on those things, which are understood and mastered, does not reduce the risk! The risk is only being suppressed and the danger is that the damage will be worse at a later time.

> Don Reinertsen and Preston G. Smith point out, that underestimating market risk can cause two new types of risk to arise (Reinertsen & Smith, 1998):
>
> 1. The fear of technical risk results in over-management through excessive reviews. These reviews delay the project, which in turn causes market risk to increase.
> 2. An initially unrecognized market risk results in changes to the project, usually too late. Marketing and/or Sales realize that the product in its current form does not match what the customer needs. The product should be redesigned and the project is delayed.

5.3.2 Quantifying Risk

Risk is made up of two components: the level of its possible impact (Risk Value) and the probability of occurrence. Using the example of the envelopes with money, the possible outcomes in the first scenario are €0, €3 and €10. In the second scenario, the possible outcomes are €0, €300,000 and €1,000,000. How relevant each outcome is dependent, among other things, on the financial situation of the player. The profit or loss probability is, however, in each scenario the same.

It makes sense to address the largest risks at the beginning, which requires the risks to be quantified. There are two possible variations to quantify risk. The first one I will designate as independent risk estimation. The second, more structured, variation is model-based estimation. Independent risk estimation is useful for large development proposals with a high degree of uncertainty at the beginning. When the proposal becomes more tangible and the degree of uncertainty is reduced, patterns emerge as part of the regular risk reviews, and it is important to know what is behind them. Model-based Estimation is the next step because it attempts to more precisely assess and measure the different risk dimensions.

5.3.2.1 Independent Risk Estimation

Larger initiatives need, in my opinion, a screening at the start of the project. In a group brainstorming session, with all those responsible present, all possible risks which could arise should be considered and written down. It's important to assess the project from as many different angles as possible, so the brainstorming group should be cross-functional. The point is to always continue asking if, in fact, both types of risk - technical and market - have been taken into account. Ideally, the list will be checked again to group together similar risks and remove redundancies.

The next step is to attempt determining the level of risk value in a monetary amount. This is, in some cases, not an objective, quantifiable value. Instead, it is similar to determining a value for Cost of Delay that depends on assumptions. The risk value will simply - also through assumptions - be assigned a probability of likelihood that it could occur. These assumptions should, in any case, be written down so they can be referred to at a later time. Let's assume risks A, B and C are identified and each are assigned a probability of occurrence:

Risk	Risk Value	Probability	Expected Value	Assumptions
A	€ 100.000	80%	80.000	
B	€ 300.000	20%	60.000	
C	€ 500.000	10%	50.000	

You can simply calculate the Expected Value to determine in which sequence the risks should be addressed in order to minimize them. In this case, despite having the smallest risk value, the higher probability of occurrence means risk A should be dealt with first.

$$ExpectedValue = RiskValue \times Probability$$

The risks, along with their values and probabilities, could also be represented as a risk profile in a diagram. Don Reinertsen and Preston G. Smith recommend defining the threshold line in such diagrams (Reinertsen, Smith 1998). This line shows the border of risks that need to be considered. All of the risks that are below or left of this threshold line do not require special attention. All of the risks that are to the right or above this threshold line must be actively managed in order to bring them under the threshold line (see Figure 5.18).

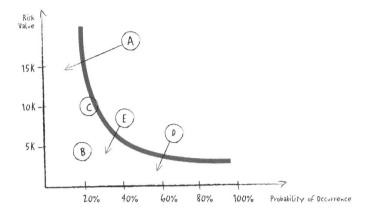

Figure 5.18: Threshold Line

The definition of this threshold is dependent on the context. It could be defined by sales figures, such as company sales, product sales, project budget, and so on. For example, if you have a project budget of €1,000,000 where half of it (€500,000) is threatened by a risk with ten percent probability of occurrence, risk management makes sense (this would be the upper-left starting point of the curve) only if managing the risk costs less than the risk itself. The other end of the curve (lower-right) could be, for instance, €1,000 risk value which has 100% probability of occurrence. From the project perspective, there would be no need for a comprehensive risk management. In this example, the threshold is the curve connecting these two points.

Reinertsen recommends careful consideration of this threshold, since each risk which needs to be managed also means overhead. It should be checked again, if all risks above the threshold really belong there. Likewise, are the risks under the curve perhaps an underestimated risk? The next step would be to make an action plan for each risk which should be managed.

Those involved should meet at fixed intervals for a risk review to discuss any developments. Has anything changed with the previously identified risks, or has something new come along? The quantifications and diagrams, along with the Kanban board, should be retained to reinforce the awareness of the risks for all those involved with this area. The important thing to remember about independent risk estimation is that the considerations do not need to be exact calculations since they are for the most part only assumptions. However, an analysis based on these calculations is better than having no analysis at all.

At the program and portfolio level, the Spice Girls must decide which large initiative - sagas or projects - will be started next. In this case, I recommend determining the Cost of Delay first, then additionally evaluating the risks of the individual initiatives and making a risk profile. Then it will be clear, in which sequence the initiatives should be started. Figure 5.19a and Figure 5.19b show the comparison of risks of two projects. Which project should be started first?

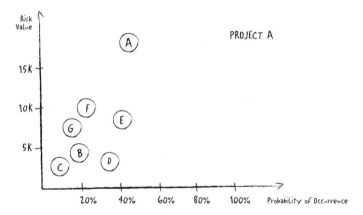

Figure 5.19a: Risk Comparison of two projects

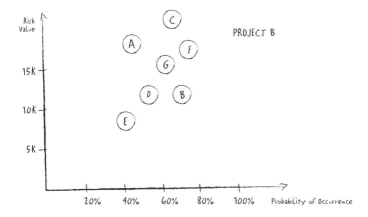

Figure 5.19b: **Risk Comparison of two projects**

The further risk moves to the right of the diagram, the more urgent it is to address these risks. Assuming it has the lower Cost of Delay per week, Project B is "riskier" and should be started first. It's important to note here that we are not deciding if a project will be implemented because the decision was already made that both initiatives will be implemented. Instead, we are only determining the order in which the implementation takes place.

In the case of sagas, as well as pieces of work, that stretch out over months, it might make sense to not start the project immediately when the risk profile is similar to the one for Project B. Instead, epics should be defined that deal with the largest risks. As soon as you have more information, the risk can be re-evaluated. It's possible the analysis will show that the preparation for the epics needs to be worked on a little more. It's also possible at this point, that the risk, in relation to the overhead and benefit of the project, is out of proportion and the project should not even be implemented. It's clear at this stage that estimations of "Cash Cows" and innovative projects should be separated. When estimating risk, the Cash Cow projects will always be chosen, but in the long-term is fatal for the innovative ability of a company. This is only a small look at how risks can be reduced in the preliminary stages of a project. The possibilities for risk management at the portfolio level alone could fill an entire book.

5.3.2.2 Model-based Estimation

Working with models for risk estimation functions well at the project level, but it can also be used for epics. You can use existing models (or build your own) to specify risks and formalize risk management. Model-based estimation asks many more questions about the product or project to those involved. In my opinion, if you are going to use this variation of risk estimation, it's important to have thoroughly discussed the topic of risk.

In order to demonstrate this, I am going to build my own model (only as an example) that is comprised of five dimensions: Cost of Delay, Effect of Cost of Delay, technical risk, market risk and product life-cycle. In the following list, you will find a number in parentheses always next to the individual sub-category of each dimension. I use this to estimate the risk of that category in order to depict it later in the risk profile.

If **Cost of Delay** was ascertained beforehand, the relevant **effects** on the business could be examined in the next step. This can be done, for example, using the following categories:

- Intangible (1): The Cost of Delay is too small to be able to determine a threat, or it cannot be defined.
- Discretionary Spending (2): The Cost of Delay is such that its effect can be covered by available reserves.
- Serious Impact (3): The Cost of Delay is so high, that other planned initiatives cannot be implemented without further investment.

- Extinction Level Event (4): The Cost of Delay is at a level where the existence of the company is in danger, even if it only gets into this situation for a short time.

These are just some examples. Risks can be categorized as such, or they can be categorized in a completely different way. Categorizing should simply provide a common basis of communication, and these will be defined differently from company to company.

Technical risk can also be roughly broken down into the following categories:

- Very Low Risk (1): These include standard tasks with low technical requirements that are routinely performed (such as updating text on a website).
- Low Risk (2): This is known technology and has already been used before - however, these experiences have not yet turned into a routine.
- Medium Risk (3): The technology was already used in one (or several) projects, although not by our company. A solution exists, but we need to build up our knowledge of the technology.
- High Risk (4): It is not known if this technical problem has been solved by someone before.

The third dimension that I need for my model is **Market Risk**, by using the Market Role Model (Anderson, 2012). The corresponding risks can be split up as follows:

- Standard Functionality (1): Without this functionality - also known as Table Stakes - there is no need to even attempt to bring your product to market. Usually, this functionality has low value and very little uncertainty. As such, you cannot differentiate yourself from your competitors with this functionality. It makes sense to invest as little energy as possible in standard functionality. It is possible that it is more efficient to just buy the standard functionality and instead invest the time in your own unique selling point (USP) and business development.

- Cost Reducing (2): This functionality is not necessarily standard functionality, but it helps to reduce the cost of a product (for instance, automating the invoicing in a web shop).
- Spoiler (3): The users find this functionality attractive and cool to the point that they become loyal customers to the platform or product from the competition. This functionality can ruin your business when you do not offer it in your platform or product. Customers are also impressed by it and we need to offer it as quickly as possible to prevent losing our customers.
- Distinguishing Features (4): With this functionality, a company distinguishes itself or its product from the competition, and this is where the USP is hidden. In order to expand and increase the know-how, investment should be made in the distinguishing features. Ideally, these products are high-value and have a large market share, but every action is also associated with a higher risk. It is an art to address the risks as soon as possible and to make the batch size as small as possible. At the same time, you should begin with the distinguishing features in order to verify their technology, as well as test them in the market and get feedback. When the difficult and complex tasks cannot be implemented, it makes no sense to work on the easier ones. Twitter didn't start by developing the functionality to use a profile picture. Instead, they first verified if potential users would write 140 character messages. Time-to-market and rapid verification feedback is everything in the case of distinguishing features.

As we know, **Product Life Cycle** describes the current phase of existence of a product on the market. Each phase of the Product Life Cycle contains its own risk.

- Introduction (4): A completely new product without users (or very few users) - the risk that the market doesn't embrace it is very high. Until now, the product has only produced costs.
- Growth Phase (3): The product is no longer completely new. There are the first early adopters and revenue is increasing.
- Maturity and Saturation (2): The cash cows of the company are located here. The risk for these products is low, but the danger is to depend on the cash cows rather than finding the right mix between new and existing products. The cash cows are actually in a downswing phase, so new cash cows must be provided at the other end.
- Degeneration (1): The product is still delivering revenue, but is gradually sliding into a loss zone. Here you must make a decision: No longer invest in the product and hasten the death of the product, or try a relaunch?

These five (possible) categories

1. Cost of Delay (you should always begin with this)
2. Effects of Cost of Delay
3. Technical Risk
4. Market Risk
5. Product Life Cycle

and their estimated subcategories can be aggregated for an applicable piece of work (often dealing with something larger - a project or saga) into a spider chart like Figure 5.20. The categories are used for the axes and the corresponding risk estimation from 1 to 4 (in parentheses) are the intercept points on each axis. Each risk category that pertains to this piece of work can be allocated in the diagram. When connecting the points, a spider web is formed. The further the spider web expands outwards, the higher the risk when starting the project. This also means that a project with this profile requires an intensive risk management. The goal is to reduce the dimension of the web. Naturally, there is not always an evenly distributed web. When the risk in the individual categories vary greatly, some of the axes will be more pronounced than the others. In such cases, it's understood that the most pronounced risk must be dealt with first. For example, the technical risk is extremely high because the product is just being developed and is completely new to the market. In this case, two things need to be verified: Is it even technically possible to implement it and will it be accepted by the users? Both of these questions can be answered by creating a prototype. Once the first information has been gathered from the prototype, you can return to the risk assessment and check if the risk has been reduced or not.

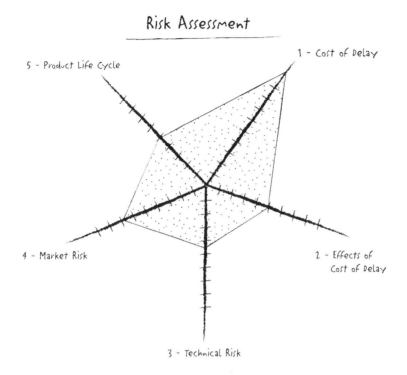

Figure 5.20: Risk Spider Chart

The important point to take away is that this model - or whichever one you come up with for your own project or product - must be a living model. With each new insight, it will be modified, so that it optimally represents the specific situation. In my ideal world, risk assessment should be a daily management task. More exactly, every decision made in a private company is a risk decision. Every schedule, every decision in a Spice Girls meeting, every forecast - everything is designed to deal with the risk that could cause a company to fail in the market. The only time a company has no risk is when then the company no longer exists. Contrary to popular belief, successful companies, just like successful extreme athletes, do not blindly take on risk. They know that risk exists, and take deliberate measures to reduce risk. If a company has the maturity to manage risk based on models, it would learn from any unexpected outcomes and adapt the model accordingly, to be better prepared the next time. Many product and project managers must first come around to this way of thinking, because they see their current duties as administrative work - but they are actually risk managers. This assumes that those responsible free themselves from the idea of prioritization and stop continually starting new projects as long as there is enough work in the system. Gut decisions should help sustain an execution sequence that is based on economic criteria. When supported by a limited, flow-based system, re-prioritizing becomes unnecessary and you can focus instead on getting work completed.

5.4 An Interview with Markus Andrezak

Markus Andrezak has been developing high traffic, high revenue internet products for more than 15 years. Before starting his product consulting company "überproduct", he worked for a broad spectrum of companies such as eBay Classifieds Group, AOL, the Scout-Gruppe, Gruner & Jahr. He has a vast experience with prioritization and risk assessment.

Klaus: You have quite a bit of experience with prioritization, Cost of Delay and risk estimation. In your opinion, where can these concepts be utilized?

Markus: From my point of view, Cost of Delay and Risk Estimation, as you also describe them, are generally applicable tools that can be used for the estimation of projects, proposals, initiatives, features, etc., in order to get away from decision making based on opinion, pure intuition or even worse: HiPPO (Highest Paid Person's Opinion). The topic is a bit like an enlightenment in this area. It is most obvious perhaps in a company's portfolio planning. A portfolio does nothing more than describe the things that you do. However, the things that you do should have a few positive characteristics, which are understood in advance. But a portfolio should be balanced with regard to risk. Risk can be determined by examining the possible opportunities and drawbacks of a proposal. The trick is to limited downside and give yourself as many opportunities as possible. Then things will thrive.

Klaus: The estimation of upsides and downsides can eventually be expressed really well with Cost of Delay, don't you think?

Markus: Yes, but now it's going further: Who needs to determine the Cost of Delay? In the case of a portfolio, it should be discussed by a group that is responsible for leading the company's path ahead. In this discussion, the exercise is to specify the Cost of Delay, simply as a learning tool. Trying to define CoD helps to ask the right questions about the proposal and to quantify the learnings. Say, I have three projects to choose from, but can only implement one based on the resources available. Then Cost of Delay and the underlying discussions can help the group to make a coherent and informed decision which option might have the best payoff. This is completely different than just saying "I believe we have to do this because the competition has it" or similar prevailing justifications. Cost of Delay has many functions. First, it is used to understand, and then decide, the value of a proposal. At the same time, you can be certain that different opinions will lead to varying estimations. Interestingly, it is exactly these diverse points of view that are valuable, because they help to understand the proposal from various perspectives. Continuous and frequent - highly frequent - discussions about this topic lead to a great amount of trust within the group, as well as a homogenous, reasonable and informed point of view. Now, not only can each individual from the group support the company's decisions, but each project or initiative can be well-justified. For that reason, it is necessary to continually have these discussions. I also take extreme care to keep these discussions away from controlling and monitoring aspects, in order to make them purely decision-making meetings.

Klaus: What constitutes "highly frequent" for you in this context?

Markus: My preferred frequency is, actually, to have these meetings weekly and to keep them short. In a company with up to 200 employees, a half-hour is adequate if the discussion is limited to only the project decisions and new information. The conciseness of the meeting is certainly a way to reduce the "one more meeting effect". Eventually, it will be clear to everyone involved that there is no other meeting as important is this one.

Klaus: It can also happen, of course, that not everyone is immediately in agreement. That's why I also recommend working with a range of values when quantifying, so these disagreements and uncertainties are made explicit. This is all well and good, but what do we do when the range is large?

Markus: When the opinions in the meetings continue to drift further apart after a month, it is a sign that orientation has been lost. There isn't enough clarity about the objectives, the vision, the strategy and the strategic goals of the company. Then, opinions must naturally drift apart. In this case, it's important to quickly clarify these points, because without clear measurements guidelines, it is unavoidable that the proposal will be estimated differently by different people.

Klaus: Can you think of an example, when the views are further apart and when they are closer together?

Markus: In product maintenance, you should arrive at a very clear estimation for Cost of Delay, otherwise you haven't done your homework. With completely new products, services and proposals, on the other hand, it is completely normal that the Cost of Delay estimations will show large ranges, uncertainty and ambiguity. There is nothing wrong with this: Something new is always uncertain, but doing new stuff is necessary. Cost of Delay simply shows that something new and uncertain is being undertaken.

Klaus: Well, the boundaries between product maintenance and new products are often not clearly drawn. In which case should Cost of

Delay be determined?

Markus: Yes, the borders get blurry. I believe, though, that Cost of Delay can be used in both cases, because Cost of Delay at least two functions. On one hand, it simply helps represent the value and risk of a proposal as a number. On the other hand, Cost of Delay is an instrument to lead a discussion and to ask the right questions. By standard procedures - as you discussed in the billing example - you need to investigate something based on quantifiable facts. You can receive qualitative data from marketing, but the data is completely anecdotal for new products, because there isn't any data available. It's necessary to do the routine work when determining Cost of Delay, and there is enough material available to assist in this. The more work that is put into determining Cost of Delay, the more exact the values become and the range of values will become smaller - the forecast becomes more accurate. The work required is different with new products. The huge starting range requires asking questions and investigating why a new product makes sense and produces value. The whole arsenal of user, market and product research exploration (Fuzzy Front End), etc., can be used. Ultimately, you learn more about the customer, their needs and their interactions. The purpose is to get information as quickly as possible through preferable frequent and cheap interactions (experiments) with the customers. The funny thing is, these little tidbits of information have great value when dealing with large uncertainty. They help us to better approximate Cost of Delay.

Klaus: Isn't there a danger, that precise measurements will always win when compared to abstract estimations with larger range?

Markus: Yes, absolutely! Cost of Delay from Fuzzy Front End projects will be measured completely different than those from production projects. The discussion is more abstract, but this is exactly the reason why they should be had and a consensus about the abstract estimations should be achieved. It's also important that the differences in the estimations are understood and forced. Otherwise, precise and safe proposals will always win over the uncertain, abstract ones. This is the death of renewal and innovation. The value of a new product is also derived from the strategy: When we want to achieve something specific for our customers, we must solve specific problems. We know there are needs, but we don't know how to satisfy those needs. When we satisfy those needs, there also should be measurable effects. Ultimately, the uncertainty, or the complete lack of knowledge at the start, drives us to search for the right questions when determining Cost of Delay. Asking questions is the common denominator. In every case, you must allow for different perceptions and, above all, see the value in the various opinions.

Klaus: We're talking the whole time about assumptions and ranges. How can you actually verify whether or not the correct decision was made?

Markus: That's an interesting question. Eric Ries would tell us, that we simply need to build our model, based on the definition of product success, and then measure it (Ries, 2011). In reality, it's quite often not that simple. In your example of process optimization in billing, it is relatively easy since the previously accrued costs could be compared with the actual outcome. With anything new, it's difficult, because, for example, new features must be explained and learned and must be established in the market. In addition, they have side-effects on other product parts and these effects are not linear. Even a Killer-Feature does not necessarily have a linear increase in the number of new users, or result in customers willing to pay more for it. It's possible the customers simply stay with what they know out of convenience, instead of trying something new. In some cases, this can only be measured after a long time, like a year. It's similar in marketing. It's obvious that marketing is important, but the relationship between the expenditures for each marketing channel and their impact can sometimes be difficult to measure. Even though there are better tracking tools for this now, much remains unclear. That is why I make the case for a more probabilistic approach. We carry out measurements at wide intervals and compare our success over this larger timeframe based on the important statistics. This way, instead of evaluating our portfolio from a detailed local perspective, we evaluate our portfolio from an across-the-board perspective over a period of time. Product managers and developers can certainly contribute a more detailed point of view. At the portfolio level, however, we should simply force ourselves to measure at a higher level. When we make well-grounded decisions, usually we are better off than always making decisions instinctively. This also helps us to see proposals as building blocks and experiments, and to avoid placing the blame for failures on the executor of the proposal. Especially since the decision to do something was made at the portfolio level.

Klaus: Cost of Delay and risk estimation are also not the one-size-fits-all approach with which everything will be okay?

Markus: That would be even nicer - a tool that would solve all problems. Even better, of course, would be an all-encompassing theory that could be used to simply calculate correct decisions. However, deliberate assessment of proposals using Cost of Delay and risk estimation is very powerful and a common tool for continuous learning within a company. Companies who are open to continuous learning, should look more closely at these concepts. Cost of Delay and risk estimation begin at the portfolio level, i.e. at the place where vision and strategy are put into operation, and continue all the way through to the feature level. The portfolio level is where the substance, or character, of the company is determined. This should be a very deliberate process, and has very little to do with guessing games. Cost of Delay and risk estimation help when discussing the substance of the company because they uncover assumptions, and they help us ask the right questions at the places where it's not yet working. All in all, companies who consistently utilize the concepts of Cost of Delay and risk estimation profit immensely on consistency, trust and efficiency.

5.5 Summary

The classical prioritization of work has one disadvantage: It rarely deals with economically accountable criteria. Through outside pressure, or through political pressure within the company, there is constant re-prioritization. The resulting bottlenecks are often countered by increasing resources, but doing this increases the complexity even more. The result: Too much work gets started and eventually, as a result, no work is finished on time. With economic assessments, balance between demand and resources can be achieved and an organized inflow to the work system established. Cost of Delay, which the Spice Girls use to assign work in the idea pool, results in an economically rational order of processing. Cost of Delay is always based on value-generating, deliverable units that give the customer tangible benefits. It is a function of the value generated by a piece of work and its urgency.

Mature companies expand their assessment to additional dimensions before deciding on the sequence of work. A significant dimension is the risk associated with a piece of work, which can be broken down into technical risk and market risk. Risk is the individual effect of uncertainty and can be quantified through the level of its possible effect (risk value) and its probability of occurrence. For risk management, a combination of existing models within the company can be used to develop suitable models (such as Cost of Delay or Product Life Cycle).

Sequences that are economically based, together with the WIP limits of a Kanban system, help a company to quickly get working on generating value. Determining both Cost of Delay and risk requires that everyone involved put personal interests aside, and focus instead on what's best for the customers and the company.

Literature

(Anderson, 2012) David J. Anderson. *Lessons in Agile Management. On the Road to Kanban.* Blue Hole Press, 2012.

(Arnold, 2015) Joshua Arnold. *The HiPPO effect.* Blog entry from February 9, 2015. http://blackswanfarming.com/the-hippo-effect

(Hubbard, 2014) Douglas W. Hubbard. *How to Measure Anything: Finding the Value of Intangibles in Business.* John Wiley & Sons Inc, 2014.

(Leopold & Kaltenecker, 2015) Klaus Leopold & Siegfried Kaltenecker. *Kanban Change Leadership: Creating a Culture of Continuous Improvement,* John Wiley & Sons Inc, 2015.

(Reinertsen & Smith, 1998) Don Reinertsen & Preston G. Smith. *Developing Products in Half the Time. New Rules, new Tools.* 2nd edition. John Wiley & Sons, 1998.

(Reinertsen, 2009) Don Reinertsen. *The Principles of Product Development Flow. Second Generation Product Development.* Celeritas Publishing, 2009.

(Ries, 2011) Eric Ries. *The Lean Startup. How Constant Innovation Creates Radically Successful Businesses.* Portfolio Penguin, 2011.

(Savage, 2012) Sam L. Savage. *The Flaw of Averages: Why We Underestimate Risk in the Face of Uncertainty,* Wiley, 2012.

(Surowiecki, 2005) James Surowiecki. *The Wisdom of Crowds.* Anchor, 2005.

(Wardley, 2015) Simon Wardley. *On Pioneers, Settlers, Town Planners and Theft.* Blog entry from March 13, 2015, http://bit.ly/1Iz2dsf.

6. Kanban in the STUTE Logistics Company

The IT Manager for STUTE Logistics, Holger Rieth, introduced his colleagues to Kanban a year ago. Since then, a momentum has developed that even impresses me. Holger Rieth's personal conviction was and is the driving force behind these changes, but the attitude of his employees has, in the meantime, also completely changed. Since implementing Kanban, the daily work of five teams has evolved into a harmonious work flow and as a result, allows employees time to work on and actively participate in resolving strategy issues. "Before, strategy development took place at the beginning of the year and the goals were derived from this strategy," Holger said. "Mid-year, at the very latest, came the realization that the goals were wrong. The employees still had to implement them, causing frustration." Today is a different situation: since the start of 2016, employees develop, within communities, their vision for the IT department based on the overall company strategy. This takes place on an internal platform called "Connect", where everyone can introduce their ideas for change. Each week, the submitted ideas are analyzed. Once the idea has matured and the goal is well-defined, it is evaluated by its cost of delay and placed in corresponding order on the Kanban board, which is viewable on large screens in each office. With the high amount of activity in the communities, Holger Rieth expects to have around 400 new ideas per year from this deliberate improvement process. "We can use this process to work on our vision, because using Kanban has shown us how to free-up capacity, supports implementation and uncovers potential improvements", stated Holger. So, what happened at STUTE?

A Leading Force in Contract Logistics

STUTE has been in business for more than 160 years. Since its start in Bremen, the company (known today as STUTE Logistics (AG & Co) KG) has become one of the most sought-after service providers for contract logistics, overland transport and ocean freight. STUTE has grown rapidly in the last few years: from 900 employees to over 2,500 in more than 40 locations across Germany. Customers such as Airbus, Hilti or Deutz, have outsourced their procurement and production logistics to STUTE, and in some cases, receive complete production kits that are put together and quality controlled by STUTE. It is a service that is tailored specifically to the requirements and needs of the customer. The IT department must provide individualized interfaces to the warehouse management system of each customer. Every software and hardware related request goes to the IT department, which is responsible for the Electronic Data Interchange (EDI), business intelligence and big data applications, as well as operating the service desk, managing and maintaining the technical infrastructure, developing and implementing special projects and processes. The IT department, however, is constantly faced with one problem: customers expect cost-savings each year. This requires the IT department to work closely with other departments. In many cases, processes need to be simplified and automated so people without specialized training can use their system. Every change on the customer side must be incorporated by the STUTE IT department as well, regardless of the nature of the change. Approximately 25,000 tickets go through the system each year and the IT department has 18 shifts per week with 24x7 on-call duty. "If you are unable to balance customer growth with internal process optimization, the customer notices immediately", says Holger. In addition to the on-going work for customer improvement, there are new projects which come up that need to be completed quickly. If a new warehouse is built, for example, the planned IT infrastructure needs to be installed and operational within days. That is why standardization is a constant issue. To complete all of these tasks, the IT department has 30 employees working in five teams located at the Bremen

Headquarters.

The End of ITIL is the Beginning of Kanban

In 2014, Holger Rieth was thinking about how the work processes in his department could be further optimized. He had been using ITIL for a long time, but no longer wanted to know simply how a process was supposed to work. Instead, Holger wanted a way to continuously improve the processes in his department. One of the problems he saw in his work culture was STUTE's "Start Policy", where new tickets were assigned to employees before the end of the day. The point of assigning a ticket was to make sure it was being worked on and the customer was being updated on the progress. But what did this policy achieve? Tickets - or rather customer requests - should be resolved rather than just looked after. Each evening, as new tickets would be added to the still unresolved tickets, employees started to jump between tickets leading to continuous task-switching. "We noticed that oversight was lost when someone had ten or more unresolved tickets", Holger stated pointedly. Holger was familiar with Kanban from the field of production logistics, but wondered if something like that existed for IT. The next logical step was to Google it. The search results brought him and two of his employees to one of my trainings. Holger recalls that the training content, and a few books, gave him enough information to reflect upon his situation. It was a guide to thinking for yourself - it showed the path to improvement, but didn't define a specific way to get there. This was exactly what Holger was looking for: direction and freedom at the same time.

Travel Companion, Skepticism and a few Departures

Each colleague was given my *Kanban Change Leadership* book (Leopold & Kaltenecker, 2015), and Holger, along with the team leaders, considered what Kanban could mean for the STUTE IT department, and thought about how they could get started. With his two travel companions and promoters of his idea, he introduced Kanban to the employees. First and foremost, he answered the following question: How does Kanban work and what problems will it solve? Holger made his intention very clear by stating, "If we launch this change process, if we get involved with it, we are in it all the way." He spoke with each employee and allowed the ideas about implementing Kanban to ripen. The team leaders discussed it amongst themselves, and decided they would also go along with this new approach. There was less resistance than expected, because the pressure on the employees increased through the use of the start policy. With the principles of Kanban, they could see a solution and understood that their personal work situation would improve. "There were also people who decided to leave during this phase, because they had defined themselves by the number of tickets they closed", Holger remembers. "A closed ticket does not necessarily mean a ticket with a quality resolution though, especially if you are just concentrating on making the numbers." These supposed "top-performers" lost their standing in relation to their colleagues, because individual performance numbers were no longer relevant.

Service Desk and Infrastructure Begin the Transition

The first Kanban systems were built for the Service Desk and the Infrastructure Team because these two areas had the most transitions and connected structures with each another. Did it go smoothly? No, it did not. There was at least a month of uncertainty because there were neither statistics nor reference data to compare. "We didn't write anything down before", explains Holger, "as such, the conversion to Kanban and its effect were interpreted as failure, since we couldn't demonstrate if our situation had improved or not." At the beginning, the team lost efficiency and speed during the changeover, and from time to time the employees would, out of habit, fall back into the old work practices. Holger readily admits that it was sometimes difficult, especially since critics spoke up during this phase. Again, there was again much reasoning and persuasion needed, and another workshop was held to help understand Kanban better. During reviews, those things which didn't work were examined. There was great enthusiasm when the teams designed their Kanban boards within a day. An essential experience for Holger was to not overwhelm his colleagues with too many details at the beginning. Therefore, in the first weeks of the transition, some team boards started only with the columns "input", "doing" and "done", and were refined step-by-step.

The transition phase lasted nine months, with plenty of skepticism and occasionally having to start at the beginning again, during which some employees left the company. "A bit long", Holger concedes, "because it was first necessary to overcome the false incentives of the past." With increasing frequency, there were successes with the new system (even if they were small successes) and each success was celebrated. Each hurdle overcome was shared in the team and gradually everyone involved saw the positive changes.

Success, as well as Inefficient Processes, become Visible

Despite the troubles at startup, within three months the gains in efficiency through Kanban were visible. The total number of open tickets dropped, backlog had been resolved and the throughput increased - the customers were getting increasingly better service. The reason: the time which was used for the administration of the tickets previously was now invested in working on and closing the tickets. As mentioned, before Kanban was implemented, a ticket was immediately assigned to an employee who would be responsible for it. Since the implementation, this requirement has changed. Now, the work time should be used as efficiently as possible to solve the customer problems. The principle of late commitment had already been established - the employees started the next task only when they had the time and resources available. In time, additional possibilities for improvement could be seen because of the process transparency that occurred with Kanban. "For the first time, we started to think about how support could be more efficient, versus taking the process as a given", said Holger Rieth. One challenge that was always present was to immediately classify and qualify the incoming tickets in order to assign them to an appropriate area of responsibility. The tickets needed to be handed over to be worked on, and already came the next hurdle: someone needed to communicate with the customer. With this process, there were many handover points, which even the customers noticed. The solution to this problem was simple. The customer received one contact person who not only gathered the information on the problem, but also worked on resolving the issue and was always the contact person for the customer.

What Creates Value for the Customer?

Changing the process to a single point of contact for the customer brought the next mental obstacle: the people who solve the technical issues for the customer prefer to do their work in the background and do not particularly like customer contact. Several employees often said, "I am a system administrator, not a helpdesk employee!" Again, it was necessary to gently remind them to change their perspectives about creating value for the customer. The customer is not interested if a command line needs to be changed, they are only concerned about their problem getting resolved, regardless what happens in the background at STUTE IT. The value created for the customer through a smooth problem-solving process is also value created for STUTE. In order to support the transition to self-awareness by the employees, a rotation principle was introduced. Everyone from trainee to administrator took turns at first level support on a weekly basis. On one hand, the trainees learned from the beginning how to communicate with customers and how to think out solutions. In addition, the original skeptics gained a different perspective about customer issues during their time at first level support, and discovered possibilities for improvements at second level support. Holger Rieth also understands that there is danger in this approach. "At some point a dynamic is reached where you have to be careful not to lose your employees. When expanding the tasks - today first level, tomorrow back to second level - the workers go from specialization to generalization in the job. We were aware, however, that we needed to go in this direction in order to handle the customer requests correctly." All of these insights were worked out in the retrospective meetings which were held every 14 days with each team and were crucial for thinking outside the box. Once a month there were also cross-team retrospectives with team leaders and delegates from each team.

Visualization and Key Figures

After being implemented in the service desk and infrastructure areas, Kanban was brought to the development, EDI and project management areas. In these areas, there was a greater understanding, or often demand, for new practices and Holger Rieth and his colleagues could dive deeper into the Kanban design after this second implementation. The topic of visualization was at the top of their list: How could information from the teams be consolidated in order to illustrate the evolution of the entire IT department? How should cumulative flow diagrams (CFD) look, where should the numbers come from, when should which number be released, etc.? There were many discussions about what should be measured, when it should be measured and how it should be measured. "These discussions were important because a uniform understanding was formed", states Holger. "Without discussion, there was always someone who would get lost in the figures." In the end, that meant all numbers were generated collectively and nobody, not even Holger Rieth as the boss, would demand different or additional figures.

Over the course of the discussions on visualization and key figures, one employee started to design a STUTE exclusive electronic Kanban board that built upon the existing ticketing system and pulled out information for the CFD. The board has become extremely flexible and each employee can adjust it to their personal needs: ordering the swim lanes, long or short descriptions, how many tickets per column displayed, and so on. New requirements for the board will be implemented in such a way that the overall view is preserved. The pull principle, transparency, WIP limits - the fundamentals of Kanban - must always remain. Every Tuesday and Thursday, Holger Rieth discusses the CFDs in a 15-minute session with the team leaders. He observed that self-awareness improved, and everyone wants to contribute to a positive overall result. The work flow - made visible through the data analysis - rather than individual work, is discussed. Daily work is discussed in the daily standups of each team, and the team leader meetings revolve around improving the overall system.

Dependencies: Visualize, Eliminate, Automate

From the very beginning there was a board for overall team coordination, in addition to the individual team boards. The goal was to have an overall view of the IT department and it became apparent that even non-IT related work needed to enter the Kanban system. Work regarding optimization and organization was especially important to have in the system, such as IT audits needing to be performed in different locations or supplying application support. An especially complex service dealt with the administration of employees joining or leaving the company. When someone joined the company, up to 14 different tickets would be generated. All pertinent information about the employee - from birthdate to promotions - is found in the PASS system. Also, what is required from the IT department, such as creating accounts, is also processed over PASS. The plethora of issues and tasks associated with personnel administration was one of the most time-consuming processes, and it received its own swim lane on the boards. It was exactly this visualization which explicitly showed how many steps in this service could be automated. "The understanding about where the work came from was not available before", said Holger Reith. One process after another was analyzed and gradually automated.

Today, an employee joining or leaving a company generates only one ticket, and the rest can be done by mouse click. This way, the service desk can commit a majority of their time to procurement, which due to compliance reasons, is also an extensive process. Even here they are examining the process, but for now the tasks are depicted in the self-developed SEPP application (STUTE Equipment Planning and Procurement) built through intensive teamwork in iterations in a little over two months. STUTE started with Kanban at the team level, but the services the IT department provided were, in effect, "Kanbanized". Team members thought about which services the IT department offered and these were pictured in swim lanes. Each service was analyzed step-by-step to determine how much "load" lay on each service and what could be automated was automated. Additional important criteria that emerged from analyzing the services and simplifying the steps were security and cost.

Holger Rieth believes the evolving nature of Kanban is what facilitated implementing all of these improvements in just one year. There is no "must" - no prescribed processes - how things need to be done, but rather the possibility to understand, to learn about and to improve yourself. For this reason, Holger Rieth does not want the path STUTE took with Kanban to be used as a model or blueprint, because the requirements for each company are unique. Automation makes sense in our context, but is not necessarily the correct solution for every other IT department in the world," he emphasizes. Working with Kanban, by the way, changed nothing in the structure of the organization: there are still five teams and five team leaders. The structure was never the object of the transformation. Naturally, it could have changed, but it wasn't necessary. The real attraction for Holger Rieth is that Kanban is nothing more than an instrument of analysis, which makes the starting points for change visible. "The surprising thing - if one can say it that way - for me is, above all, that there is not much needed for these changes. This is a marked contrast to ITIL, which requires unnecessary amount of data to be produced." Once the processes are stabilized and the services (newly) defined, according to Holger, the possibility for meaningful economic consideration and further optimization happen on their own. You have a steady-state system on which you can build. Holger is no longer interested in strict frameworks and standardized process models. For STUTE IT, it was important to go from quantitative statements to qualitative thinking, and as such, the Kanban approach was exactly the right method.

Maximum Transparency for the Customer

Since the processes identified above were running smoothly, the IT department at STUTE was able to think about forecasting. The basis information was already available: timestamps, Cumulative Flow Diagram, cycle time and throughput. The focus of these improvements was still the customer. Before Kanban was implemented, a service desk dispatcher was responsible for assigning the customer requests to the appropriate group. If the dispatcher didn't keep an eye on things, customer requests would be left unattended. Actually, a prioritization should have occurred at this point. The customer requests were analyzed in the retrospectives and it became clear that much of the work could be automated and the system would be more transparent for the customer. Through the analysis of requests at the service desk, approximately 300 use cases were derived and were allocated to each service. The use cases are connected to the "Helpdesk Launcher" tool. The customer can enter text in the search function of the Launcher and the auto complete suggests matching use cases. As soon as the customer selects the matching use case, the appropriate process will be automatically started.

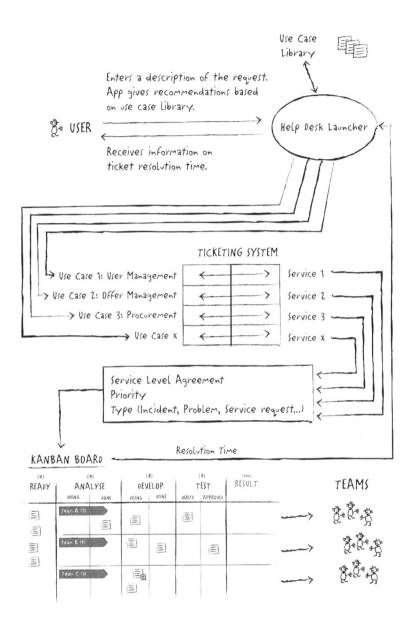

Figure 6.1: Helpdesk Launcher Mode of Operation

Holger Rieth and his team quickly saw that there was even more potential for transparency in the Helpdesk Launcher. The customer should receive at the same time their request has been entered, information on the forecasted time for implementing the solution. Holger Rieth talks about the earliest development. "We bought the book *Actionable Agile Metrics for Predictability*, written by Daniel Vacanti (Vacanti, 2015), worked through it and assumed an 80% probability of occurrence. The forecasts are delivered at the service level and depicted on the individual swim lanes of the Kanban board - the colleagues are impressed. The solution time is automatically calculated backwards till the forecasted due date. In the Helpdesk Launcher, the customer can, at any time, see how far the implementation is as well as when it is expected to be finished."

Away from Prioritization and Towards Cost of Delay

How does STUTE IT decide which customer request will be worked on next in each service? For the daily business, a model was developed for the Helpdesk Launcher. A sequence is calculated based on classification of business impact (for the use case) along with the age (target date) of the ticket. The classification goes from severity 1 (where the customer only requires information) to severity 5 (when the complete fallout of a location is imminent). The combination of these two factors - business impact and age - determines the order of the tickets within the individual services (as can be seen in the swim lanes on the board), as well as across all services. By automatically calculating the order of tickets in the system, it prohibits the employees from cherry-picking their tasks, since the order of requests to be worked on is already determined. Aside from the daily work, attention is given to the strategic issues. To keep them from being constantly pushed aside, a minimum amount of these strategic issues must be worked on. Usually Fridays are reserved as a time for the teams to work on intangibles, which are assessed once a week by the team leaders in a 30-minute meeting according to their weighted cost of delay. Is there always consensus in these meetings? Not by any means, since it deals with the estimations given by team leaders, and these can sometimes be quite far apart. It is clear to everyone, however, that there is a principle of common understanding about the impact of the measures which are or aren't achieved, so a way is always found. At the moment, thought is being given as to how an early-warning system could function, so tasks on the Kanban board will automatically be put higher on the list when the target date is getting close. The necessary forecasting already exists.

Personal Transformation improves Economic Performance For me, it is impressive the level of maturity STUTE IT has achieved in just one year. The insights which were reached in this short time are fascinating to me and the meaning behind the simple phrase "live your workflow" becomes tangible. The visualization only reveals its power, however, when - as STUTE IT did - the acquired information is worked on with focus and intention. Here is a short summary:

- We know which processes/services exist and how they look.
- We know which services are already stable and which are not.
- We know how the system has developed since the implementation of Kanban.
- We measure the cycle time of our services and can give a forecast without needing to use estimations.
- We measure how much effort is in a service, and based on that effort, we think about what can be automated.
- We have seen that manual classification of tickets at the service desk could be assigned and ranked more quickly by using a model.

These are results which have a direct impact on the economic performance of the IT department. Holger Rieth points out once more the most important steps that, without question, had a positive effect on the economic performance of the department:

- The *procurement process* was a process full of interfaces and was, for the most part, processed over a manual ticket system. A purchasing tool was developed so that parts of the process were passed on to the individual subsidiaries, and a large part of the interfaces were eliminated.
- By using the Helpdesk Launcher, *the quality of the input information* improved considerably, because the customer can easily input very precise details. Many processes have been reduced because of this.
- The IT infrastructure was split into a first and second level in order to offer the customer *faster* technical *solutions*. The solution times have been reduced dramatically and many requests could be answered immediately on the telephone.

Holger Rieth is convinced, however, that the economic successes are due to the personal development of the employees that in turn fires up the dynamic of the improvements. This simply goes hand-in-hand, he says. In a review, the team leaders collected their impressions:

- There is positive feedback from the employees, the idea was understood and accepted.
- Cherry-picking was able to be reduced.
- The transfer of knowledge (know-how) improved.
- New topics are worked on with impartiality.
- Transparency from the department outwards, within the teams and between the teams, improved.
- Ticket load per employee decreased dramatically, while productivity and quality have noticeably improved.
- Employees actively take part in the improvements and hold to them.

Holger Rieth realizes, after a year of Kanban, how the employees deal with the processes and their work within their processes:

The personal involvement is a new dimension for everyone. Above all else, it occurs to me that ritualization is a factor not to be underestimated, because it forces the employees to focus for a particular moment during the working day. You stand up, literally, to set something in motion. We have, for example, a Prio-5 board: when a location has an outage, everyone - including me - stands up and goes to the board. By standing up and going to the board, it signals that something important has happened, which has a completely different effect than just a by-the-way announcement.

As such, all Kanban meetings at STUTE IT are, out of principle, held with everyone standing. For Holger, there is nothing more important than the meetings with team leaders every Tuesday and Thursday from 8:45 am till 9:00 am, period.

The adoption and following of Kanban goes along with a change in culture and that, for Holger Rieth, makes the difference between a successful company and an unsuccessful company. He sees himself, as well as his leadership team, obligated to do the following:

When someone in a leadership position is not confident about Kanban; when they do not follow and defend it, then it will not succeed because the employees will not follow such a large change project pertaining to their way of working.

Literature

(Leopold & Kaltenecker, 2015) Klaus Leopold & Siegfried Kaltenecker. *Kanban Change Leadership: Creating a Culture of Continuous Improvement*, John Wiley & Sons Inc, 2015.

(Vacanti, 2015) Daniel S. Vacanti. *Actionable Agile Metrics for Predictability: An Introduction*, Actionable Agile Press, 2015. {width="100%"}

Terms used in this book

Activity is a step that is established in a work system in order to create value. On a Kanban board, a column represents an activity.

Cost of Delay is a function of the performance over a specific period of time, and is best expressed as a monetary unit per week. It represents the costs, as well as economic effects over time, that occur when the completion of work is delayed or doesn't respond quickly enough to the market. Cost of Delay includes not only actual costs incurred, but also all lost revenues which are incurred, regardless if a project is worked on or not.

Customers refers to either internal customers or external customers.

Definition of Done describes which result must be delivered by an activity in order for a ticket to go from "In Progress" to Completed.

Forecasting is the attempt to determine the manifestation of future events using model-based prediction.

Kanban Flight Levels are an instrument of communication to clearly identify the implementation possibilities for Kanban, as well as to find out where it's possible, or makes sense, to start an improvement process within an organization.

Flow efficiency designates the amount of time in which a work item is actively worked on within the entire cycle time.

kanban is literally a tag that not only enables, but also ensures, Just in Time (JIT) production. Seen as a totality, it is a system of time management for production companies that helps decide what, when, and how much is to be produced. In knowledge work, we use virtual kanban systems to represent work items.

Kanban is a management method for knowledge work. It supports change in an evolutionary sense, by successively optimizing existing processes. I use a capital 'K' when referring to the Kanban method in order to distinguish it from the production kanban and the virtual kanban system.

Kanban board is the physical, tangible representation of a Kanban system consisting of columns and lanes to varying degrees.

Monte Carlo Simulation uses random numbers within a predefined possible range of numbers to conduct several iterations for a defined model. A Monte Carlo simulation helps calculate the distribution of possible results and their probability of occurrence.

Quantile are threshold values which divide a probability distribution (in this book, it is used in terms of the cumulative probability of occurrence), meaning a certain amount of the values are smaller than the quantile and the remaining values are larger.

Spice Girls are those colleagues in the company who are responsible for supplying work into the system. They serve two roles. First, they are the bouncers of the system and determine who is allowed in and who has to stay out. Second, they place work in a reasonable sequence based on an evaluation of the Cost of Delay.

What do I mean by system?[1]

> **System** in ancient Greek means "body, organized whole, that which is connected". In contemporary sociology, it describes a meaningful unity of elements that differentiates itself from the surrounding environment. According to Niklas Luhmann, who is considered the father of sociological systems theory, "a system is an organized complexity".

[1] see also Klaus Leopold & Siegfried Kaltenecker. *Kanban Change Leadership: Creating a Culture of Continuous Improvement*, John Wiley & Sons Inc, 2015.

Social systems are complex bodies produced and reproduced via communication. Society and all its organizations and interactions are "communication network(s)". This makes them living beings but also incalculable.

Psychological systems operate in the form of processes of self-awareness that can be described as a meaningful unity of perception, thought, feeling and desire. They are inseparably connected with social systems although they are not a part of them.

Technical systems unite elements whose interaction likewise forms a unity. This interaction-based unity however is not defined in terms of meaning, but rather in terms of function. It is highly structured and mathematically predictable just like, for example, a computer or operational system.

Kanban systems (capital 'K') describe the complex interrelation between social, psychological and technical elements geared for continual improvement. Kaizen— the Japanese term for "change for the better"—demands a goal-oriented bond between the organization, the employees and the work processes.

By **technical kanban system**, in the narrow sense, I mean the form of visualization of the work process (e.g., via a board) and the individual instruments (e.g., tickets, meetings) that help provide insights into your own processes. The visualization simultaneously indicates the specific individual in the particular value-creation chain we wish to optimize. The most important characteristic of a technical kanban system is that it quantitatively limits the work in progress.

Throughput is the amount of work completed in a given period of time. Throughput is an economic measurement.

Value is the monetary amount that can be generated from work.

Value Creation Chain (Value Generation Chain) is the set of activities in the system that generate value for the customer.

Visualization is a core practice in Kanban which makes the value stream visible.

WIP is the acronym for Work in Progress. This refers to any item actively being worked on in the system.

WIP Limit denotes the limit for the number of items that can be actively worked on in the system at any given time.

Work Item (Work) is either a subtask or a complete task that passes through the activities which create value.

About the Author

Dr. Klaus Leopold is computer scientist and Kanban pioneer with many years of experience in helping organizations from different industries on their improvement journey with Lean and Kanban. He is one of the first Lean Kanban trainers and coaches worldwide. He was awarded with the Brickell Key Award for "outstanding achievement and leadership" within the Lean Kanban community in San Francisco, 2014. His main interest is establishing lean business agility by improving organizations beyond the team level, especially in large environments from 50 to 5,000 people. Klaus speaks regularly at renowned Lean and Kanban conferences worldwide. He publishes his current thoughts on his blog www.LEANability.com and you can follow him on Twitter at @klausleopold.

Acknowledgements

It's a wrap! This time, it took almost two years exactly from the time the first line was written until the book was published. It took approximately another year after that for the English version to be completed and made available in its entirety. Thanks to the contributions of many people, I was able to get this book past the finish line.

First and foremost, I want to thank my life and business partner, Katrin Dietze, who must constantly endure my unripe visions and ideas. She is my most important sparring partner and thanks to her, ideas don't just ripen and mature in my head, they become reality. Katrin also contributed enormously to the fantastic illustrations in this book.

I would also like to thank my text fairy, Dolores Omann, who really understands how to translate my thoughts and texts into German that is readable. Working with her is both humorous and professional, a combination I really appreciate. Dolores also always finds the right places to put commas in my text (and most certainly has put her touches on this paragraph, too.)

A big thank-you goes to Holger Rieth, who was willing to tell his story as IT Director at STUTE Logistics (AG & Co.) KG in this book. It also seems that Holger thoroughly read the text because his comments during the review process went well beyond what was expected. I would like to say a special thank-you to mathematic professionals Ralf Männel from RME and Horst Eidenberger from the Technical University of Vienna. These two elevated the mathematical correctness of the chapter on Forecasting without it becoming an unreadable jumble of mathematical formulas. It all began with a terse remark from Horst: "Now you have to show me that 11 samples are enough." The result was innumerable discussions and emails with my good friend and forecasting guru Troy Magennis. In the end, I also consulted my "uncle-in-law" Ralf Männel, who ultimately gave the mathematical proof that 19, and not 11, was the correct sample size in the given context. My friends, that was fantastic! I would also like to give an extra thanks to Troy: For years, he has been setting the bar continuously higher on the subjects of metrics and forecasting, and he allowed me to interview him for this book as well.

Forecasting without metrics is like soup without salt. I am extremely lucky to count Daniel Vacanti as one of my friends because he is the salt in the forecasting soup. I really appreciate his (mathematical) precision, since his scrupulous feedback kept me from losing the necessary accuracy, despite my requirement for an easy-to-understand presentation. Dan also gave a fascinating interview for this book. Heartfelt thanks go to my long-time friend and Kanban companion Markus Andrezak. Above all, his viewpoint on innovation and business strategy helped me to determine which content belonged in this book and which content should be saved for the next book. In the interview, we worked out a more exact delineation of the content.

Many thanks to Andreas Haugeneder and Hans-Oliver Ruoß from Bosch Automotive Electronics. We definitely practice Kanban on a large scale there. Andreas and Oliver are in charge of implementing Kanban in Germany, China, India, Hungary and the USA. Their often very ambitious goals require me to push my own limits and spur me on to perform better. In the interview, they offer a look at what has happened in their Kanban initiative.

Matthew Philip was one of the first users of my blocker-clustering method outside of my clientele. He talks about his experiences during the interview in Chapter 2—thank you so much, Matt!

You might think with so much support already recognized, there wouldn't be anyone left, but that is not the case with this book. I repeatedly received feedback from my reviewers Andreas Schliep, Anton Spitzer, Arne Roock, Daniel Dorion, Eric-Jan Kaak, Florian Eisenberg, Oliver Finker, Michael Beyer, Siegfried Kaltenecker, Stefan Rook and Wolfgang Wiedenroth. Thank you!

For the English translation, I would like to thank Jennifer Minnich and Dan Vacanti. Jennifer didn't just give a good translation of the book, she also managed to transfer the spirit of the book into the English version. Dan watched over the text with hawk-eyed precision and during review phone calls, Dan and Jennifer had many suggestions about translating terms correctly. Thank you both—it was a pleasure to work with such professionalism!

27810405R00193

Made in the USA
Columbia, SC
30 September 2018